DIRECTIONS IN
FUNDAMENTAL MORAL THEOLOGY

Books by Charles E. Curran Published by the
University of Notre Dame Press

Directions in
Fundamental Moral Theology

CHARLES E. CURRAN

UNIVERSITY OF NOTRE DAME PRESS
NOTRE DAME, INDIANA 46556

Library of Congress Cataloging in Publication Data

Curran, Charles E.
    Directions in fundamental moral theology.

    Includes index.
    Contents: A methodological overview of fundamen-
tal moral theology — The Stance of moral theology —
The person as moral agent and subject — [etc.]
        1. Christian ethics — Catholic authors — Addresses,
essays, lectures. I. Title.
BJ1249.C817   1985   241'.042   85-2543
ISBN 0-268-00854-1-X

In gratitude to
students, colleagues, and friends
especially
F.A.C.T., Past Presidents of the CTSA, faculty colleagues
and all who have expressed support
for my theological endeavors

In tribute to
Tom, Tony, and others
who have suffered unjustly for their theological work

In memory of
Emily and Rosemary
who with their team and associates
shared the practical struggles of Catholic theology

Contents

Introduction

In 1977 the University of Notre Dame Press published my *Themes in Fundamental Moral Theology*. This book brought together eight different essays dealing with fundamental moral theology and touched on most of the important issues involved in that subject area of moral theology.

The continued use of *Themes* in connection with courses in fundamental moral theology raised the question about a new edition or a revision of that work. This present volume, *Directions in Fundamental Moral Theology*, attempts to serve the same purpose today that *Themes* did a few years ago. The title has been changed because about half of the volume consists of different essays; five of the chapters originally appeared in *Themes* but have been updated for this volume. *Directions in Fundamental Moral Theology* thus brings together nine of my essays. The volume is not a systematic treatment of fundamental moral theology as such; however, the essays gathered together here do consider the most important issues involved in that area of theology. In addition there is an overriding methodological approach which runs through all the chapters.

There is no need for a long introduction, for the first chapter basically fulfills that purpose. It provides an overview of fundamental moral theology and summarizes the method which is then developed at much greater length in subsequent chapters. The first chapter by its very nature is somewhat sketchy and jejune, but it should provide the reader with the necessary framework and map for more easily assimilating

1

what is later explained in much greater depth.

All of these essays except one have already appeared in recent volumes of my writings published by the University of Notre Dame Press. Chapter 3, "The Person as Moral Agent and Subject," originally was presented at the 1984 Villanova Theology Institute and was published in *Called to Love: Towards a Contemporary Christian Ethic*, ed. Francis A. Eigo (Villanova, PA: Villanova University Press, 1985).

Finally, I am grateful to all of those who have helped me in my research and writing. Special thanks are due to the following: my colleagues in the Department of Theology at The Catholic University of America, especially John T. Ford and C. Gerard Austin, who have served as chair of the department, and Johann F. Klodzen, the administrative assistant; the librarians at Mullen Library of Catholic University, in particular Carolyn Lee, Bruce Miller, David Gilson, and Mary Liu; my graduate assistants, especially Mark O'Keefe, who prepared the index; the many different people who have graciously helped with the typing of the manuscript; my editor at the University of Notre Dame Press, John Ehmann, who suggested this project and has seen it through to completion.

1. A Methodological Overview of Fundamental Moral Theology

Moral theology, like all theology, bases its reflections on the Word of God in the scriptures, on tradition, on the teaching of the church, on the signs of the times, and on the eschatological pull of the future. In the last few years great attention has been paid to the signs of the times. The signs of the times, which are important for moral theology in the United States, include both the cultural milieu with its understanding of moral problems and the thematic and systematic reflection, which is the discipline of ethics, both in its religious and philosophical contexts.

To read the signs of the times always involves a prudential discernment and the risk of being wrong. Traditionally American life and ethos have given great importance to freedom in all aspects of life, but there has also been a recognition of the limits of freedom which has especially come to the fore in recent years. The contemporary American scene has witnessed the end of an era in which easy optimism and even naïveté characterized much of the country's self-understanding. Self-criticism and doubt have been more apparent ever since the Vietnam War, Watergate, continuing world crises, and the energy shortage. At times there is a feeling of pessimism and even helplessness, but this self-critical attitude has raised in the public consciousness a greater interest in ethics and the morality of the decisions that must be made to guide our future life. No one is unaware of the multitude of problems calling out for a solution: nuclear energy and weapons; poverty throughout the world and at home; hunger in the world; human rights and wars of liberation; the contemporary trouble spots in the globe — the Near East, Indochina, Africa, Central and South America; world trade and economic policies; multinational corporations; technology; energy; the environment. There appears to be a widespread feeling that Americans must be willing to face these problems and also to change their own life styles away from the consumerism and materialism which have so often characterized our society. At the same time there exists a great interest in contemplation, in the personal struggle for growth, and in the meaning of life and death.

The influence of specifically Catholic thought and theology on the American cultural and intellectual life has not been great. Over twenty years ago John Tracy Ellis criticized American Catholicism for its failures in making any noticeable contribution to the wider scene of American intellectual and cultural life.[1] Since that time individual Catholics and groups have made some contributions, but generally speaking there has been little that is specifically theological in these individual contributions.

On the reflective level of ethics as such, Catholic moral theology in the United States is related to and influenced by religious ethics, especially Protestant Christian ethics, and philosophical ethics. Protestant ethics has had a significant influence in the United States. Perhaps there is no intellectual figure who had a greater impact on American foreign policy in the middle years of the twentieth century than theologian Reinhold Niebuhr.[2] Before the Second Vatican Council there was little or no dialogue between Protestant and Catholic ethicists, but that situation has changed dramatically since the 1960s. Not only dialogue but also rapprochement characterizes the relationship between Catholic moral theology and Protestant ethics. As one very knowledgeable and competent Protestant scholar has pointed out, Catholic moral theology now gives more stress to aspects of ethics that were previously identified as typically Protestant emphases — becoming, process, dynamism, change, freedom, history, grace, and gospel. On the other hand, Protestants have striven to give more importance to Catholic concerns such as being, structure, order, continuity, nature, and law.[3] Close contact and dialogue with Protestant Christian ethics characterizes moral theology in the United States, but moral theology still attempts to remain firmly rooted in its own tradition. At the same time there is increasing communication with philosophical ethics both on methodological and on substantive questions. Philosophical ethics is no longer dominated by an analytic approach which shuns substantive and content questions. Now there is a growing interest of philosophers in the ethical questions facing society and in theoretical issues such as justice and the justification of moral norms.[4] Catholic moral theology exists in an intellectual milieu in the United States in which it is in contact and dialogue with Protestant and philosophical ethics. In the light of these signs of the times this chapter will discuss method in moral theology.

I approach the question of method in moral theology with the presupposition that errors and mistakes in method generally arise not so much from positive error as from the failure to consider all the aspects which deserve discussion. In moral theology itself in the last few years there has been an unfortunate tendency, readily understandable in the light of the contemporary controversies, to reduce moral theology merely to the question of norms and the morality of specific actions. The questions of specific actions and of norms are significant questions in moral theology, but there are other questions which are of greater or equal importance. In my judgment the following areas must be investigated in any systematic reflection on Christian moral life: the perspective or stance; the ethical model; Christian anthropology; concrete Christian decision-making and norms. These different aspects will now be discussed in greater detail.

I. Stance

The question of stance or perspective is the most fundamental and logically first consideration in moral theology. Catholic moral theology has not explicitly posed the question of stance, but in the American Protestant tradition James Sellers has insisted on stance as the first consideration and the source of other criteria.[5] James Gustafson employs a similar concept of perspective or posture to indicate the fundamental angle of vision which directs the entire enterprise of Christian ethics.[6]

Two cautions should be kept in mind in any discussion of stance. First, it is impossible to say that one stance is right and another wrong. The adequacy of the stance depends on how well it accomplishes its purpose as being the logically prior step which structures our understanding of moral reality, serves as a critique of other approaches, and is a source of other ethical criteria. Second, although stance as a logically prior step seems to have something of the apriori about it, in reality my own stance developed in an aposteriori way based on a critique of other positions. To properly fulfill its critical function and be proved adequate, the stance cannot rest merely on an apriori deduction or assumption.

My stance consists of a perspective based on the fivefold Christian mysteries of creation, sin, incarnation, redemption, and resurrection destiny. The reason for accepting these as aspects of the stance are obvious for the Christian, but the adequacy of this fivefold stance must be shown. The stance functions both methodologically and substantively. From a methodological viewpoint the stance both serves as a negative critique of other methodologies and provides a positive approach of its own.

Roman Catholic natural law theory rightly recognizes that the Christian finds ethical wisdom and knowledge not only in the scriptures and in Jesus Christ but also in human nature and human reason. On the basis of creation by a good and gracious God, human reason reflecting on human nature can arrive at ethical wisdom and knowledge. Insistence on the goodness of the natural and the human, with its corollary that grace builds on nature and is not opposed to nature, stands as a hallmark of the Catholic theological tradition. Some Protestant theologians deny the goodness of creation and the possibility of ethical wisdom and knowledge based on human nature and human reason for a number of different reasons — scripture alone is the source of ethical wisdom for the Christian; a narrow Christomonism sees Christ as the only way into the ethical problem; sin so affects human nature and human reason that they cannot serve as the basis of true knowledge; an unwillingness to accept an analogy between creation and the creator.

However, from the viewpoint of the proposed stance, the natural-law approach is deficient because it does not integrate the natural or creation into the total Christian perspective. The natural-law theory rightly recognizes creation and incarnation, but sin, redemption, and resurrection destiny do not receive their due. Catholic moral theology may have overstressed sin in terms of particular actions, but it never paid sufficient attention to the reality of sin as present in the world and affecting, without however destroying, human nature and human reason. Likewise, natural-law theory gives no place to grace, or redemption and resurrection destiny as the stance describes this reality, so that often Catholic moral theology became based exclusively on the natural to the neglect of what was then called the supernatural.

On the contrary, a Lutheran two-realm theory recognizes the reality of sin but overemphasizes sin and fails to give enough importance to the reality of creation and to moral wisdom based on it, to the integrating effect of the incarnation, to the recognition that redemption also affects the world in which we live, and to a more positive appreciation of the relationship between resurrection destiny and the present world.

Protestant liberalism arose in the nineteenth century, and its most significant ethical manifestation in the United States was the Social Gospel school.[7] This approach, especially in its more extreme forms, stressed the goodness of creation, the integrating effect of the incarnation on all reality, and the presence of redemption in the world, but sin and resurrection destiny as a future gift at the end of time were neglected.

Liberalism was succeeded in Protestant theology by neo-orthodoxy with its Barthian and Niebuhrian approaches. Barthian ethics flourished in Europe, but its most significant American exponent is Paul Lehmann.[8] Barthian ethics emphasized the centrality of redemption and of Christ and made Christ the sole way into the ethical problem. There was no place for philosophical ethics or natural law for the Christian. Within such a perspective, sin, incarnation, redemption, and resurrection destiny could all be given due importance, but creation and its ethical ramifications in terms of human reason were denied. Niebuhrian Christian realism, which ultimately exerted such a great influence on American thought and foreign policy, recognized some ethical import in creation even though it was infected by sin, but in the final analysis gave too much to the presence of sin and failed to appreciate the effects of incarnation, redemption, and a more positive relationship between the world of the present and the fullness of resurrection destiny in the eschaton. However, in many ways Niebuhr tried to account for all the elements in the stance but overemphasized the role of sin and downplayed the others.

In the 1960s in Protestant theology some approaches similar to the older liberalism came to the fore in the form of the theologies of the death of God and of secularization. Once again there was a tendency to overstress creation, incarnation, and redemption and to neglect the reality of sin and the fact that resurrection destiny is future and its fullness comes only as God's gracious gift at the end of time. In the light of the proposed stance subsequent developments were healthy. A theology of secularization gave way to a theology of hope with the primacy on resurrection destiny as future. However, at times there was still not enough emphasis on sin and on some discontinuity between this world and the next. Moltmann as a Protestant and Metz as a Catholic both went through a development similar to that outlined above and then put greater emphasis on discontinuity by highlighting the role of suffering as Moltmann wrote about *The Crucified God* and Metz talked about the future *"ex memoria passionis eius."*[9]

In the 1960s in conjunction with the Second Vatican Council, Roman Catholic theology rightly attempted to overcome the dichotomy between nature and grace, between gospel and daily life, between church and world. But in overcoming the dichotomy there emerged the danger of making everything grace and the supernatural. In other words, there was a tendency to forget sin and the fact that resurrection destiny is future and exists always in discontinuity, as well as in continuity, with present reality. Catholic thinking in this period often suffered from a collapsed eschaton because of which people thought that the fullness of the kingdom would come quickly, readily, and without struggle or suffering.

In contemporary Catholic theology, liberation theology, with its attempt to integrate redemption and the gospel into our understanding of political and economic life in society, marks an improvement over the exclusive natural-law approach that formerly characterized Catholic social ethics as exemplified in the papal social encyclicals. However, in liberation theology there exists among some a tendency to forget the reality of sin as affecting to some extent all reality (too often the impression is given that sin is all on one side) and a tendency to think that the fullness of the eschaton will come too readily and quickly. On the contrary, liberation will involve a long, hard, difficult struggle and will never be fully present in this world. At times liberation theology fails to recognize complexity in this world, for among some there is a great confidence in being able to know quite easily what God is doing in this world. The opposite danger maintains that reality is complex, and sin so affects all reality that one cannot know what God is doing in the world. I want to avoid both these extremes.

Not only does the stance embracing the fivefold mysteries of creation, sin, incarnation, redemption, and resurrection destiny serve as a critique of many other theories in moral theology as pointed out above, but at the same time it provides a positive methodology and perspective for approaching moral theology. Creation indicates the goodness of the human and human reason; but sin touches all reality, without, however, destroying the basic goodness of creation. Incarnation integrates all reality into the plan of God's kingdom. Redemption as already present affects all reality, while resurrection destiny as future exists in continuity with the redeemed present but also in discontinuity because the fullness of the kingdom remains God's gracious gift at the end of time.

The stance also addresses some substantive issues; but since the stance is the logically prior step in moral theology and by definition remains somewhat general, one cannot expect the stance to provide specific and detailed substantive content. A primary contribution of the stance is in giving a direction and general perspective to our understanding of some of the most basic issues in Christian ethics. The first question concerns the meaning of human existence in this world and the relationship between this world and the kingdom. In the past Protestant theology often addressed the same basic question in terms of the relationship between Christ and culture as illustrated in the work of H. Richard Niebuhr, who points out five different typologies for understanding this relationship.[10] The position derived from the stance corresponds to Niebuhr's type of Christ-transforming culture. The fullness of the kingdom will only come at the end, but in this world the kingdom strives to make itself more present. The individual Christian and the mission of the church and of the gospel calls for them to struggle for peace and justice in the world.

The stance also sheds light on the meaning of death for the Christian. Death seems to point to total discontinuity between this world and the next for the individual person, but in the light of the stance death can be seen in a transformationist perspective. All created reality will die, but sin has added an important negative dimension to the Christian understanding of death. Even more importantly, death is understood in the light of the mystery of the incarnation, death, and resurrection of Jesus, so that death is neither the end nor the beginning of something totally discontinuous but rather the transformation of earthly life and reality into the fullness of life and love.

The stance serves as an interpretive tool in understanding the basic mysteries of the Christian life. Especially in a sacramental and mystical perspective the Christian life is often described in terms of living out the paschal mystery of Jesus into which we are baptized. The paschal mystery can be interpreted in different ways depending on the stance. Some have interpreted it in paradoxical terms to show that life is present in the midst of death, joy in the midst of sorrow, and light in darkness. A transformationist understanding recognizes that there are some paradoxical aspects to the Christian life, but also at times God's life is known in human life, God's love in human love, God's light in human light, and God's joy in human joy. The paschal mystery understood in this perspective gives us a better understanding of Christian life and death and the relationship between the two. Life involves a constant dying to selfishness and sin to enter more fully into the resurrection, and so death itself can be seen as the moment of growth par excellence — dying to the present to enter most fully into life itself. Chapter 2 will develop the meaning of stance in greater detail.

Perhaps this is the best place to mention briefly the debate about a distinctive Christian ethic. I deny that on the level of material content (actions, virtues, attitudes, and dispositions) there is anything distinctively Christian because non-Christians can and do share the same material content of morality even to the point of such attitudes as self-sacrificing love. Unlike some others, I base this, not on a common human nature abstractly considered, but rather on the fact that in the present existential order all are called to share in the fullness of God's love. However, Christians thematize their understanding in a specifically Christian way. Since ethics, as distinguished from morality, is a thematic and systematic reflection, moral theology and Christian ethics must be based on Christian realities even though some of these (e.g., creation) are not distinctively Christian.

II. Ethical Model

The second logical step in the systematic reflection, which is moral theology, concerns the model in view of which one understands the Christian life. Three different models have been proposed in both philosophical and theological literature. The teleological model views the ethical life in terms of the goal or end to be achieved, but in the complexity of existence one distinguishes ultimate goals from intermediate and subordinate goals. Something is morally good if it is conducive to achieving the goal and is evil if it prevents the attainment of the goal. It should be pointed out that these models are very broad umbrellas. Thomas Aquinas, who begins his ethical consideration with a discussion of the last end, serves as a good example of the teleological model, but utilitarians also fit under the same model. A deontological model views the moral life primarily in terms of duty, law, or obligation. The categorical imperative of Immanuel Kant well illustrates a deontological approach to ethics. Popular Christian piety frequently adopts such an approach by making the ten commandments the basis of the moral life. The manuals of moral theology, although thinking they were in the tradition of Thomas Aquinas, by their heavy emphasis on law as the objective norm of morality and conscience as the subjective norm, belong to the deontological model. A relationality-responsibility model views the moral life primarily in terms of the person's multiple relationships with God, neighbor, world, and self and the subject's actions in this context.

I opt for a relationality-responsibility model as the primary ethical model. Such an option does not exclude some place for teleological and deontological concerns, but the relationality-responsibility model is primary and forms the perimeters within which the ethical life is discussed. There are a number of significant reasons supporting the primacy of such a model. Contemporary scriptural studies indicate that the primary ethical concept in the Old Testament is not law but covenant. The New Testament emphasis on love as at least an important ethical concern, despite its different understandings by different authors, argues for a relationality-responsibility approach. The scriptures often describe the moral life as our response to the gracious gift of God. Contemporary hermeneutics reminds us of the difficulty of finding universal moral norms in the scriptures.[11] Among Protestants a Barthian approach argued against a fundamentalistic reading of the scriptures often associated with legalism and replaced it with an understanding of the scriptures as the description of the mighty acts of God to which the believer responds. The stance reminds us of the call for the Christian to respond creatively to the contemporary situation and to make the kingdom more present. Philosophical emphases on historical consciousness, the importance of the subject, and personalism argue against the more static notion of morality as the plan of God worked out for all eternity which so often characterized Catholic understanding in the past. Although the teleological model might be more open to historicity, personalism, and the importance of the subject, still one does not have as much control over one's life as this model often supposes.

Within a relationality-responsibility model one must avoid

the danger of a narrow personalism which views the moral life only in terms of the perspective of an "I-thou" relationship. The Christian is related to God, neighbor, the world, and self. The failure to give due weight to all these relationships will distort the meaning of the Christian life. The basic reality of the Christian life has been described in different ways—love, conversion, life in Christ, the law of the Spirit. All of these descriptions can be used, but they must be understood in terms of a relationality model which includes all the aspects mentioned above.

Just as the fundamental, positive understanding of the Christian life is viewed in relational terms, so too the negative aspect of sin should be seen in the same perspective. A deontological model defines sin as an act against the law of God. A teleological model views sin as going against God, the ultimate end. But from the earliest pages of Genesis sin is described in terms of our relationship with God, neighbor, the world, and self. A contemporary theology of sin in terms of the fundamental option should also be interpreted in relational terms. Mortal sin is primarily, not an act against the law of God or going against the ultimate end, but rather the breaking of our relationship of love with God, neighbor, world, and self. Venial sin is the diminishing of these fundamental relationships. In this perspective which will be further explained in chapter 4 all the aspects of sin become apparent, especially social sin and its influence on our political, social, and economic structures.

Changes in the understanding of the sacrament of penance well illustrate the shift to a more relational model of the Christian life. In the context of a deontological ethical model the sacrament of penance was called confession from the name of the primary act—the confession of sins according to number and species. Today the sacrament is called reconciliation—a relational term which includes our multiple relationships with God, neighbor, world, and self.

The general notion of relationality-responsibility needs to be developed and spelled out as accurately as possible. On the American scene H. Richard Niebuhr has attempted a further elucidation of this basic concept. Niebuhr understands

responsibility as involving four elements—response, interpretation, accountability, and social solidarity.[12] My own development of relationality-responsibility, especially in com-
parison with Niebuhr, gives more significance to the ontological grounding of relationality and to the creative role of
the subject. Without using the term relationality-responsibility,
Daniel C. Maguire has recently proposed a method which fits
under such a model. According to Maguire one seeks to dis-
cover the moral reality on the basis of four sets of questions—
What?; Why? How? Who? When? Where?; Foreseeable effects?; Viable alternatives? The evaluation of this moral reality
involves a number of factors including creative imagination,
reason and analysis, principles, affectivity, individual experience, group experience, authority, comedy, and tragedy.[13]

A relationality-responsibility model also influences our approach to particular questions. Take the example of lying.
An older approach, based on the teleology inscribed by nature
in the faculty of speech, defined the malice of lying as frus-
trating the God-given purpose of the faculty of speech, which
according to God's plan is to express on one's lips what is in
one's mind. Within such a context it was necessary to resort
to a casuistry of mental reservations to deal with some of the
problems that arise. Lately a different approach employing
a relationality model has seen the malice of lying in the violation of my neighbor's right to truth. There are cases in which
the neighbor does not have the right to truth, and my false
speech does not involve the moral malice of lying. Similarly,
in questions of sexuality, contraception and sterilization were
condemned on the basis of the innate teleology inscribed in
the sexual faculty. To go directly against the procreative purpose of the sexual faculty is always wrong. A more relational
approach sees the sexual faculty related to the human person
and the person related to others, especially to the marriage
partner. For the good of the marriage relationship contraception or sterilization can be justified. A relationality-responsibility model not only determines our understanding of basic
moral considerations but also results in different solutions to
concrete ethical questions. Subsequent chapters make frequent
reference to this model.

III. Christian Anthropology

A third step in the development of a method for moral theology concerns Christian anthropology, or the subject existing in the midst of these multiple relationships. In ethics the basic importance of the person is twofold. First, individual actions come from the person and are expressive of the person. Actions are ethically grounded in the person placing the actions. As the scriptures remind us, the good tree brings forth good fruit, or those who live in the Spirit should produce the fruits of the Spirit. Second, the person, through one's actions, develops and constitutes oneself as a moral subject. In the transcendental terms to be developed later, through one's actions one fulfills the drive to authentic self-transcendence. Individual acts are not the most fundamental ethical category because they are both expressive of the moral subject and constitutive of the moral being of the subject.

The importance of the moral subject underscores the place of growth and development in the Christian life. The Christian is called to be perfect even as the heavenly Parent is perfect. Although the fullness of response to God's gracious gift will never be achieved, the Christian strives to grow in wisdom, age, and grace before God and human beings. The call to continual conversion also highlights the importance of growth in the Christian life. Philosophically this growth is grounded in the drive of the subject toward authentic self-transcendence. Through actions the subject continually transcends self and thereby contributes to true growth. Psychologists, too, have been paying much attention to the importance of moral growth in human life. Lawrence Kohlberg has proposed his theory of moral development involving six stages, with the last stage exemplifying postconventional morality and described as the full development of an interior, self-directed moral sense with an orientation of conscience toward ethical principles which appeal to logical comprehensiveness, universality, and consistency.[14] Catholic thinkers are appreciative of Kohlberg's work but are beginning to deal with Kohlberg in a critical way.[15] In my judgment Kohlberg's basic limits come from the formal aspect of his approach which is conditioned both by his Kantian philosophy and by his attempt to come up with a model of moral development acceptable and usable in a pluralistic context. As a result, his approach is based on the formalities of justice but does not give enough importance to content, to questions of dispositions and virtues, and to aspects other than a rationalistic understanding of justice. The critique of Kohlberg and other matters discussed in this section will be considered in greater depth in chapter 3.

Intimately connected with the person are attitudes, virtues, and dispositions, which are expressed in action and which also constitute the subject as morally good and form an essential part of the growth and development of the moral subject.[16] These dispositions or virtues affect the various relationships within which the subject finds oneself. It is impossible to describe in detail all the dispositions which should characterize the different relationships within which the Christian person exists as subject, but some of the more significant ones can be mentioned.

Traditionally the relationship of the individual to God is characterized by the three theological virtues of faith, hope, and charity. In the light of a better integrated view of the moral life of the Christian based on the stance, some other important dispositions and attitudes should be developed. The attitude of worship and thanksgiving must characterize the Christian, who recognizes God as the author of love, life, and all good gifts. The Christian is primarily a worshipper. Here one can see the intimate connection between liturgy and the moral life of the Christian. The liturgy with its celebration of the encounter of God's giving and of human response mirrors the basic structure of life. A second very fundamental attitude for the Christian is openness and receptivity to the word and work of God. The scriptures frequently allude to the importance of this basic virtue—be it done unto me according to your will. This disposition is the true humility of spirit which the scriptures portray as the great characteristic of the poor of Yahweh. The privileged people in the kingdom—the poor, children, and sinners—underscore the importance of this disposition of openness to God's saving gift. A self-sufficiency, which so often characterizes the rich, the proud, and the important, is the antithesis of the disposition of openness or true humility of spirit.

Within the traditional triad of faith, hope, and charity more importance must be given to hope than was true in the manuals of moral theology. This emphasis comes from the contemporary theological highlighting of eschatology and of the pilgrim nature of our existence. Struggle and suffering are an integral part of our existence.

Relationships to neighbor are characterized by the generic dispositions of love and justice. These general attitudes are then specified by the different relationships one has to specific neighbors — parent, friend, teacher, coworker, client, supervisor, employer, person in authority. In this context one cannot underscore enough the Christian insistence on love for the poor, the needy, and the outcast. This habitual attitude constantly calls one out of one's own narrowness and selfishness and strives to make ever broader and more universal the horizons of our love.

The relationship to the world and to earthly realities involves a number of specific relationships. The basic Christian attitude is that the goods of creation exist to serve the needs of all. The purpose of the goods of creation is to serve all God's people, and no one has a right to arrogate superfluous goods to oneself at the expense of the neighbor in need. Unfortunately an overemphasis on private property has too often blinded us to the basic attitude toward the goods of creation.[17] Selfishness and sinfulness have too often turned the goods of creation into the means of personal gratification and aggrandizement at the expense of others. The question of the best economic system is complex, but the guiding principle must be how well the system fulfills the basic principle that the goods of creation exist to serve the needs of all. An attitude of respectful gratitude for the gifts of creation serves as the basis for an environmental ethics. Our relationships with the different types of material goods will make more specific and spell out this general understanding of their universal destiny.

Our relationship to self is governed by the basic attitude of stewardship, using our gifts, talents, and selves in the living out of the Christian life. Here, too, the individual must always struggle against the opposite attitude of selfishness. As in our other relationships there is place for a proper Christian asceticism, which uses our lives, our gifts, and our bodies for the service of the kingdom and our own proper development.

IV. Decision Making and Norms

The fourth and final level of ethical reflection in describing a method for moral theology concerns concrete decision making and the morality of particular actions. In the contemporary context the two most important questions are the grounding of moral norms and the role and function of conscience, both of which will be treated at length in subsequent chapters.

There has been much discussion in Catholic moral theology, in Protestant Christian ethics, and in contemporary philosophical ethics about norms and the grounding of moral norms. Among a good number of Roman Catholic theologians throughout the world there has been a dissatisfaction with the existence of certain negative moral absolutes and the grounding of these norms in a particular understanding of natural law. In my judgment the problem arises from a concept of natural law as coinciding with the physical structure of the act, so that the physical structure of the act becomes morally normative — an act described in physical terms is said to be always and everywhere wrong. I am not saying that the physical structure of the act and the moral reality of the act cannot coincide, but the moral must include much more than merely the physical structure of the act and the grounding of the moral meaning involves more than merely a consideration of the physical structure of the act.

Many revisionist Catholic moral theologians at the present time solve the problem by distinguishing between moral evil and premoral, physical, or ontic evil, which, in the understanding of the manuals on questions such as double effect or sterilization, was called moral evil. Physical, ontic, or premoral evil can be justified if there is a commensurate or proportionate reason.[18]

In my view such an approach is in the right vein but does not go far enough. The physical is but one aspect of the moral, which is the ultimate human judgment and includes all the other aspects — the psychological, the sociological, the pedagogical, the hygenic, etc. It is necessary to unravel what is meant by premoral or ontic evil and commensurate reason. This raises the question of the different values involved. In general, norms exist to protect and promote values. But the question arises of how norms are arrived at and grounded?

Before discussing the precise way in which norms as the safeguard of values are to be grounded, a word should be said about the source of conflict situations, which bring about the tensions existing between and among different values. Again, in keeping with a general presumption in favor of complexity, there appear to be numerous sources for the conflict situations that arise and might call for modifications or exceptions in moral norms. From a strictly ethical perspective Catholic moral theology has recognized one source of conflict in its distinction between the objective moral order and the subjective. Objectively a particular act is morally wrong (e.g., drunkenness), but for this individual subject in these particular circumstances (e.g., an alcoholic) there is no subjective guilt or the guilt is greatly diminished. Philosophical ethics recognizes the same reality in its distinction between circumstances which justify an act (make it right) and circumstances which excuse an act (take away guilt without making it right).

There exist other sources of conflict situations in moral theology which can be reduced to three — eschatological tension, the presence of sin, and human finitude. Eschatological tension results from the fact that the fullness of the eschaton is not here, and in this pilgrim existence the eschatological exigencies cannot always be fully met. In this light I have argued against an absolute prohibition of divorce and remarriage.

The presence of sin in the world also causes some conflict situations. There can be no doubt that the presence of sin in the world has justified certain moral actions which would not be acceptable if there were no sin. Think of the justifications given for war, capital punishment, revolution, occult compensation. An older Catholic theology explicity recognized that the justification of private property was grounded in the fact of original sin and not in human nature as such. In the light of my stance and contention that at times Catholic moral theology has not explicitly given enough importance to the reality of sin, it seems there might be other cases in which the presence of sin might justify an action which could not be justified if sin and its effects were not present. In the past I have referred to this as the theory of compromise. Such a theory is more a theological explanation of the source of the conflict and tension rather than a tightly reasoned ethical analysis of how it is to be applied in practice. Compromise was chosen to describe this reality in order to recognize the tension between justifying such actions because of the presence of sin and the Christian obligation to try to overcome sin and its effects. However, at times in this world sin and its presence cannot be overcome — a fact which the Catholic tradition has recognized in its discussion of war and private property; but perhaps a greater emphasis on the compromise aspect of these two ethical realities might have made us more cautious in dealing with them.

A third source of tension and conflict in establishing moral norms as preservers of values stems from human finitude. Values will at times conflict and clash because it is impossible to obtain or safeguard one value without losing or diminishing another value. At the very least moral theology should recognize the sources of the conflict situations which often arise in questions involving norms. However, the recognition of the different sources of conflict does not help to resolve the question of modifications or exceptions in some norms that have been accepted as absolute in the manuals of moral theology.

In approaching the question of grounding norms much can be learned from a dialogue with contemporary philosophical ethics. The question is often phrased in terms of a deontological or teleological grounding of norms. According to the deontological grounding of norms certain actions are right or wrong no matter what the consequences. No matter how much good might result, suicide, for example, is always morally wrong. Such an approach has been called a Catholic position and certainly coincides with what has often been presented in Catholic philosophy and theology. However, some revisionist Catholic moralists maintain that norms are derived teleologically and this was true even for the Catholic understanding in the past. Norms were based on whether or not the particular action was judged good or evil for the human person and for society.

Many of the revisionist Catholic theologians, who have proposed a teleological grounding for norms, have employed an approach according to which commensurate reason can justify premoral or ontic evil and, thereby, have challenged some of the absolute norms defended in the manuals of moral theology. As a result some other Catholic theoreticians claim that such approaches are consequentialist, basing morality solely on the consequences of the action.[19]

An overview of the contemporary philosophical discussion about the grounding of norms indicates there are three different positions and not just two, but the terminology is confusing and not uniform. The one position is clearly deontological — some actions are always wrong no matter what the consequences. A second position is truly consequentialist, utilitarian, or strictly teleological and derives norms and the morality of actions solely on the basis of consequences. In this context there has been much debate about the difference between act and rule utilitarianism.

However, it is evident that there also exists a third position mediating between the two and called by different names including teleology and *prima facie* obligationalism.[20] This position rejects deontology but also disagrees with a strict teleology or consequentialism. In disagreement with strict consequentialists or utilitarians this middle position maintains the following three points: (1) moral obligations arise from elements other than consequences, e.g., promises, previous acts of gratitude or evil; (2) the good is not separate from the right; (3) the way in which the good or the evil is obtained by the agent and not just the end result is a moral consideration.

The existence of three different positions on the grounding of the moral norm indicates there are more than just two different approaches to this question. In my judgment the middle position is best described as a distinct approach based on a relationality-responsibility grounding of norms. Such a position grounds the norm on the basis of what is experienced as good for the person and for the total human society, and this on the basis of a relational criterion which gives importance to consequences but also gives moral value to aspects other than consequences.

In general, a relational grounding of the norms sees the norm as protecting and promoting values. Such an approach avoids the absolutism of a deontological approach and also the simplistic approach of a consequentialism which gives moral significance only to consequences. By highlighting the continued importance of the social dimension of human existence, such an approach recognizes that often norms are required for the good of all living together in human society.

The difference between my approach and that of Germain Grisez, a contemporary Catholic deontologist, helps to give a clearer understanding of how my approach works. According to Grisez there are eight basic human goods which the individual person can never directly go against.[21] My relational approach does not see the individual face to face with eight separate, basic goods but rather views the individual in multiple relationships with others and sees these goods as also related among themselves. At times there might be a conflict among these eight basic goods, and one might have to be sacrificed for other important values. In my methodology a relationality-responsibility model not only serves as the basic model of the Christian moral life but also grounds and establishes moral norms.

Conscience is the guide and director of the moral life of the individual. The understanding of conscience found in the manuals of moral theology can be criticized for being legalistic, minimalistic, overly rational, and too deductive. A better notion of conscience must be integrated within the understanding of the stance, model, and anthropology described above. For example, a relational model will not accept as primary the deontological understanding of conscience as the subjective norm of morality trying to conform to the objective norm of morality which is law in all its different aspects — divine, natural, and positive. Conscience is grounded in the subject, who is called to respond to the gospel message in the midst of the multiple relationships of human existence and thereby live out the thrust for authentic self-transcendence. Conscience thus partakes of the dynamism of the self-transcending subject.[22] The authentic life of the person as subject calls for self-transcendence which on the moral level reaches its fulfillment when the subject exists in a loving relationship with God, neighbor, the world, and self. An older faculty metaphysics situated conscience in the practical intellect. In my perspective conscience should be seen as an operation of the subject. In this way one can better integrate the creative and affective aspects of conscience and avoid a one-sided rationalism.

Conscience is the operation of the subject guiding and directing the moral life. Conscience is stimulated in many different ways — through parables, stories,[23] symbols, the liturgy, through the example of others as models, and through a myriad of life experiences. In its pursuit of values and self-transcendence the subject in many different ways comes to know, appreciate, love, and create the attitudes which should mark the life of the Christian. Conscience is seriously impoverished when it is reduced merely to a knowledge of the law, for it should be seen as an operation of the self-transcending subject trying to live out the fullness of the relationship with God, neighbor, the world, and self.

What about the decision of conscience about a particular action to be done here and now? In accord with a transcendental approach in the context of a relational model of ethics, the judgment of conscience is grounded ultimately in the self-transcending subject. The ultimate criterion of the truth of conscience is not conformity to the truth existing out there but is the self-transcendence of the human subject striving for authentic development. Authentic subjectivity is genuine objectivity.

The judgment of conscience is virtually unconditioned. The self-transcending subject with its thrust towards the true and the good constantly asks questions. The criterion of a true judgment exists when the subject rests at peace because there are no more pertinent questions to ask. The subject is always dealing with the data and reality before it and asking questions precisely to comprehend the moral meaning. Of course, there are dangers that the drive for authentic self-transcendence and the questioning based on it will be blunted and short-circuited, but the mature moral subject will be aware of these possible pitfalls and struggle against them.

The Christian tradition has talked about the peace and joy

of conscience as being the sign of a good conscience. A transcendental theory grounds this peace and joy in the judgment of conscience as a virtually unconditioned in which the subject, constituted by its dynamic thrust toward self-transcendence, arrives at the true and the good and is at peace. The subject rests in the achievement of the true and the good. In this whole process the self is constantly asking questions about the entire moral act, end and circumstances, and takes all the steps which are appropriate in a discerning process including prayer, reflection, and counsel.

The dilemma of conscience has always arisen from the recognition that the individual must act in accord with one's own conscience, but conscience might be wrong. The generic limitations of conscience, especially in the light of the stance, are finitude and sinfulness. The person striving for true self-transcendence must be aware of these limitations and strive to overcome them. In this context, from a purely ethical viewpoint, which is obviously strengthened in the light of Catholic ecclesiology, one can see the importance of the church as a moral teacher because by definition the community of believers guided by the Spirit through various offices and charisms exists in diverse times and places and is aided in the struggle against sin. The church helps to overcome the twofold generic limitation of human conscience.

This study has attempted to sketch the method which should be employed in moral theology, especially in the light of the cultural and academic situation in the United States. On the basis of a presupposition recognizing great complexity in the moral life in general and in the systematic reflection on that experience, four general areas of reflection have been considered — the stance, the ethical model, anthropology, and norms and concrete decision making. This chapter has attempted to compress into a few pages an overview of the approach I propose for moral theology. The reader should not expect to understand fully all that is mentioned here. The following eight chapters will try to expand and explain this approach in greater detail.

NOTES

1. John Tracy Ellis, "American Catholics and the Intellectual Life," *Thought* 30 (1955), 351-388.

2. See Ronald Stone, *Reinhold Niebuhr: Prophet to Politicians* (Nashville: Abingdon Press, 1971); also *Reinhold Niebuhr: His Religious, Social and Political Thought*, ed. Charles W. Kegley and Robert W. Bretall (New York: Macmillan Co., 1956).

3. James M. Gustafson, *Protestant and Roman Catholic Ethics: Prospects for Rapprochement* (Chicago: University of Chicago Press, 1978).

4. See, for example, *Ethics and Problems of the 21st Century*, ed. K.E. Goodpaster and K.M. Sayre (Notre Dame, Indiana: University of Notre Dame Press, 1979). On questions of justice much discussion has been sparked by John Rawls, *A Theory of Justice* (Cambridge, Mass.: Harvard University Press, 1971).

5. James Sellers, *Theological Ethics* (New York: Macmillan, 1966), pp. 29-68.

6. James M. Gustafson, *Christ and the Moral Life* (New York: Harper and Row, 1968), pp. 240-248.

7. The standard account of this movement remains Charles Howard Hopkins, *The Rise of the Social Gospel in American Protestantism, 1865-1915* (New Haven, Conn.: Yale University Press, 1940).

8. Paul Lehmann, *Ethics in a Christian Context* (New York: Harper and Row, 1963); Lehmann, *The Transfiguration of Politics* (New York: Harper and Row, 1975).

9. Jürgen Moltmann, *The Theology of Hope* (New York: Harper and Row, 1967); Moltmann, *The Crucified God* (New York: Harper and Row, 1974); Johannes B. Metz *Theology of the World* (New York: The Seabury Press, 1969); Metz, "The Future in the Memory of Suffering," *New Concilium* 76 (1972), 9-25.

10. H. Richard Niebuhr, *Christ and Culture* (New York: Harper Torchbook, 1956).

11. The way in which moral theology employs the scriptures in moral theology constitutes another very significant methodological question. I distinguish different ways in which the scriptures have an impact on the four levels discussed here — stance, ethical model, anthropology, and concrete actions and norms. For a recent discussion of this question in American Christian ethics, see Bruce C. Birch and Larry L. Rasmussen, *Bible and Ethics in the Christian Life* (Minneapolis, Minn.: Augsburg Publishing House, 1976). These authors do not consider any Catholic literature coming from outside the United States.

12. H. Richard Niebuhr, *The Responsible Self: An Essay in Christian Moral Philosophy* (New York: Harper and Row, 1963).

13. Daniel C. Maguire, *The Moral Choice* (Garden City, New York: Doubleday, 1978).

14. Kohlberg has published his stages of moral development in many

different places. For a recent elucidation, see Lawrence Kohlberg, "The Implications of Moral Stages for Adult Education," *Religious Education* 72, 2 (March-April 1977), 183-201.

15. Illustrative of this critical approach are the following: Paul J. Philibert, "Conscience: Developmental Perspectives from Rogers and Kohlberg," *Horizons* 6 (1979), 1-25; Walter E. Conn, "Post-conventional Morality: An Exposition and Critique of Lawrence Kohlberg's Analysis of Moral Development in the Adolescent and Adult," *Lumen Vitae* 30 (1975), 213-230.

16. A significant factor on the American scene is the interest by Protestant ethicians in the subject and in character. See James M. Gustafson, *Christian Ethics and the Community* (Philadelphia: Pilgrim Press, 1971), pp. 151-216; also in his *Christ and the Moral Life;* Stanley Hauerwas, *Character and the Christian Life: A Study in Theological Ethics* (San Antonio, Texas: Trinity University Press, 1975).

17. The universal destiny of the goods of creation to serve the needs of all has been highlighted in more recent statements of the hierarchical magisterium; but John A. Ryan, the leading figure in American Catholic social ethics in the first half of the twentieth century, insisted on such a first principle in his discussions of the goods of creation and the system of private property. See John A. Ryan, *Distributive Justice* (New York: Macmillan, 1916), pp. 56-60. See also Reginald G. Bender, "The Doctrine of Private Property in the Writings of Monsignor John A. Ryan" (S.T.D. dissertation, The Catholic University of America, 1973).

18. For a book of readings in English of significant articles originally written on this topic in various languages, see *Readings in Moral Theology, No. 1: Moral Norms and the Catholic Tradition*, ed. Charles E. Curran and Richard A. McCormick (New York: Paulist Press, 1979). On the American scene Richard A. McCormick has done the most to carry on a dialogue on this question of norms both with Catholic moral theologians throughout the world and with Protestant and philosophical ethicians in the United States. See especially his "Notes on Moral Theology" which appear regularly in *Theological Studies* and also *Doing Evil to Achieve Good: Moral Choice in Conflict Situations*, ed. Richard A. McCormick and Paul Ramsey (Chicago: Loyola University Press, 1978).

19. John R. Connery, "Morality of Consequences: A Theological Appraisal," *Theological Studies* 34 (1973), 396-414; reprinted in *Readings in Moral Theology, No. 1*, pp. 244-266.

20. This third or mediating position is held by a large number of philosophers. See, for example, Rawls, *A Theory of Justice,* pp. 25ff; William K. Frankena, *Ethics* (Englewood Cliffs, New Jersey: Prentice-Hall, 1963), pp. 13ff.

21. Germain Grisez, *Abortion: The Myths, the Realities and the Arguments* (New York: Corpus Books, 1970), pp. 311-321; Germain Grisez and Russell Shaw, *Beyond the New Morality: The Responsibilities of Freedom* (Notre Dame, Indiana: University of Notre Dame Press, 1974). For his critique of what he calls consequentialism, see Germain Grisez, "Against Consequentialism," *The American Journal of Jurisprudence* 23 (1978), 21-72.

22. For a detailed development of this notion of conscience, see Walter E. Conn, *Conscience, Development and Self-Transcendence* (Birmingham, Alabama: Religious Education Press, 1981).

23. For a strong insistence on the importance of story, see Stanley Hauerwas, with Richard Bondi and David B. Burrell, *Truthfulness and Tragedy: Further Investigations into Christian Ethics* (Notre Dame, Indiana: University of Notre Dame Press, 1977), especially pp. 15-98.

2. The Stance of Moral Theology

This chapter concerns the most fundamental question in moral theology — the stance which serves as the starting point of moral theology by forming the perspective with which Christian ethics or moral theology reflects on human life and actions in the world. The same stance or horizon plays a similarly important role in the practical life of the Christian so that the question pursued here has both theoretical and practical importance.

Some Proposed Stances

In his *Theological Ethics*, James Sellers raises the question of the stance of Christian ethics as logically the first consideration.[1] Sellers admits that one does not necessarily have to begin ethics with this question, as is exemplified in the case of Reinhold Niebuhr, who began with temporal actions and especially the injustices existing in the life of society. Not only is stance the most fundamental question in Christian ethics, but it serves as a source of other ethical criteria. Sellers, however, would not maintain that the other criteria are merely deduced from the stance. Sellers also describes the stance as the servant of the gospel although it can never be adequate to the whole gospel. Finally, the stance is always subject to revision in the light of the gospel and of the changing times.[2]

Sellers rejects the more traditional approach by Orthodox Protestantism which made faith the stance for Christian ethics. *Sola fide* (By faith alone) was a most fundamental considera-

tion even in Protestant ethics. Faith as a stance is rejected
by Sellers for two reasons: 1) *Sola fide* implies an altogether
passive view of human beings who merely receive the gift of
God, but it does not pay enough attention to the active and
creative role women and men are called upon to play in our
ageric society. 2) Faith as a stance introduces a cleavage between faith and the cultural and the social life. The theologian
today places more stress on the worldly and temporal aspects
of life in the world.[3]

The standard alternative to faith as a stance in Protestant
ethics has been love, but Sellers also rejects love as the stance.
The word love has been battered and poorly understood on
the one hand by the biblical theologians who have made love
something almost humanly impossible and, on the other hand,
by the sentimentalists who have reduced love to trivialities.
The ultimate reality in the Christian life is not love but
redemption, and love is the qualitatively highest mode of attaining the goal of redemption.[4]

Love continues to be proposed very often as the stance for
Christian ethics, but there are also other problems connected
with love as the stance for moral theology. No one can deny
the high priority which Christian ethics should give to love,
but love as the fundamental stance is another question. One
aspect of the problem is the nature of the stance itself. As the
logical starting point for ethical reflection the stance must be
comprehensive enough to include all the aspects of Christian
ethics and yet limited enough to serve as a foundational point
and a source of further criteria. One wonders if any content
aspect of the Christian experience, whether it be love, hope,
humility, or any particular virtue can ever serve as the stance
for moral theology. H. Richard Niebuhr realized the difficulty
of finding any one virtue which gives the key to the life of
Jesus and his followers. Niebuhr see the uniqueness of Jesus
in terms not of any one virtue but in terms of his unique relationship with God. Thus Niebuhr disagrees with much of
Protestant liberalism which had equivalently made love the
stance for Christian ethics.[5]

The question of love as stance was raised a few years ago
in the light of the situation ethics debate especially as centered
on the ethics proposed by Joseph Fletcher. On a popular level

there is an untested assumption that love is the stance for moral theology, but again there remains here the danger of not understanding precisely what is the meaning and function of stance. Fletcher unhesitating makes love the starting point, the boss principle, and the only thing that ultimately counts in his ethics. He succinctly summarized his approach in six propositions.[6] The debate on situation ethics occasioned by Fletcher's book has brought to light some problems and difficulties with love as the fundamental stance for moral theology.[7]

If love is to have such an all encompassing role, then it seems to take on many different and even contradictory meanings. Donald Evans, who is basically sympathetic to a situational approach to morality, claims that Fletcher gives four conflicting accounts of love. The one moral test of an action is whether it increases love. Secondly, love is an attitude of good will. Thirdly, love is what the agent does. Fourthly, love is a faculty by means of which the agent discerns what one is to do.[8] Basil Mitchell argues that in ethics love is not enough. Love requires thought, and specifically moral thought; but also love requires some decision as to what human ends are or are not worth seeking.[9] Mitchell begins his essay with the common sense observation, illustrated by a parlor game, that one is faced with two possible alternatives neither of which is helpful to the ethicist who wants to enshrine love as the stance for Christian ethics — either there are some sorts of actions that cannot be performed lovingly or there are no actions that cannot be performed lovingly.[10]

These comments generally work from the same basic assumption that love, or for that matter any one virtue, cannot encompass all the things that go into ethical considerations. It is too simplistic to reduce all morality to love. Evans and Mitchell are not speaking specifically about love as the stance understood in our exact sense, but their criticisms stem from the fact that it is too simplistic to reduce everything to love. I cannot accept love as the stance for Christian ethics precisely for the same basic reason — the stance really cannot be equated with any one aspect or any one attitude of the Christian life no matter how important it is.

Another set of problems arises from the fact that there is great disagreement about the exact meaning of love and the different elements involved in love. Fletcher, for example, claims that he is talking about love as *agape* and not love as *philia* (friendship love) or *eros* (romantic love).[11] I would argue that love must contain all three of these aspects and cannot be just pure *agape* as separated from and distinquished from any concept of reciprocity and self-fulfillment. Although in his description Fletcher draws a very exalted concept of *agape*, in practice it does not seem to be all that different from other forms of human wisdom.

The fact remains that love is a very complicated reality and includes many different aspects. Some theories of love appear inadequate precisely because they do not include certain elements that cannot be excluded. There has been a long debate in the history of Christian ethics about the exact relationship of human love and Christian love which shares in the *agape* of God. The Catholic tradition following in the footsteps of Augustine has always seen Christian love as incorporating the best of human love.[12] In the strict position of Lutheran Protestantism, Anders Nygren sees Christian love as altogether different from human love.[13] One can also ask if love of God and love of neighbor are the same thing. The seemingly simply reality of Christian love raises a number of significant and important questions about its precise meaning and the elements it includes.

After rejecting love as the stance, Sellers proposes his own stance. Salvation or redemption for contemporary human beings is best understood in terms of wholeness, but the pilgrim as yet does not fully possess this wholeness and is searching for it. Our way to wholeness has been presented in the Scriptures as pilgrimage. "The Judaeo-Christian faith, then, offers a distinctive understanding of what is happening to man: he is moving from promise to fulfillment."[14] The stance for Christian ethics is thus promise and fulfillment.

I have difficulty accepting the stance proposed by Sellers for the precise reason that he gives too great a role to fulfillment in Christian ethics. Perhaps the ultimate reason for the difference lies in two different views of eschatology and the possibility of fulfillment in this world. Sellers insists in a number of places that this fulfillment will take place in finitude, temporality and spatiality — in the world.[15] At times Sellers is willing to admit that there might be something beyond this life in terms of fulfillment, but he is interested in fulfillment only in this world.[16] I would hold for fulfillment only outside time and beyond history. In this world there seems to be more promise than fulfillment both in terms of the biblical witness and in the light of human experience.

One could interpret the biblical message as being opposed to the stance proposed by Sellers. Paul Ramsey, for example, on the basis of biblical considerations refuses to accept any ethical methodology that depends on the Christian's attaining certain goals or ends. Ramsey is opposed to any teleological basis for Christian ethics. "Eschatology has at least this significance for Christian ethics in all ages: that reliance on producing *teloi*, or on doing good consequences, or on goal seeking has been decisively set aside. The meaning of obligation or of right action is not to be derived from any of these ends-in-view in an age that is fast being liquidated."[17] Ramsey also understands the biblical concept of covenant as emphasizing the aspect of promise and fidelity much more than the note of fulfillment.[18]

I would interpret both these eschatologies as somewhat extreme. With Sellers I would give more importance than Ramsey to this world, its continuity with the future and the human vocation to work for building the new heaven and the new earth. But I think Sellers has wrongly collapsed the eschatological tension into a realized eschatology, for human fulfillment lies ultimately outside time, history and space. There is also discontinuity between this world and the next. Sellers has too optimistic a view of the possibility of true human fulfillment in this world, and thus his proposed stance seems inadequate.

James M. Gustafson raises the same basic question in terms of the perspective or the posture as the fundamental angle of vision which the Christian gospel requires. The words perspective and posture each refer to something which is basic. Perspective, drawn from the visual experience, ultimately refers to the state of the viewing subject. Posture has developed from its use in describing the arrangement of the parts of the body to now suggest the basic characteristic of a person, one's fundamental state or frame of mind.[19] The perspective or posture for the Christian is Jesus Christ. Jesus Christ as the revealer of God is the One through whom the ultimate meaning of life is known and understood. Jesus Christ is the focal point of the Christian community, and he remains the common object of loyalty for all Christians.[20]

I have some difficulties in accepting Jesus Christ as the basic stance, posture or perspective of Christian ethics. Some Protestant theologians (not Gustafson) employing, at least implicitly, Jesus Christ as the stance of Christian ethics adopt an unacceptable Christological monism. A Christological monism so emphasizes the centrality and importance of Jesus Christ that it does not give enough importance to other aspects of the moral perspective of the Christian. If Jesus Christ becomes the only way into the ethical question not enough importance is given to the reality of creation and all those things that have some meaning and intelligibility even apart from the explicit redemption in Jesus Christ. Some Christian ethics thus rule out any other source of ethical wisdom and knowledge for the Christian except Jesus Christ. Such a vision (which, I repeat, is not Gustafson's) is too narrow and exclusive.

There is no doubt that in a certain sense Jesus Christ is what is most distinctive about Christian life and ethics, but there is a danger that too exclusive an emphasis on what is distinctive in Christian ethics will not do justice to what the Christian shares with all humanity. Especially with the realization that Christians constitute a minority of humankind, one might be somewhat hesitant to take as the perspective of Christian ethics what could be construed in so exclusive a way as to neglect the elements which Christians share with all others.

The fact that there can be different ways of understanding Jesus Christ as the stance or posture of Christian ethics points to a problem which is even true with regard to Gustafson's use of Jesus Christ. As such, Jesus Christ as stance needs some further elaboration and development. Obviously any stance would need such elaboration, but one wonders if this stance says both too much and too little.

In reflecting on this whole question of stance it might seem quite unusual that faith, love and Jesus Christ have all been rejected as the proper stance for Christian ethics. In no way does this deny the importance of all these realities, but the stance has some specific functions to fulfill. It is the logically prior first question in ethics which is comprehensive enough to include all that should be included and yet gives some direction and guidance in terms of developing other ethical criteria. There will never be the perfect stance, but some seem more adequate than others in terms of the function the stance should fulfill in moral theology. To adequately judge any stance it is necessary to see precisely how it does function in practice, but the ones proposed thus far do not seem to fulfill the role of stance as well as the one about to be proposed.

In talking about the stance, posture or perspective of moral theology, I would add the term horizon to try to further clarify the meaning and function of what is being discussed. Bernard Lonergan understands horizon as a maximum field of vision from a determinate viewpoint. Horizon thus includes both an objective pole and a subjective pole.[21] The use of the term horizon allows one to emphasize the importance of the subject as well as the object in the question of stance. The horizon forms the way in which the subject looks at reality and structures one's understanding of the world and reality. Horizon indicates that what we are talking about is not necessarily in terms primarily of content or of object, but rather a formal structuring of the way in which the individual views reality. Christian ethics and the Christian in my judgment must view reality in terms of the Christian mysteries of creation, sin, incarnation, redemption and resurrection destiny.

The stance or horizon must be comprehensive enough to include all the elements which enter into the way in which the Christian understands reality and the world. Problems arise whenever one adopts a stance which does not include all the elements which should enter into the Christian perspective on life in this world. These five mysteries point to the five aspects which together form the proper stance or horizon for Christian ethics and for the individual Christian in one's life. This chapter will explicate and develop the horizon of Christian ethics in terms of this fivefold aspect of creation, sin, incarnation, redemption and resurrection destiny. This stance must serve as a critique of ethical approaches and as a criterion for developing more adequate approaches in moral theology. The stance is not the only question to be considered in the methodology of moral theology, but it is logically the first and primary consideration. One must judge the ultimate adequacy of the stance in terms of how it does fulfill its function. Obviously there are many theological and ethical presuppositions which also influence the stance which one employs, but the following description and application of the stance should bring to light many of the presuppositions involved in the proposed stance.

The five aspects taken together form the horizon for moral theology. This essay will proceed by investigating each of the aspects and showing the insufficiency of those approaches which have forgotten one of the aspects or have given proportionately too much importance to what is only one aspect of the total horizon. Thus in the course of the development the way in which the five aspects are related to one another should become clarified.

Creation

The Christian believes that God has created this world and that creation is good. The work of creation then serves as a basis for ethical wisdom and knowledge for the Christian. All people share the same humanity and world created by God, and by reflecting on the work of God they can arrive at some ethical wisdom and knowledge. The Christian who accepts the basic goodness of creation and its continuing validity has a source of ethical wisdom which exists outside the pale of explicit Christianity and which one thus shares with all humanity. In Roman Catholic theology, the theological presuppositions of the natural law theory accepted such an understanding of creation. The natural law is the participation of the eternal law in the rational creature. God has implanted and written God's law in the hearts of all human beings.[22] The terminology appears to me to be too deontological in tone, but it points to the basic understanding of a common ground morality based on creation. In such a generic approach the Scriptures are not the only source of ethical wisdom for the Christian.

The realization that on the basis of creation the Christian

shares ethical wisdom and insights with non-Christians has important ramifications both theoretically and practically. Theoretically such an approach affects the basic methodology of moral theology, for the Scriptures or Jesus Christ are not the only way into the ethical questions for the Christian. Catholic teaching and theology have followed such a generic approach in using the ethical wisdom and knowledge common to all because of their human nature. Many of the recent papal encyclicals especially in the area of social justice have been addressed to all people of good will.[23] The methodological tone of these teachings is such that non-Christians could find them congenial, and even if they might not agree they could argue on human and rational grounds with the teaching proposed by the Popes. In *Pacem in Terris* John XXIII explicitly explains the methodological approach of the encyclical in terms of the law which the creator has written in the hearts of all human beings.[24] Such an ethical methodology does not usually begin with the Scriptures or Jesus Christ, even though these may be used in a confirming and supplemental way.

The Declaration on Religious Freedom of the Second Vatican Council well illustrates this type of methodology. The teaching on religious liberty is based on the dignity of the human person existing in civil society. The first chapter of the document proves the right to religious liberty on the basis of reason and does not invoke revelation or the Scriptures. The second and final chapter tries to show that the teaching on religious liberty has its roots in divine revelation, and for that reason Christians are bound to respect it all the more conscientiously.

The methodology of Vatican II differs from the approach of the documents of the World Council of Churches which treat of religious liberty. The World Council of Churches teaching antedates the Vatican Council teaching by many years, but also employs a different approach. The "Declaration on Religious Liberty" of the Amsterdam Assembly of 1948 sees religious liberty as an implication of the Christian faith and of the world-wide nature of Christianity. The rights which Christian discipleship demands are such as are good for all people. Religious freedom is required as an outward protection and an expression of that freedom by which Christ has set us free.[25] The "Statement on Religious Liberty" issued at New Delhi in 1961 holds a distinctive Christian basis for religious liberty which is still regàrded as a fundamental right for people existing everywhere. The Christian basis is the fact that God's redemptive dealing with us is not coercive. The freedom given us by God in Christ Jesus implies a free response on our part.[26]

Interestingly, in the course of Vatican II a number of bishops wanted to change the proposed draft on religious freedom so that it would be more firmly rooted in the Scriptures and in revelation. These bishops were committed to the newer approach to religious liberty, but they wanted a methodology which would be more expressly Christian and biblical. These bishops were unsuccessful in their attempt.[27] The approaches of Vatican II and the World Council of Churches with their different starting points on religious liberty well illustrate the two different approàches, but there could be some convergence depending on the way in which the other source of ethical wisdom is employed. Some Protestant theologians, for example, would add no arguments or reasons based on things common to all women and men, whereas others would be willing to introduce these arguments, but usually in a more secondary role.

The practical implications of the recognition that Christians share ethical wisdom and knowledge with all humanity because they share the same human nature involve the recognition that Christians do not have a monopoly on ethical insights and wisdom, but rather Christians must constantly be in dialogue with all other people. The acceptance of the goodness of creation and the possibility of deriving ethical knowledge from God's creation gives to moral theology a universalism. At times in practice the Roman Catholic Church has forgotten this basic insight implied in its theological methodology. An authoritarian approach to natural law coupled with an overemphasis on the rights of the Church as the authentic interpreter of the natural law prevented the type of dialogue and discussion with science, philosophy, art and culture which in principle was accepted by the ethical methodology proposed in the Catholic tradition. If one takes seriously the fact that all human beings share the same humanity and can arrive at some true ethical conclusions, then dialogue becomes an absolutely necessary aspect of our existence as Christians. Of course, this does not imply that one blindly accepts what others or a majority of people are doing.

I maintain that Roman Catholic theology was correct in asserting that Christians share a great deal of ethical wisdom with all humankind on the basis of creation, but unfortunately the Catholic tradition has not always satisfactorily solved the problem of the relationship between this ethical wisdom and the knowledge which is derived from the specifically Christian source of revelation. Too often the natural was distinguished from the supernatural as the bottom layer common to all, on top of which is now added a layer of the supernatural. This poor concept of the relationship between the two contributed to the fact that human life in the world and society was seen primarily in terms of the natural law but did not appear to have much bearing on our supernatural destiny. The somewhat rigid separation of the past between the natural and the supernatural has had disastrous effects both in theory and in practice in the life of the Roman Church. There are many attempts being made today to develop a better understanding of this relationship in general and specifically the relationship between the ethical wisdom and knowledge which is common to all and that which is specifically Christian.

Those theologians who deny the existence for the Christian of a source of ethical wisdom and knowledge which the Christian shares with all people have proposed different reasons. Three of the more fundamental reasons will be considered here.

The first reason stems from the overinsistence in Protestant theology on the famous axiom *Scriptura sola*, Scripture alone. There is an obvious connection between the insistence on Scripture alone and the insistence on faith alone as the stance for moral theology. Sellers recognizes such a connection and rejects both of them.[28] Some Protestant theologians have so interpreted the Scripture alone axiom as to deny the possibility of any true ethical wisdom being derived from a non-Scriptural source. It seems that to a certain extent Martin Luther, but especially John Calvin, did not entirely reject the idea of a natural law, but in both scientific and popular expression Protestant thought has in some cases denied the existence of any ethical wisdom which does not come from the Scripture.[29] Roman Catholic theology, with its emphasis on faith and reason, Scripture and tradition, has never in theory denied the existence of ethical wisdom outside the Scriptures. The major problem in Roman Catholic ethics has been the failure to give enough importance to the scriptural aspect in its reflection on the Christian life.

A second reason for denying a source of ethical wisdom based on the creation which all creatures share stems from a theology of sin. Sin has affected the world and human reason. Christian theology readily acknowledges that creation no longer exists in its state of goodness but has been affected by sin. Even our everyday experience reminds us how sin continues to affect our reason so that often our prejudices and biases are rationalized away. Some theologians in the Protestant tradition, especially the Lutheran tradition, claim that sin has so affected creation and human reason that these can no longer serve as a source of positive ethical knowledge for the Christian. "In this whole problem of the natural, and specifically in the question of the possibility or the impossibility of a recognizable order of being, I see a basic difference between Roman Catholic and Reformation theology. For the possibility or impossibility of working back to the eternal order depends upon the understanding of sin, upon the degree to which we think the being of our world is altered and impaired by the rest of the fall."[30]

Thielicke here expresses quite succinctly the difference between Roman Catholic and some forms of Protestant theology, but there would be many other Protestants who would not accept Thielicke's approach. For Thielicke the natural law is not the participation of the eternal law in the rational creature so that creation is a source of positive ethical information even for the Christian, but rather in the *sinful* world in which we live we can at least negatively learn what we should not do if we want to preserve our existence in the fallen world. What Catholic theology calls the natural law, Thielicke would call the orders of preservation in this sinful world.[31] In my judgment Thielicke overemphasizes the reality of sin so that it completely takes away the basic goodness and positive meaning of creation. Roman Catholic theology, as will be explained later, has distorted reality by not giving enough importance to sin and its effects in our world.

A third theological reason for denying the existence of true moral wisdom which the Christian shares with all women and men on the basis of creation derives from a fundamental presupposition of Barthian theology and ethics. Paul Lehmann also advocates such an approach to Christian ethics. Lehmann summarizes the Barthian position that the difference between Christian and philosophical ethics is unbridgeable not because Christian ethics rejects philosophical ethics but because philosophical ethics rejects Christian ethics. The grace of God protests against every humanly established ethic as such. For Barth, a theological ethic must include all ethical truth under the rubric of the grace of God.[32] The later Barth, however, does not see this grace of God as denying and condemning the human but rather as affirming and saying yes to the human.[33]

The position that includes all ethical wisdom under Christ and the grace of God in Christ Jesus is in keeping with a basic Barthian assumption that one must begin theology with God and not with any creature. Barth staunchly maintains that one cannot go from creation to God, but rather must begin with God and God's Word to us. Barth is thus opposed to natural law, natural theology and even religion. In the Barthian understanding religion is the creation of humanity's own wants, needs, hopes, and desires. Religion, by beginning with the human, commits the great blasphemy of ultimately making God into the image and likeness of human beings. Once Barthian theology refuses to go from the human to God, the only possible procedure is to start with God and God's revelation to obtain a proper understanding of humanity and the world.[34]

Again, there is some truth in the fact that distortions do occasionally arise in going from the creature and the human to God if one forgets the discontinuity that exists between the human and the divine. Think for example of how we usually think of God in terms of our own culture, our own sex and our own racial color. Barthian theology, however, goes too far in denying the possibility of any valid moral truth that can be derived from creation and human nature and by insisting that we arrive at ethical wisdom only by hearing the Word and command of God.

In recent theology especially in the United States there appears to be a growing convergence even among Protestant theologians on the existence of a common ground morality which the Christian shares with all humanity.[35] This also indicates a similarity in the ethical methodology employed by both Protestant and Catholic theologians thus overcoming some of the differences of the past. The Christian horizon with its acceptance of creation recognizes the basic goodness of creation and its continuing validity because of which it can serve as a source of moral wisdom, but at the same time such a vision must also realize the imperfections, limitations and sinfulness of the creation as it exists today.

Sin

The second aspect of the stance for Christian ethics concerns the reality of sin and its effects on human beings and the world in which we live. The Christian faith has pointed out the sinful condition of humanity which serves as the backdrop for the redeeming act of God. Even after redemption the Christian fails to live in accord with the fullness of the new life received through Christ Jesus. Protestant theology has constantly reminded us of the sinful condition of the believer even after one has responded in faith to God's loving gift. In the more Orthodox forms of Protestantism the stress on the sinfulness of the believer and one's inability to perform good deeds cohered with its *sola fide* and *sola Scriptura* approach. The emphasis was on the transcendence and power of God while the human being was considered to be incapable of good works on one's own. Whatever good works the believer performed were the gift of God and from God's grace. By exalting the transcendence of God, a much less positive role was given to human beings. Even after baptism the believer was viewed as *simul justus et peccator* (at the same time sinner and justified) who is saved by faith and not by works.[36]

The Roman Catholic theology of justification has argued for a transformation and change of the person so that one now becomes a new creature. Contemporary Catholic scholars realize, however, that there is truth in the realization that the Christian remains *simul justus et peccator*, and they are striving to understand this in a way which is compatible with the Roman Catholic tradition and belief.[37] In general, one might summarize the theological approaches to the reality of sin by noting that while some forms of Orthodox Protestantism have overstressed the totality and effects of sin, Catholic theology has generally not given enough importance to sin. This essay will now illustrate how Catholic theology, together with some aspects of Protestant theology, and Catholic life especially in the decade of the 1960s failed to give enough importance to the reality of sin.

The encyclical *Pacem in Terris* well illustrates the failure of Roman Catholic theology to realize the existence of sin in the world. A theology which does not come to grips with the existence of sin will tend to be dangerously naive and romantically optimistic — dangers which are to some extent present in *Pacem in Terris*. The very title of the encyclical indicates the penchant for a too one-sidedly optimistic understanding. I do not think there will ever be perfect peace on earth. History reminds us that humanity has constantly known the lack of peace, and our own experience of the last few years shows that peace on earth is still far distant from the world in which we live. The Christian vision with its understanding of eschatology and the realization that sin will always be part of our human existence will never hope to find the fullness of peace within history.

For one who acknowledges the continuing reality of sin in our world, there is need to recognize that the existence of sin can never become an excuse for an easy acceptance of the situation as we know it. Christians are called upon to continue to struggle against sin and in the power of the Risen Jesus to overcome the reality of sin if at all possible. Christians can never use the existence of sin as an excuse for acquiescing in the injustices and ills that afflict our contemporary world. As human beings and Christians we are called upon to work for peace, and can and should do much more than is now being done. The fullness of peace in all its ramifications, however, will always elude our grasp. The very title of Pope John's encyclical thus appears somewhat distorted in the light of the full Christian vision of reality. The 1983 pastoral letter of the American bishops has a more appropriate title — *The Challenge of Peace: God's Promise and Our Response.*

In the Introduction Pope John explains the methodology which he will employ in the encyclical. The creator of the world has imprinted in human hearts an order which conscience reveals to us and enjoins us to obey. The laws governing the relationships between human beings and states are to be found in human nature where the Parent of all things wrote them.[38] In the final introductory paragraph the Pope explains that these laws teach citizens how to conduct their mutual dealings, show how the relationships between citizens and public authority should be regulated, indicate how states should deal with one another, and finally manifest how individual citizens, states and the community of all people should act towards each other.[39] These four considerations are the skeleton outline of the encyclical which then develops the teaching on each of these points in the four main parts of the encyclical.

In a certain sense what Pope John says is true, but there is something else in the heart of human beings — disorder or what Christians have called sin. A glance at the world around us only too easily confirms the existence of these disorders even in the four areas in which the encyclical stresses the existence of order. The vision of the papal teaching is somewhat unreal if it does not take into account this sinful aspect of reality. There is definitely order and the possibility for a greater order in the world, but there remains the obstacle of sin which any realistic ethic must consider. One perhaps could argue that Pope John was talking about the ideal and urging people to live up to that ideal without descending into the very concrete ways in which this is to be accomplished. Perhaps there is some validity in such a defense of *Pacem in Terris*, but if the encyclical is to serve as a realistic guide for life in our society, then it must at least recognize the persistent reality of sin and how sin will affect our world and our actions. One must always talk about the ideal towards which all must strive, but a realistic assessment of the obstacles is necessary for the completeness of the teaching.

Whereas some forms of Protestant theology have overemphasized the reality of sin, Catholic theology generally has not given enough importance to sin. In ethics the natural law theory tended to forget sin. A poor understanding of nature and supernature understood sin as depriving human beings of our supernature, but leaving our nature intact. Thus sin did not really affect human nature. In parts of the Catholic theological tradition it was constantly maintained that through sin the individual was wounded in things pertaining to human nature (*vulneratus in naturalibus*), but this did not completely destroy one's humanity.[40] However, in moral theology this wounded nature was not given enough attention.

The better part of the Catholic theological tradition realized that nature did not refer to what is historically existing at the present time after the fall, but rather to that metaphysical understanding of what humanity is in all possible states of salvation history. This basic nature was then modified by the historical circumstances of the state in which it exists; for example, the state of fallen nature or the state of redeemed nature.[41] Even in such an understanding it appears that not enough importance is given to the realities of sin and grace in the history of salvation. In the more popular understanding, which was generally presupposed in the manuals of moral theology, the effects of sin on humanity were definitely underdeveloped. Such a theology was poorly equipped for coming to grips with the presence of sin and the surd in our human life.

There have been aspects of Protestant theology which have also forgotten the reality of sin. Twice in the present century trends in Protestant theology have ignored to their own peril the reality of sin. Protestant liberal theology arose in the nineteenth century in reaction to the somewhat negative approach of Orthodox Protestantism with its stress on the transcendence of God and the sinfulness of human beings.[42] A very popular form of liberal theology was the social gospel movement which reached its zenith in the United States in the early decades of the twentieth century.[43] Liberalism stressed the humanity of Jesus and understood him primarily in ethical terms. The individual Christian is no longer thought of as a sinner who passively receives the gift of salvation but rather as a free person with responsibility to build the kingdom of God on earth. The notions of evolution and progressive development fit in with the liberal conception of an optimistic eschatology which inclined towards a progressivistic view of history. The kingdom of God and its progress readily become identified with human and scientific progress. Liberal theology looked to the prophets and Jesus as the great biblical figures who call human beings to work for bringing about the kingdom of God in history.[44]

In general this teaching with its emphasis on immanence, progressivism and human moral effort and responsibility forgot the reality of sin. H. Richard Niebuhr in a somewhat exaggerated way pointed out the one-sidedness of liberal Protestant theology. "In its one-sided view of progress which saw the growth of the wheat but not that of the tares, the gathering of the grain but not the burning of the chaff, this liberalism was indeed naively optimistic. A God without wrath brought men without sin into a kingdom without judgment through the ministrations of a Christ without a cross."[45]

The omissions of liberal theology became even more glaring in the light of the historical circumstances of the day. The First World War burst the bubble of any progressivistic dream of a world that was becoming better and better in every way and every day. The war was the sign of inhumanity, human greed, selfishness and inability to live in peace with others. It was no mere accident that in Europe Karl Barth reacted against the liberal theology in his commentary on the Epistle to the Romans which was first published in 1919. The naively optimistic theology of liberal Protestantism was not all that convincing in the aftermath of World War I. The early Barth reemphasized the transcendence of God and saw the Word of God as a negative judgment on human existence. A short time later while still holding on to transcendence Barth saw the Word of God not so much as judging but rather affirming and saying "Yes" to the human.[46]

In the United States the major theological attack against Liberalism and the social gospel was launched by Reinhold Niebuhr in his *Moral Man and Immoral Society* published in 1932. "Insofar as this treatise has a polemic interest it is directed against the moralists, both religious and secular, who imagine that the egoism of individuals is being progressively checked by the development of rationality or the growth of a religiously inspired goodwill and that nothing but the continuance of this process is necessary to establish social harmony between all the human societies and collectivities."[47] Niebuhr castigates this liberal theology for its failure to realize the brutal character of human behavior especially in terms of class egoism.[48]

The tendency within liberal Protestant theology to forget the reality of sin became evident again in the 1960s. In some versions of a theology of the secular and in the death of God movement there was a denial or at least a downplaying of the role of sin with the resulting overly optimistic view of reality and the world, as well as human capabilities for bringing about quick and radical change. Harvey Cox, for example, did not deny the fact of sin, but he interpreted it in such a way that sin was viewed primarily in terms of apathy or failure to take responsibility for the world. Sloth is the traditional name for this sin.[49] This remains one aspect of sin, but one must also recognize that human beings too often use their power for the exploitation of others and for their own aggrandizement. Pride is the traditional name for such an understanding of sin.

Others went much further than Cox in reducing the emphasis on sin. Perhaps the most illustrative example of this approach is William Hamilton's essay, "The New Optimism — from Prufrock to Ringo." Hamilton believes that pessimism does not persuade anymore, for there is an increased sense of the possibilities of human action, human happiness, human decency in this life. Hamilton wants to establish a new mood of optimism based not on grace but on a worldly optimism that believes it can change the human conditions that bring about fear and despair.[50] Hamilton sees the "State of the Union" address of President Lyndon B. Johnson in January 1965 as an example of this new optimism and the new possibilities open to humanity. Allowing for political rhetoric, Hamilton still claims that Johnson's invitation to accept revolutionary changes in the world was believable.[51] A few intervening years have apparently decimated Hamilton's thesis. Theologians such as John Macquarrie[52] and Roger Shinn[53] have called attention to the failure of secular theology to give enough attention to human sinfulness.

Not only Catholic theology and some trends in Protestant theology but also Catholic life especially in the aftermath of Vatican II tended to deny in practice sin and its effects. A naive optimism often characterized Catholic life in the 1960s. The encouraging reforms of Vatican II seemingly provided an impetus for the possibilities of massive reform and renewal both within and outside the Church. Disillusionment, however, quickly followed as this reform movement was not able to accomplish such grandiose schemes. The whole process of reform and growth is much more complicated and difficult to attain than many had realized in the warm afterglow of Vatican II.

A romantic understanding of reality with its over-optimism tends to idealize and easily forgets about the harsh and difficult side of reality. Romanticism frequently has a tendency to idealize the past as the perfect time in which there was no tension, frustration or division. In Christianity this romanticization often takes the form of an uncritical understanding of the circumstances of the primitive Church.

A few years ago I was asked to criticize a paper which set forth the plans and rationale for the senate of priests in one of the large archdioceses of the United States. The document began with a consideration of the Church as found in the Acts of the Apostles with the implication that this should be somehow normative for the way in which the Church functions today. The priests' senate is a vehicle for the bishop in union with the priests to serve the people of God. The Acts of the Apostles bears witness to the great unity and community existing in the early Church. Christians were known by their service of others and by their love. They gathered together for the breaking of the bread as the sign of that unity of love which they lived out in their daily existence. So too the Church today on the local level must be this community of love and service united around the bishop and characterized by their mutual sharing and service which is symbolically represented in their breaking the bread together.

Again there is some truth in such a picture, but it is not the whole story even as this is recorded for us in the literature of the primitive Church community. Also such a naively romantic view of the past can too easily occasion disillusionment when the reality of the present falls so far short of such a picture. The primitive Church obviously knew the struggles and tensions which the Church community will always experience.

Paul felt the need to stand up to Peter and rebuke him for his attitude towards the Gentile converts (Gal. 2:11–21). Ananias and Sapphira are reported as lying to Peter and holding back some of their funds for themselves, all the while giving others the impression that they were sharing their goods with the community (Acts 5:1–11). Paul and Barnabas were unable to agree on whom they wanted to accompany them on their missionary journeys so they were forced to split up (Acts 15:36–41). Apparently at times there also arose problems at the meetings of the early community in terms of some members not being willing to share with others and thus seemingly acting against the real meaning of *agape* (1 Cor. 11:20–22). One must avoid a naive romanticism that enshrines the past as an ideal time, when in reality the past, like the present and the future, will always know the problems and tensions of life in the Christian community, which Christian tradition sees as affected by human sinfulness.

To acknowledge the reality and effects of sin does not demand a negative, pessimistic and despairing worldview. By no means. Sin is not so total in its effects that it destroys the goodness of creation. Some forms of Orthodox Protestant theology, especially in the Lutheran tradition, have overemphasized the reality of sin so that it pervades and even destroys the goodness of creation. Creation remains as a true but limited source of ethical wisdom for the Christian existing today. Sin can never be the last word or the ultimate or the most influential word for the Christian who believes that the redemptive love of Jesus Christ has conquered and overcome sin. Even now by our participation in the paschal mystery we are called upon to share in Christ's struggle with sin but also in this world to some extent we can also partially share in Christ's triumph over sin. The fullness of redemption will only come outside history, but in the meantime we are called to share in the fellowship of Jesus' sufferings and in the power of his resurrection. Sin thus has an important but somewhat limited place in the Christian view of reality.

The failure of Roman Catholic theology and life to give

enough importance to sin not only produces at times an overly simplistic view of progress and development with a corresponding failure to consider all the elements and obstacles which are present, but also has influenced the way in which Catholic moral theology deals with certain concrete ethical problems. Elsewhere I have developed a theory of compromise theology precisely because of the inadequacy of Catholic ethics to come to grips with sin-filled situations. Sometimes the presence of sin in the world will force one to do something which, if there were no sin present, should not be done.[54] This is just another illustration of the fact that in Roman Catholic theology there has been a built-in tendency not to give enough importance to the reality of sin.

Incarnation

The third aspect of the stance for moral theology is furnished by the Christian mystery of the incarnation. The incarnation by proclaiming that God has united God's self to humanity in the person of Jesus Christ gives a value and an importance to all that is human and material in this world. The very fact that God has joined God's self to humanity argues against any depreciation of the material, the corporeal and the worldly. The sacramental celebration of the Christian mysteries is a constant reminder of the incarnational principle, for the common elements of human existence — wine, water, bread and oil — are part and parcel of the sacramental celebration and have their meaning transformed in this mystery of faith.

In our contemporary world there seems to be no danger of forgetting this aspect of the basic goodness of the material and the worldly and its incorporation into the whole mystery of God's union with humanity, but the history of Christian thought reveals the various forms of dualism which have existed in the Church and have exerted their influence on theology and practical life. Any attempt to belittle or condemn the material or earthly as being evil or a total obstacle to the higher calling of human beings fails to appreciate the reality and meaning of the incarnation.

In Roman Catholic spirituality in the decades immediately preceding the Second Vatican Council there were two different schools of spirituality — the one called the incarnational and the other, the eschatological.[55] The incarnational approach emphasized the responsibility of the Christian to make incarnate in daily life the Christian gospel and to take seriously earthly existence with the vocation to transform the human into the divine. The eschatological approach tended to think more of the future life and de-emphasized the importance and place of life in this world. The incarnational approach marked the attempt of recent theology to try to develop a spirituality for Christians living in the world which had been a lacuna in Christian thinking. Even the spirituality proposed for diocesan priests was modeled on a monastic spirituality and unadapted to the needs of ministering the Word and Work of Jesus in the world.[56] These decades before Vatican II also saw the increase of theological literature on the value and meaning of earthly realities.[57]

Time has now bypassed this historical discussion although the basic question of a Christian spirituality for the contemporary believer has not been solved. The dangers in the older discussion were an either-or approach which tended to exclude one aspect and the poor understanding of eschatology which viewed eschatology as referring only to the last things and not really present in any way here and now. The entire horizon as described in this essay can serve for the development of a more adequate spirituality which will avoid some of the shortcomings of the past debate especially by seeing the incarnation also in terms of the other important realities and by not opposing incarnational and eschatological reflections.

The failure of Catholic theology to develop a spirituality for Christians living in the world does indicate the fact that such a theology did not give enough importance to the earthly aspects of our existence. In earlier periods in Church history the failure was even more noticeable in terms of the various forms of dualism which tended to look down upon the earthly, the material and the corporeal as being evil. Such a dualistic mentality often, for example, misinterpreted the Pauline dichotomy between spirit and flesh as if Paul were referring to the spiritual part of human beings in opposition to the material or lower part of our being. Such an understanding was far from the mind of Paul who understood spirit to refer to the whole person insofar as one is under the Spirit and flesh to refer to the whole person insofar as one is under the power of sin. The Pauline dichotomy did not refer to the body-soul relationship in human beings. A theologically unacceptable dualism paved the way for such a misinterpretation of Paul.[58] Today, however, there does not seem to be a pressing problem resulting from a failure to accept the implications of the incarnation. If anything, the problem is a failure to recognize the reality of transcendence in our human existence.

Redemption and Resurrection Destiny

The Christian ethical horizon is also formed by the mysteries of redemption and resurrection destiny. In a sense one can and should speak of two different realities in this case, but both can be considered together with the realization that the resurrection destiny of all brings to fulfillment the work of redemption. There would be a problem in considering the two together if redemption were so identified with resurrection destiny that there would be no tension between the now and the future.

Redemption and resurrection destiny in the Christian ethical horizon serve to point to the danger of absolutizing any present structures, institutions or ideals. Resurrection destiny and the future serve as a negative critique on everything existing at the present time. The presence of sin and the limited aspects of creation reinforce the same relativizing tendency. As a result the Christian can never absolutize the present, but a critical assessment calls to mind the need for constant change and development with the realization that the eschatological perfection will never be arrived at in this world, and it will always be necessary to live with imperfections and limitations.[59]

Too often in the past Catholic theology tended to absolutize what was only a very limited and historically conditioned reality. The accepted natural law theory spoke in terms of the immutable order of God and the unchanging essences of things. Thus existing social arrangements or structures could very easily be mistaken for the eternally willed order of God. The tendency of such a vision was conservative in the bad sense of failing to see any need for change and development.

One specific example concerns the outlook of the Church on the whole area of new developments arising in the nineteenth century. Here there were new developments in philosophy, science, politics, forms of government and understanding of the freedom and rights of citizens. In all these areas the reaction of the Catholic Church tended to be one of fear of these newer developments and an effort to turn back the clock to an older historical period with the assumption that this was the order willed by God.[60]

The nineteenth century witnessed an explosion of new philosophical ideas and major developments in science such as the theory of evolution. There was a stirring in some segments of the Catholic Church to bring Catholic theology and thought abreast of these modern developments. A congress for this purpose was organized by Döllinger in Munich in 1863, but the reaction of Rome to such an approach was negative.[61] The Pope, in a letter to the Archbishop of Munich, stressed the need to continue to follow the traditional and accepted theologians and writers, who for centuries have shown the true way of explaining and defending the faith. At the same time, Pius IX insisted on the need for all Catholics to obey the papal magisterium and also the decisions of the Roman congregations. The general tone of the letter was negative to any real dialogue with the contemporary world and urged a return to the safe teaching of the past.[62]

In this context of the nineteenth century Thomas Aquinas was declared to be the patron of Catholic theology and philosophy which was to be taught in Catholic schools according to the plan, the principles and the teaching of Thomas Aquinas.[63] One cannot deny that many benefits have accrued to the Catholic church and to humankind through the Thomistic renewal sparked by Leo XIII and his successors, but there were also harmful effects. Ironically the nineteenth and twentieth century popes used Thomas Aquinas for exactly the opposite of what Thomas himself had accomplished in his own lifetime. The return to Thomas was an obvious attempt to cut off dialogue with the contemporary world of philosophy and science, but the genius of Aquinas consisted in his successfully trying to express the Christian message in the thought patterns of Greek philosophy which had just been entering the university world of the Europe of his day. Thomas was not content merely with repeating and handing down what had been said in the past, but in a very creative way he tried to use the contemporary philosophical insights for a more profound understanding of the Christian faith. This tendency to turn back the clock and to avoid dialogue with the contemporary world characterized much of Catholic life and thought until Vatican II.

Perhaps the most significant expression of the condemnation of the thought of the nineteenth century is found in the "Syllabus of Errors" which Pius IX published in 1864 and which collected some of the more important condemnations which the Pope had earlier made about various new trends in the philosophical and political worlds. The severity of the document was somewhat modified by Dupanloup's famous interpretation based on the difference between thesis and hypothesis. The Pope condemned all these things in thesis; i.e., what roughly corresponds to the ideal world. But in hypothesis, or in what corresponds roughly to the actual historical world in which we live, some of these things may be tolerated. In theory things should be different, but we can tolerate and live with the real situation.[64]

Specifically in the area of social ethics the hierarchical magisterium in the nineteenth century continued to argue for the union of Church and State as the immutable order willed by God and at the same time rejected the emphasis on freedom which was manifesting itself in many different areas of concern including of course political freedom, freedom of conscience and freedom of religion.[65] New political forms of government based on freedom were being espoused. I do not think that the Catholic Church should have uncritically accepted the new political thought, for there were many shortcomings in such new theories as was pointed out from a different perspective by Karl Marx.

The general problem was that Catholic theology looked

upon the union of Church and State as the eternal plan of God when in reality as later changes made clear it was only a very historically and culturally conditioned reality. This furnishes an example of that unacceptable conservatism in Catholic social ethics which proceeds from the basic error of identifying an historically limited and conditioned reality with the eternal and immutable order willed by God. In fairness to Catholic social ethics there was also a great willingness, especially in the area of economic ethics, to point out the failures and injustices of the existing order although here too the impression also persisted among some Catholics that a solution could be found by returning to an older social form such as the guild system.[66]

The danger of false conservatism arising from absolutizing existing or previously existing structures is even greater in the rapidly changing circumstances of contemporary existence. A law and order mentality tends to absolutize the present structures and fails to notice the imperfections and even the positive sinfulness and injustice present in the existing social order. The individual Christian looking forward to the fullness of resurrection destiny can never be content with the present. This realization calls for the necessity of growth and constant conversion in the life of the individual Christian who can never be smug or content about his or her response to the good news of God's loving call. In the light of resurrection destiny the Christian realizes one's own sinfulness and lack of response, the hardness of one's heart and the Christian imperative of growth and change.

In the area of social ethics the fullness of resurrection destiny likewise emphasizes the imperfections of the present and the need for change and growth. The Christian can never be content with the status quo and can never identify the existing order or structure as the perfect reflection of the eternal plan of God. This does not mean that every proposed change is necessarily good and to be embraced, for this would be the most naive of approaches and in its own way be against the horizon of Christian ethics which tends to point out the ambiguities of all existing and proposed orders and structures. In the light of redemption and resurrection destiny social change and the constant improvement of existing structures remains an imperative for the Christian.

There is another important function which redemption and resurrection destiny serve as part of the horizon of moral theology. This aspect exists in tension with the function of resurrection destiny serving as a negative critique on all orders and structures and a spur for growth and change. Resurrection destiny also reminds us that the escatological fullness will never be present until the end of history. The Christian always lives in the tension between the imperfections of the now and the perfection of the future. One can wrongly destroy that tension either by absolutizing the present and seeing no need for change or by thinking that the fullness of resurrection destiny will come easily and quickly. The danger in the 1960s both in theory and in practice consisted in collapsing the eschaton and thinking that the fullness of resurrection destiny will arrive shortly.

The question of redemption and resurrection destiny entails a theory of eschatology. In general I would adopt a theory of eschatology in the process of realization. This argues for continuity between the present world and the next but also for discontinuity. Human beings by their efforts must try to cooperate in bringing about the new heaven and the new earth, but our efforts will always fall short. The naive optimism seen in the failure to appreciate the fact of sin also tends to think of human progress in an evolving way that progressively and somewhat easily becomes better and better. Some of the frustration and malaise both in the world and in the Church at the present time appears due to the fact that people naively expected progress and fulfillment to come too easily and too quickly. When the social structures do not change overnight, there is a tendency to abandon the effort and commitment needed to bring about such change in the real order.

It is helpful to see progress and growth in the social order according to the paradigm of growth and progress in our individual lives. Christians must honestly admit their own sinfulness and failure to fully respond to the gift of God and the needs of our neighbor. The eschatological fullness of the gospel challenges us to continual conversion and growth. However, the process of growth and change is a constant struggle that seems at times not to progress at all. In honesty, we willingly confess how slow we are at changing our hearts and responding more fully to God and neighbor. Growth and progress in the social order will likewise be a slow and painful process. One might argue that growth in the social order will be even more difficult than in the personal realm because of the greater complexity involved in social relationships.

Such a realistic view of progress and development will not place primary emphasis on fulfillment and accomplishment but rather sees the reality of struggle and the consequent Christian emphasis on hope which comes from the promise God has made to us and not primarily from our own deeds and accomplishments. The paschal mystery as another paradigm of growth reminds us of the need to suffer and die in order to live. The Christian with the proper horizon avoids a naive expectation that change will be rapid and easy. The Christian struggles for growth and progress because of hope in the power and presence of the living God and does not ultimately base this hope on one's own accomplishments and deeds although these do retain a secondary but still important role in the Christian understanding of ethics.

The life of the individual person and the paschal mystery as paradigms for social progress also remind us that there is no perfect continuity between this world and the next. Death is an important reality which too often has been pushed to the background in modern life and theology. Death for the Christian does not constitute a reason for despair or a denial of all that has gone before. There certainly is an aspect of death as break between the past and the future, and a sorrowful break that on the surface appears to deny any continuity between past and future. But death for the Christian is also a transformation which ultimately does transform the past and the present into the fullness of resurrection destiny.[67] The ultimate work of transformation at the end of life serves as a reminder of the discontinuity between this world and the next and the fact that it is the power of God that will usher in the fullness of resurrection destiny.

Redemption and resurrection destiny thus serve to create the proper tension by which the Christian is constantly reminded of the need for change and growth in individual life and in the life of society, but at the same time realizes that the fullness of growth and progress will only come at the end of time and in some discontinuity with the present. In the times in between the comings of Jesus, the Christian lives in hope and struggle as one cooperates in the joyful work of redemption and resurrection destiny.

One final word of explanation is necessary. The stance proposed in this chapter presupposes an explicitly Christian understanding of reality and is based on what the believer properly calls five Christian mysteries. A very important problem concerns the relationship of Christian ethics to other ethics. For now, it is sufficient to note that I believe the realities referred to as redemption and resurrection destiny are also in some way available to those who are not Christian. In the same context it should be noted that contemporary theology realizes there is no longer in actuality a clear distinction between creation and redemption. In the last few years Roman Catholic theology has rightly tried to overcome the older distinction and even dichotomy between the natural and the supernatural. But in so doing there is the danger of seeing everything as supernatural, grace or the kingdom. Catholic and Protestant theology in the 1960s too easily forgot the limitations and finitude of creation, the fallenness of sin and the future aspect of resurrection destiny.

This completes the analysis of the various elements which make up the horizon or stance for moral theology. One ultimately has to judge the adequacy of this or any other model by the way in which it accomplishes its function. I have tried to indicate that a stance for moral theology involving the aspects of creation, sin, incarnation, redemption and resurrection destiny adequately serves as the first logical consideration in moral theology and is a standard or criterion which can be effectively employed to criticize other ethical approaches and thus contribute to a more adequate methodology for moral theology.

NOTES

1. James Sellers, *Theological Ethics* (New York: Macmillan, 1968), pp. 31-68.

2. Ibid., pp. 31-38.

3. Ibid., pp. 39-53.

4. Ibid., pp. 54, 55.

5. H. Richard Niebuhr, *Christ and Culture* (New York: Harper Torchbook, 1956), pp. 14-19.

6. Joseph Fletcher, *Situation Ethics* (Philadelphia: Westminster Press, 1966). Also see Fletcher, *Moral Responsibility: Situation Ethics at Work* (Philadelphia: Westminster Press, 1967).

7. For a variety of reactions to Fletcher see John C. Bennett et al., *Storm Over Ethics* (n.p.: United Church Press, 1967); *The Situation Ethics Debate*, ed. Harvey Cox (Philadelphia: Westminster Press, 1968).

8. Donald Evans, "Love, Situations and Rules," in *Norm and Context in Christian Ethics*, ed. Gene H. Outka and Paul Ramsey (New York: Charles Scribner's Sons, 1968), pp. 369-375.

9. Basil Mitchell, "Ideals, Roles and Rules," in *Norm and Context in Christian Ethics*, p. 363.

10. Ibid., p. 353.

11. Fletcher, *Situation Ethics*, p. 79.

12. M.C. D'Arcy, S.J., *The Mind and Heart of Love* (New York: Meridian Books, 1956); Jules Toner, *The Experience of Love* (Washington/Cleveland: Corpus Books, 1968).

13. Anders Nygren, *Agape and Eros* (New York: Harper Torchbook, 1969). For a fine contribution to this whole debate see Gene Outka, *Agape: An Ethical Analysis* (New Haven: Yale University Press, 1972).

14. Sellers, *Theological Ethics*, p. 63.

15. Ibid., pp. 62-64.

16. Ibid., pp. 55,63.

17. Paul Ramsey, *Deeds and Rules in Christian Ethics* (New York: Charles Scribner's Sons, 1967), p. 108.

18. Paul Ramsey, *Basic Christian Ethics* (New York: Charles Scribner's Sons, 1950), pp. 2-24.

19. James M. Gustafson, *Christ and the Moral Life* (New York: Harper and Row, 1968), p. 242.

20. Ibid., p. 241.

21. David W. Tracy, "Horizon Analysis and Eschatology," *Continuum* 6 (1968): 166-172.

22. Josef Fuchs, S.J., *Natural Law: A Theological Investigation* (New York: Sheed and Ward, 1965). Fuchs rightly points out that the natural does not correspond with creation as it exists today, but rather the natural refers to what would be true of human beings in all possible states of existence in salvation history.

23. E.g., *Pacem in Terris, Acta Apostolicae Sedis* 55 (1963): 257. *Populorum*

Progressio, A.A.S. 59 (1967): 257. *The Pastoral Constitution on the Church in the Modern World*, n. 2, follows the same approach. References to the documents of the Second Vatican Council are from *The Documents of Vatican II*, ed. Walter M. Abbott, S.J., trans. ed. Joseph Gallagher (New York: Guild Press, 1966).

24. *Pacem in Terris*, n. 1-7, *A.A.S.* 55 (1963): 257–259.

25. A.F. Carillo de Albornoz, *The Basis of Religious Liberty* (New York: Association Press, 1963), p. 157. The author has an appendix containing the main ecumenical statements on religious liberty.

26. Ibid., p. 159.

27. Richard J. Regan, S.J., *Conflict and Consensus: Religious Freedom and the Second Vatican Council* (New York: Macmillan, 1967), pp. 117-119.

28. Sellers, *Theological Ethics*, pp. 85-92.

29. Ernst Troeltsch, *The Social Teaching of the Christian Churches* (New York: Harper Torchbook, 1960), II: 528-544, 602-616; Arthur C. Cochrane, "Natural Law in the Teachings of John Calvin," in *Church-State Relations in Ecumenical Perspective*, ed. Elwyn A. Smith (Pittsburgh: Duquesne University Press, 1966), pp. 176-217; David Little, "Calvin and the Prospects for a Christian Theory of Natural Law," in *Norm and Context in Christian Ethics*, pp. 175-197.

30. Helmut Thielicke, *Theological Ethics*, vol 1: *Foundations*, ed. William H. Lazareth (Philadelphia: Fortress Press, 1966), p. 398.

31. Ibid., pp. 420-451.

32. Paul L. Lehmann, *Ethics in a Christian Context* (New York: Harper and Row, 1963), pp. 269-277.

33. Will Herberg, "The Social Philosophy of Karl Barth," in *Karl Barth, Community, State and Church* (Garden City: Doubleday Anchor Books, 1960), pp. 17-18.

34. For a concise summary of Barth's moral thought in these matters see Gustafson, *Christ and the Moral Life*, pp. 13-60.

35. John C. Bennett, "Issues for the Ecumenical Dialogue," in *Christian Social Ethics in a Changing World*, ed. John C. Bennett (New York: Association Press, 1966), pp. 377-378; James M. Gustafson, *Protestant and Roman Catholic Ethics: Prospects for Rapprochement* (Chicago: University of Chicago Press, 1978).

36. John Dillenberger and Claude Welch, *Protestant Christianity* (New York: Charles Scribner's Sons, 1954), pp. 255-283.

37. Karl Rahner, S.J., "Justified and Sinner at the Same Time," *Theological Investigations* (Baltimore: Helicon, 1969), VI: 218-230; Bernard Häring, C.Ss.R., "Conversion," in P. Delhayee et al., *Pastoral Treatment of Sin* (New York: Desclée, 1968), pp. 90-92.

38. *Pacem in Terris*, n. 1-6, *A.A.S.* 55 (1963): 257-258.

39. Ibid., n. 7, *A.A.S.* 55 (1963): 259.

40. Severinus Gonzalez, S.J., *Sacrae theologiae summa* (3rd ed.; Madrid: Biblioteca de Autores Cristianos, 1956), III: 521-542.

41. Fuchs, *Natural Law*, pp. 42-52.

42. Dillenberger and Welch, *Protestant Christianity*, pp. 179-254.

43. Robert T. Handy, ed., *The Social Gospel in America 1870-1920* (New

York: Oxford University Press, 1966).

44. Lloyd J. Averill, *American Theology in the Liberal Tradition* (Philadelphia: Westminster Press, 1967).

45. H. Richard Niebuhr, *The Kingdom of God in America* (New York: Harper Torchbook, 1959), p. 193.

46. Herberg, "The Social Philosophy of Karl Barth," pp. 13-21.

47. Reinhold Niebuhr, *Moral Man and Immoral Society* (New York: Charles Scribner's Sons, 1960), p. xii.

48. Ibid., p. xx.

49. Harvey G. Cox, *On Not Leaving It to the Snake* (New York: Macmillan, 1967), pp. ix-xix.

50. William Hamilton, "The New Optimism—from Prufrock to Ringo," in Thomas J.J. Altizer and William Hamilton, *Radical Theology and The Death of God* (Indianapolis: Bobbs-Merrill, 1966), pp. 157-169.

51. Ibid., pp. 159-160.

52. John Macquarrie, *God and Secularity* ("New Directions in Theology Today," III; Philadelphia: Westminster Press, 1967), pp. 81-85.

53. Roger Lincoln Shinn, *Man: The New Humanism* ("New Directions in Theology Today," V; Philadelphia: Westminster Press, 1968), pp. 145-164.

54. Charles E. Curran, *A New Look at Christian Morality* (Notre Dame, Indiana: Fides Publishers, 1968), pp. 169-173, 232-233; see also chapter 6.

55. Bernard Besret, S.O.Cist., *Incarnation ou eschatologie?* (Paris: Éditions du Cerf, 1964).

56. Eugene Masure, *Parish Priest* (Notre Dame, Indiana: Fides Publishers, 1955); Gustave Thils, *The Diocesan Priest* (Notre Dame, Indiana: Fides Publishers, 1964).

57. Gustave Thils, *Théologie des réalités terrestres, I. Préludes. II. Théologie de l'histoire* (Bruges: Desclée de Brouwer, 1946, 1949); Thils, *Théologie et réalité sociale* (Tournai: Casterman, 1952); John Courtney Murray, S.J., "Is It Basketweaving?" in *We Hold These Truths* (New York: Sheed and Ward, 1960), pp. 175-196.

58. A. Humbert, C.Ss.R., "La morale de saint Paul," *Mélanges de Science Religieuse* 15 (1958): 12-13.

59. Edward Schillebeeckx, *God The Future of Man* (New York: Sheed and Ward, 1968), pp. 169-207.

60. For the best historical description of this period see Roger Aubert, *Le pontificat de Pie IX* (Histoire de l'Église depuis les origines jusqu'a nos jours, XXI; Paris: Bloud & Gay, 1952).

61. Ibid., pp. 240-242.

62. *Acta Sanctae Sedis* 8 (1974/5): 438ff.

63. Ibid. 3 (1867/8): 168ff. Leo XIII in his encyclical letter *Aeterni Patris* of August 4, 1879, *Acta Sanctae Sedis*, 11 (1878/9): 98ff., prescribed the restoration in Catholic schools of Christian philosophy in the spirit of St. Thomas Aquinas. For subsequent papal directives on following the philosophy and theology of St. Thomas see Pius X, *Doctoris Angelici, Acta Apostolicae Sedis*, 6 (1914): 384ff.; Pius XI, *Officiorum Omnium, A.A.S.,* 14 (1922): 449ff.; Pius XI, *Studiorum Ducem, A.A.S.* 15 (1923): 323ff.; various

allocutions of Pius XII: *A.A.S.*, 31 (1939): 246ff.; 38 (1946): 387ff.; 45 (1953): 684ff. According to Canon 1366 of the Code of Canon Law promulgated in 1917, rational philosophy and theology should be taught "*ad Angelici Doctrois rationem, doctrinam, et principia.* . . ."

64. Aubert, *Le pontificat de Pie IX*, pp. 254-261.

65. Heinrich A. Rommen, *The State in Catholic Thought* (St. Louis: B. Herder, 1945), pp. 507-612.

66. Richard L. Camp, *The Papal Ideology of Social Reform* (Leiden: E.J. Brill, 1969), pp. 26-27, 38-40.

67. Ladislaus Boros, S.J., *The Mystery of Death* (New York: Herder and Herder, 1965); Karl Rahner, S.J., *On the Theology of Death* (New York: Herder and Herder, 1961); Roger Troisfontaines, S.J., *I Do Not Die* (New York: Desclée, 1963).

3. The Person as Moral Agent and Subject

Catholic moral theology in the last two decades has recognized the importance of the person. Morality and moral theology, which reflects systematically on the moral life, involve more than just moral norms and moral acts viewed in themselves apart from the person.

The person plays a significant moral role as agent and subject, but these two functions should not be totally separated. Human actions are ultimately rooted and grounded in the person who places these actions. The person and the attributes or dispositions of the person affect one's actions. The dispositions and virtues are more permanent than the individual actions which come and go. The good tree brings forth good fruit; the evil tree brings forth evil fruit. The person is not only the agent who performs actions but also the subject who perfects oneself in and through' these actions. Every action can contribute to the growth of the individual person as a subject. One becomes a loyal, faithful, hopeful, and good person. This chapter will concentrate on how to understand the person and the person's role in moral theology with special emphasis given to the insights drawn from contemporary Christology.

In attempting to describe and understand more accurately the role of the person and the dispositions or virtues of the person, moral theology has been helped by contributions from a number of different dialogue partners. The tradition of moral theology itself, based on the theology of Thomas Aquinas, developed a theory of virtues.[1] Although the manuals of moral theology concentrated on the morality of acts in their preparation of ministers to act as judges in the sacrament of penance, the older Thomistic tradition gave a more central and significant role to virtues than to law. Attempts to renew moral theology in the twentieth century before Vatican II often appealed to this Thomistic tradition to ground a morality that is intrinsic, dynamic, and person-centered.[2] Through grace the person is changed and now becomes the new creation. The virtues are habits which dispose the powers of the person to act for good. The theological virtues of faith, hope, and charity come with the gift of grace and dispose the person to act in accord with them. The cardinal virtues of prudence, justice, fortitude, and temperance constitute the framework for understanding all the other moral virtues. These are called cardinal virtues because they are the best illustrations of the virtues modifying the four principal human powers — intellect (prudence), will (justice), the irascible appetites (fortitude), and the concupiscible appetites (temperance).

Some contemporary philosophers, especially Alasdair MacIntyre, have emphasized the importance of the person and the virtues in the moral life.[3] On the theological scene Stanley Hauerwas, writing out of a Protestant tradition, has developed a narrative understanding of the moral life which emphasizes the virtues, vision, and character of the Christian person who belongs to the community of the church.[4]

There have been other significant contributions toward a better understanding of the person as moral agent and moral subject. Bernard Häring has constantly employed the biblical concept of conversion with special emphasis on the need for continuing conversion and growth in the Christian life.[5] Walter Conn has creatively used the philosophy of Bernard Lonergan together with contemporary psychological approaches to develop his own notion of conversion.[6] Contemporary psychologists have paid much attention to the growth and development of the person as a moral agent and subject. Within Catholic moral theology itself one of the most popular ways of overcoming an older emphasis on disparate acts has been the employment of the theory of fundamental option. There is a growing literature in contemporary moral theology on the moral person as agent and subject.

I. Contemporary Christological Perspectives

The aim of this study is to explore the contribution that contemporary Christology can make to the understanding of the person as moral agent and subject. At first thought one might question whether Christology can throw much light on the question of the moral person. However, a glance at contemporary Christologies shows that the moral factor is very much a part of their approaches. Hans Küng devotes one of the four sections of his Christology to practice, and even much of his third section on "The Program" deals with moral topics about the way in which the disciple should respond to Jesus.[7] Edward Schillebeeckx's Christological project has a definite ethical character about it. According to Leo O'Donovan, Schillebeeckx's basic Christological question "Who do you say that I am?" can be transformed into the ethical form "Can we live humanly before God?" The search for a meaningful way of life is central to the predicament and quest of contemporary human beings who are trying to find an answer in the gift of redemption brought by Jesus the Christ.[8] Leonardo Boff and other liberation theologians see an intrinsic relationship between Jesus and the struggle of all oppressed people for liberation on the spiritual, historical, political, and social levels.[9] Enda McDonagh is one contemporary Catholic moral theologian who has already recognized the significance of Christology for moral theology. The first chapter of his book *The Making of Disciples* relates contemporary Christological developments to moral theology and serves as the basis for this collection of his essays gathered around the theme of discipleship as characterizing the community of the followers of Jesus.[10]

Perhaps the most significant reason why contemporary Christology has much to contribute to our understanding of the person as moral agent and subject stems from the soteriological intent of contemporary Christology. The understanding of the Christian person is intimately connected with one's understanding of justification and sanctificaton. Roman Catholic theology has traditionally recognized that salvation involves an ontological change in the person who now becomes a new creature through regeneration by the Spirit. This newly changed person is now called to bring forth the fruits of the Spirit in life. Catholics frequently have understood the indicative and imperative in Pauline thought in these terms. Those who are now baptized in Christ Jesus and under the life of the Spirit must now act in accord with this new life. Stanley Hauerwas has perceptively pointed out that one reason why many Protestants never developed the role of the person as agent in Christian ethics stems from a theory of extrinsic justification.[11] If justification does not truly bring about a change in the person, then one cannot speak about the person as a new creature existing in the Spirit and mystically incorporated into Jesus. Soteriology obviously has very significant ramifications for an understanding of the Christian person.

The so-called traditional Catholic Christology fails to link Christology with soteriology. One model of Christology based on the Johannine approach became the primary and almost exclusive way of dealing with Christology from the Nicene period onward. This Christology can be described as metaphysical and ontological as distinguished from a functional Christology with emphasis above all on the redeeming function of Jesus who brings God's salvation to human beings in a definitive saving encounter. The definition of the Council of Chalcedon in 451 concentrated on the ontological understanding of Jesus Christ, who is complete in divinity and complete in humanity, truly God and truly human. The Chalcedonian definition goes on to explain that the one and the same Christ, Son, Lord, and Only Begotten, is recognized in two natures. Chalcedon thus insists on the hypostatic union of the two distinct natures.[12] Subsequent Christology concentrated on the constitution of Christ and used the understanding of one person and two natures to develop its approach.

In the Chalcedonian formula the soteriological aspect of Christology is hardly mentioned. Chalcedon does speak of the one and the same Son, our Lord Jesus Christ, as regards his humanity begotten for us and for our salvation. However, nothing more is said about soteriology within the larger framework dealing with the ontological constitution of Jesus Christ as true God and true human being. Such a Christology would have little significance for moral theology and the understanding of the Christian person. A soteriological Christology, however, stresses redemption and what we become as Christian persons through redemption. The sin and evil from which Christians have been redeemed also help to describe the reality of redemption shared by believers in Jesus. A soteriological Christology can say much about the Christian person and what it means for a Christian person to receive and act in accord with the redeeming gift of God in Christ Jesus.

How is our redemption in Jesus the Christ to be understood? Contemporary Christology has emphasized the importance of a Christology from below — a Christology that begins with the life, ministry, death, and resurrection of the man Jesus of Nazareth. The Christology from above as elaborated in John, in Chalcedon, and in most of the tradition begins with the presence of the preexisting Logos who is consubstantial with the Father. Soteriology is explained by the fact that the Logos takes on a human nature and saves us by dying and rising. The exact relationship between the two Christologies lies beyond the scope of this chapter. It is sufficient for our purposes to note that a Christology from below does not necessarily deny any aspect of the Christian faith testimony about Jesus the Christ. Such a Christology from below tries to explain and understand better the Christian faith in Jesus the Christ.

The shift to a Christology from below has had many significant consequences.[13] More importance is given to the humanity of Jesus than was true in an older Christology. Contemporary Christologies often differ from the more traditional Christology in their dealing with the human knowledge of Jesus and the question of the human personality in Jesus. This study will concentrate on the meaning and greater importance which a Christology from below gives to the soteriological function of Jesus.

In turning to the historical Jesus as the starting point of

Christology, contemporary approaches are very conscious of the current developments in critical biblical and exegetical scholarship. To understand the historical Jesus one must get behind the Scripture text as we have it now, since the Scriptures were obviously colored by the Easter faith of believers and by the situations of the communities in which they were told, composed, and finally written down in different accounts. This shift has brought contemporary Christology into heavy dependence on the work of Scripture scholars. Raymond Brown has commented that much of Schillebeeckx's book on Jesus is really the work of biblical scholarship and not of theology as such.[14]

An older soteriology associated with Christology from above tended to be private, extrinsic, and abstract. Individual souls shared in the satisfaction which Jesus won on the cross. Grace and the supernatural often tended to be understood in an extrinsic fashion as poured into the soul through the sacraments. This view of redemption was isolated from a relation to society, for it primarily involved the spiritual salvation of individual souls.

A Christology from below understands redemption as social, intrinsic, and very concrete. Redemption through Jesus is seen in the light of God's salvific gift as found in all the Scriptures, with its basis in the Hebrew Scripture. Redemption is understood in the light of the life, ministry, death, and resurrection of Jesus. In this context Jesus is a victim who was unjustly put to death and stands in solidarity with all those who are victims of oppression and injustice. Jesus sided with the poor and oppressed and was put to death because of the way in which he lived. Redemption is thus recognized as having concrete social dimensions and is not merely a private and spiritual reality. Liberation or redemption involves more than the spiritual, and the Christian person must live out the manifold dimensions of the new life received from Jesus.

The shift to a Christology from below has focused attention on the concept of discipleship and its implications for understanding the moral life of the Christian believer. Critical biblical scholarship indicates the different concepts of discipleship found in the Gospels. Just as there are different Christologies in the New Testament, so too there are different understandings of discipleship.[15] Mark understands discipleship in terms of belonging to a new and radical family. The family of Jesus — the mother, the sisters, and the brothers of Jesus — are those who do the will of God and follow Jesus. The radical nature of the following of Jesus on the part of the disciples as family is stressed throughout Mark's Gospel. The disciple must suffer as Jesus suffered and carry the cross. The values and the roles which are often prized by many people can be obstacles in the way of discipleship. The follower of Jesus is to serve and not to be served; the first shall be last, and the last first; the disciples are to be as children.

Luke in Acts uses the term "the Way" to describe the Christian community. Luke is particularly strong in his emphasis on the correct use of material goods and possessions. Unlike the other Synoptic Gospels, Luke insists that the disciples sell "all they have" (Luke 18:22) and leave "everything" (Luke 5:11) to follow Jesus. Luke's beatitudes retain the apparently earlier understanding of the materially poor and do not spiritualize the concept into the poor in spirit. Luke sees discipleship as following in the footsteps of Jesus.

Matthew in his own way is a catechist and teacher of morality for the community of disciples which he understands primarily as the community of justice. The greek word *dikaiosuné* (justice) plays a very central role in Matthew's Sermon on the Mount. Justice refers both to God's saving acts and to the Christian's actions in doing God's will. The disciples of Jesus hunger and thirst for justice and then suffer persecution for justice's sake. The whole thrust of Matthew's Gospel makes Jesus appear as a second Moses who has come not to destroy the law but to fulfill it. The spiritualizing and moralizing additions to the beatitudes (poor in spirit, clean of heart, hunger and thirst for justice) indicate the primary concern of Matthew. The disciples of Jesus are called to live out the new justice in all its ramifications.

Discipleship in John's Gospel is ultimately linked with faith. Faith is the fundamental decision made by the person when confronted with Jesus. The image of discipleship in terms of the sheep who belong to the shepherd and the branches which belong to the vine underscores the role of faith in discipleship. Since John's community was living much later than the historical Jesus, the time of seeing was long past. Faith is now the central reality, and in many ways the Paraclete has taken the role of the earthly Jesus.

There can be no doubt that each of the individual evangelists understands discipleship in a particular way, with emphases which fit into the whole direction and meaning of the particular Gospel. However, there are also factors that are common to the accounts of discipleship found in the Gospels. First of all, discipleship involves God's gracious gift and call. The call and the gift come first — Jesus came preaching the Good News, change your heart and believe in the Good News. Discipleship and faith remain God's gracious gift to us. There can be no discipleship without the first step being taken by God in Jesus. The nonvalue in the eyes of a secular world of the recipients of God's reign — children, the poor, and sinners — proves that discipleship is God's gracious gift.

The relational aspect of discipleship is highlighted, for discipleship is the response of the individual and the community to the gift of God in Jesus. The call-response theme is central to the Christian message and has been developed at great length by Bernard Häring in his attempts to renew moral theology.[16] The response to God's gift in discipleship is not based on fear but is the grateful response to the Good News.

Discipleship not only involves the relationship through Jesus with the loving God who is mother and father to all of us but also involves relationships within the community of disciples. The disciple of Jesus is never an isolated individual but a member of a community who shares faith and love in that community. In addition, discipleship involves relationships with all other people and with the world. The disciples who follow Jesus are called to live for and share with others as Jesus first lived for and shared with them. Love, mercy, and forgiveness must characterize the life of the Christian person who recognizes that one's sins are forgiven only to the extent that the individual is willing to forgive others. The reversal of roles within the Christian community stresses service rather than power. The following of Jesus calls for the same option for the poor and the outcasts which Jesus showed. Discipleship calls for fundamental change in our relationship with others — the poor, the needy, the enemy. The great love commandment in the synoptic Gospels has intrinsically and inevitably bound together the love of God and the love of neighbor. As John reminds us, we cannot love the God we do. not see if we do not love the neighbor whom we do see. Discipleship by its very nature involves not only the relationship to God but also relationships within the community of disciples and relationships with all God's people.

Totality and radicalness constitute other characteristics of Christian discipleship. The following of Jesus especially in suffering and death well illustrates the radical meaning of discipleship. The reign of God is the pearl of great price for which everything else must be sold. This discipleship must be the primary reality that colors, transforms, and directs all the other commitments and values in the life of the disciple. The radicalness of discipleship at the very minimum demands that all else be seen in the light of this basic commitment.

Discipleship involves the continuing call for growth. The Gospel accounts, even though colored by later attempts to build up the close followers of Jesus, do not hide the weakness of Jesus' disciples. The disciples are often pictured as vacillating, unable to understand, unwilling to follow fully in the footsteps of Jesus, and even quarreling among themselves about first place. Thus even the early disciples of Jesus are shown in their weakness and their need for greater growth. Discipleship is a gift but also a challenge which can never fully be met. The radical demands of discipleship are a constant invitation to growth. The disciple needs to grow in the manifold commitments that mark the following of Jesus. These general characteristics of discipleship are found in the New Testament, especially in the Gospel narrative despite the various particularities in each evangelist's understanding of both the community of the followers of Jesus and the meaning of discipleship in that community. Any adequate understanding of the Christian moral person as agent and subject must incorporate these general characteristics of discipleship.

In interpreting the biblical understanding of discipleship today, one must call explicit attention to eschatology. There can be no doubt that especially in the sayings of Jesus and in earlier New Testament writings there was a tendency to think the fullness of the reign of God would come rather soon.

Such an eschatology readily colors one's approach to ethics. My eschatological perspective today recognizes the need to live out the tensions of the already, but not yet, aspects of Christian eschatology. Redemption in Jesus has already occurred, but the fullness of resurrection destiny is not yet here and will only come at the end. An imminent expectation of the end time will definitely influence one's approach to particular questions such as marriage and sexuality. The general characteristics of discipleship are less subject to differing interpretations based on different eschatologies, but here too one must explicitly recognize the eschatological perspectives which are being employed. The understanding of growth developed in the preceding paragraph is logically consistent with the tension present in my eschatology and with the stance developed in the preceding chapter.

Theological methodology will have a great effect on how one understands Christology and discipleship. A Christology from below rightly gives much more importance to the historical Jesus and to the scriptural understanding of the ministry, life, death, and resurrection of Jesus. The older approach to Christology in the Catholic tradition did not give enough importance to the scriptural witness, but it rightly recognized some need for other sources of Christological wisdom and knowledge. In general the Roman Catholic tradition has always given more importance to nonbiblical sources than many Protestant theological approaches. Contemporary Catholic approaches to Christology and discipleship, while giving great importance to the scriptural witness and to the historical Jesus, recognize the place of nonscriptural sources. Edward Schillebeeckx emphasizes the role of contemporary experience and in the light of this insists that the contemporary Christian must write the fifth gospel today.[17] Elisabeth Schüssler Fiorenza maintains that most liberation theologians follow a neo-Orthodox methodology because the Scriptures are interpreted primarily on the basis of what is found only in the Scriptures themselves. Schüssler Fiorenza wants to use the contemporary experience of women to interpret and criticize the scriptural message.[18] My purpose is not to argue for the truth of Catholic methodological approaches but only to indicate that such approaches will not depend only on the scriptural witness.

A good example of Catholic theological methodology at work can be found in the Christology of Gerald O'Collins. A comprehensive Christology, according to O'Collins, needs to respect the full range of Christian and Catholic experience, expectations, teachings, reflections, and activity with the recognition of some privileged sources such as the New Testament and the early Christological confessions. O'Collins develops four aspects in the light of these sources — the Christ of the present, the Christ of the future, the Christ of the Christian tradition, and the Christ of Christian origins.[19]

The Anabaptist tradition, the left wing of the Protestant Reformation, has given central importance to the role of discipleship. However, the understanding of discipleship in this tradition has definitely been affected by a theological methodology which concentrates almost exclusively on the scriptural witness. This tradition emphasizes the radicalness of discipleship, the need for a believer's baptism which grounds this radical commitment, and a continuing conflict and struggle with most of the world. The Mennonite tradition in its purist form has called for separation from the world because of the dangers of contamination and the impossibility of living out the radical Gospel ethic of peace, nonviolence, and no oath taking in the world.[20] In the light of the stance proposed in the last chapter such an approach does not give enough importance to creation and incarnation. Any theological methodology which gives greater importance to tradition, reason, and contemporary experience tends to arrive at different understandings of discipleship, for it does not see such conflict and opposition between Christian discipleship and all other human beings. If history, culture, and experience can help us to a better understanding of Christology, then Christ cannot stand in total opposition to what is happening in history, culture, and the world.

This methodological question is intimately associated with a very significant substantive question — the relationship between Jesus Christ and the universality of salvation. Contemporary Christology has emphasized the life, ministry, death, and resurrection of Jesus, an outlook which certainly stresses the concrete, the particular, and the historically limited. At the same time, however, contemporary Christology has had to deal with a perennial soteriological question—the universality of salvation. Catholic theology has traditionally recognized the universal salvific will of God—God wills to save all people. But how does this relate to the belief that Jesus is the sole and unique mediator of redemption? The question is often phrased today in terms of the relationship between Christianity and the other religions of the world. What is the soteriological aspect of these religions? Are people saved or redeemed despite their allegiance to these religions or because of it? Various solutions have been proposed to these questions. Karl Rahner's theory of anonymous Christianity is quite well-known and often accepted today. All people are offered the gift of redemption, and those who receive it and respond are anonymous Christians even though they have never explicitly declared belief in Jesus and have never categorically experienced salvation as coming from Jesus.[21] Raimundo Panikkar, reflecting on his experience with the Hindu religion, understands Christ as the universal Logos. Jesus is Christ, but Christ is not Jesus exclusively.[22] These and other theories will continue to be debated, but the final resolution of these questions lies beyond the scope of this paper. Salvation and redemption are somehow offered to all human beings. Consequently, the Christian person and the disciple of Jesus will not necessarily be totally different from many other human beings. If redemption is offered to all, the Christian person will share much with many other people who are not Christians. The disciples of Jesus will not find themselves totally differentiated from and opposed to all other people living in the world. Redeemed people include many who are not Christians and explicit disciples of Jesus.

II. The Christian Person as Moral Agent and Subject

The Christological and soteriological aspects just addressed have much to tell about the proper understanding of the Christian person who is both the moral agent and moral subject. There are, of course, other disciplines that also shed light on the Christian person, but Christian ethics should be heavily influenced by Christological considerations of the redeemed person who is a disciple of Jesus.

The Christological considerations discussed above strongly underscore the fact that faith and morality are intimately connected. Belief in Jesus means that one belongs to and follows "the Way." The disciple of Jesus responds by a way of life. The changed relationship of the disciple of Jesus to God involves a changed relationship with others — fellow believers in the community, friends, enemies, the poor. The Catholic understanding of the evangelical command to love God and neighbor as oneself has always insisted on bringing together the proper love of God, neighbor, and self. All agree that love of God is intimately connected with love of neighbor, but the Catholic theological tradition has insisted on a proper love of self that can and should be integrated with love of God and neighbor.[23]

Contemporary Christology with its emphasis on the concrete and intrinsic aspects of soteriology has emphasized the inseparable union between belief in Jesus and working to overcome oppression in all its forms. An understanding of redemption which insists on its connection with a commitment to social justice emphasizes more the sin of the world and does not reduce sin only to the realm of the private and the individual. Liberation and redemption by their very nature call for freedom from every form of oppression and injustice. This understanding of redemption and sin grounds the assertion of Justice in the World, the document of the 1971 Synod of Bishops, which maintains, "Action on behalf of justice and participation in the transformation of the world fully appear to us a constitutive dimension of the preaching of the Gospel, or, in other words, of the church's mission for the redemption of the human race and its liberation from every oppressive situation."[24] There has been much discussion about the meaning of this passage, but the sentence remains the most frequently cited passage from any contemporary official Catholic Church document.[25] Such an approach argues strongly against separation or dualism between faith and daily life, between the sacred and the secular, between the private and the public, between preaching the Gospel and working for social justice.

All these considerations point to the need to understand the Christian person as moral agent and subject in terms of the multiple relationships within which the Christian disciple finds oneself. Specifically, the Christian person as moral agent and subject should be understood in terms of one's relationships with God, neighbor, world, and self. By simultaneously holding on to all these multiple relationships one does justice to all the different aspects of Christian discipleship and avoids any unnecessary dualisms or separations.

There are other reasons that also argue for understanding the person in relational terms. In general I have argued that a relationality-responsibility understanding of moral theology furnishes a more adequate model of the moral life in general and the Christian moral life in particular than either the deontological or the teleological models. By opting for such an ethical model I see the moral person primarily in terms of that model. Some philosophical anthropologies come to the same conclusion of seeing the human person primarily in relational terms. In this context an older Catholic understanding of the person as an incommunicable individual substance of a rational nature no longer seems adequate. In contemporary Christology Edward Schillebeeckx opts for a relational understanding of the person and then applies this to Jesus. Schillebeeckx maintains that modern phenomenology supports such a relational approach.[26] And important to note is that traditional Catholic theology has understood the persons of the Trinity in terms of relations.

A relational view of the person enables moral theology to keep together the multiple dimensions of Christian existence and to more adequately do justice to all the aspects of redemption which are emphasized in contemporary Christology. Specifically it seems that the Christian person must be understood in light of the fourfold relationship to God, neighbor, world, and self.

Character has been used to describe the basic orientation of the person. In common parlance people often speak of the good character or the bad character of a particular individual. Virtues refer to the different attitudes and dispositions that should be present in the Christian person and direct the way in which that person acts. In the light of a relational understanding of the person a theory of the virtues should develop those general virtues which characterize the person in all basic relationships and the specific virtues which relate to the different individual relationships.

The traditional triad of theological virtues — faith, hope, and charity — should be understood as general virtues affecting the person in all these multiple relationships. To restrict these attitudes only to our relationship to God tends to separate too much our relationship to God from our other relationships. Redemption would thus only affect our relationship with God and would not affect the total person in the midst of all one's multiple relationships. To describe these theological virtues in great detail lies beyond the scope of this paper, but contemporary theology has given great significance to the virtue of hope.

The basic reason for the emphasis on the virtue of hope stems from the importance given to historicity and eschatology in contemporary theology. A more static approach to theology did not give much importance to hope, but hope is truly a very important virtue for the pilgrim who is on the journey. Eschatology recognizes that the Christian lives out the tension between the already and the not yet. Redemption has already taken place. We are redeemed and incorporated into the family of disciples of Jesus, but the fullness of God's reign is not yet here. The eschatological fullness lies beyond history and will never be fully achieved in this world.

Hope is the virtue of the struggling Christian. Christians must take seriously the Marxist critique that Christianity and religion have at times been the opium of the people by promising an eternal reward in heaven if people put up with suffering and injustice in this world. An opposite danger is to expect that the fullness of God's reign will come quickly, readily, and without too great personal inconvenience. The eschatological tension means that the Christian will always be struggling. Hope provides the power to continue the struggle even though there seems to be no success or growth. The Christian hopes in the power of life over death, of light over darkness, of love over hate, of truth over falsehood. Hope enables the Christian and the entire Christian community to be faithful to its commitment even in the midst of failure and problems. A realistic hope recognizes that suffering will always be part of our human existence, but such a hope also strongly believes that such suffering can and should be redemptive for all concerned. The life, death, and resurrection of Jesus constitute the source of our hope. Hope thus affects all our relationships and all that we do.

There are other significant general virtues that affect the person in all the multiple relationships of existence. Bernard Häring has recently called attention to two such significant virtues — freedom and fidelity. Häring rightly sees the need to bring these two attitudes together so as to avoid a dangerous one-sidedness that so stresses freedom that continuity is lost or that so emphasizes fidelity that there is no possibility for risk and change.[27] Here it is important to recall that the Catholic tradition has never made freedom an absolute, nor has it understood freedom as the ability to do either good or evil. Freedom is the freedom to do the good. In the past Catholic theology unfortunately thought it knew too readily and easily what was the good. In general, freedom stresses the discontinuity aspect in life, whereas fidelity expresses the aspect of continuity. However, fidelity by its very nature is not opposed to creativity, for fidelity can and should be very creative. At times the Christian will feel the tension between freedom and fidelity, even though in theory there should be no incompatibility between the two. The one who is free and faithful can learn from Jesus that there is no ultimate incompatibility between being both free and faithful.

In addition to the general virtues that should characterize the person in one's multiple relationships there are particular virtues that affect one particular relationship. A brief sketch of the more significant virtues disposing and affecting each of these relationships will be presented. God's call and gift come first, then the response of the disciple. This understanding of the relationship of the disciple to God puts heavy emphasis on the disposition of openness on the part of the disciple to hear and respond to the call of God. Such an attitude might be characterized by a proper understanding of the virtue of humility as the poverty of spirit which marks the followers of Jesus. If redemption is a gift, then the Christian must be ever ready and open to receive that gift. From Abraham and Sarah down to the present the great believers were those who were ready to hear the call of God and willing to leave everything else behind in order to respond to the call of God. Jesus himself came to do the will of his gracious parent. Mary the model of all believers is the one who was most open to receive God's summons — be it done unto me according to your will.

The basic openness stands in opposition to a closed self-centeredness and a self-contained attitude. The person who is closed in on oneself can never hear the call of the Spirit. One who is concerned and preoccupied with one's own perspectives and ambitions will never hear the summons of God. This basic openness to the coming of God is something that must be present throughout the life of the disciple and not only at the beginning. The disciple is alert and vigilant, awaiting the coming of the bridegroom. The disciple knows there are certain times and opportunities which the alert Christian can and should grasp. God is continuing to be present to us in history and in our lives, and the disciple of Jesus must be ever vigilant to discern what God is doing. The *kairos* is a technical term for this type of time — not the time of measurement (so many minutes, hours, days, or years) but the time of opportunity — the opportune moment which comes and which will never come again. Recent Catholic theology has stressed the signs of the times and insisted on the need for the individual Christian and the Christian community to be open to discern and respond to the signs of the times.[28] Openness, receptivity, and vigilance then must characterize the Christian who tries to live out the gift-response rhythm of the relationship of the believer to God as revealed through Jesus in the Spirit.

A second important virtue that characterizes the Christian's relationship with God is thankfulness. Gratitude stems from the very nature of this relationship with its characteristic emphasis on the divine initiative. The Christian gratefully and thankfully receives the gracious gift of God. Christians are worshippers — people who gather to give thanks and praise for redemption and liberation. Individuals and the community of disciples are called to be worshippers in spirit and in truth. Liturgy is a constitutive dimension of the moral life of the disciples of Jesus.

The Christian's relationship to neighbor gives a special but not exclusive emphasis to the neighbor in need and to the needs of the neighbor. The parable of the Good Samaritan in Luke points out that the need of the neighbor who had been attacked and was lying at the side of the road comes first. The Christian tradition has seen our relationship with God as a paradigm of our relationship with neighbor. Just as the gracious God has come to us in our need, so too we are to be conscious of the needs of the neighbor and come to assist them. Mercy and forgiveness are very strongly inculcated attitudes that should belong to the Christian, but they are ultimately rooted in the fact that God has acted in this way toward us. In fact, our sins will be forgiven only to the extent that we are willing to forgive others.

God's relationship to the poor also is paradigmatic for the Christian's relationship to the poor. Again the needs of the poor call out to the Christian for help. Some contemporary Church statements highlight the option for the poor but recognize that such a preferential option is not exclusive. The concern and option for the poor must characterize the Christian person.[29]

In terms of justice very often there is a tendency grounded in individualistic perspectives to stress commutative justice based on an arithmetic equality of what one individual owes to another. However, the Catholic tradition has insisted on the importance of distributive justice as all important in social relationships.[30] According to distributive justice the goods of the society should be distributed with a stress on need and burdens should be apportioned with a heavy consideration given to abilities. The traditional virtue of distributive justice in the Catholic tradition, although formulated in philosophical language, shows the influence of the Christian preference for the poor and the needy. Note that distributive justice does not aim at arithmetic equality, or *quid pro quo*, but rather proportional equality. Society thus has an obligation to provide decent housing, food, and living conditions for all its citizens, whereas burdens such as taxation should be based heavily on one's ability to pay, with the rich paying a much greater percentage of their income than the poor.

One very significant aspect of our relations with others is based on the needs of others, but in my interpretation of the

Christian message this is not the only or the exclusive aspect of our relationship with others. Christian personal relationships at times must also emphasize the role of mutuality and reciprocity. Love of enemies is not the only form of Christian love. Love also involves union, togetherness, and sharing. Roman Catholic theology has continually recognized that the divine love of the three persons in God is based not on need but on mutuality and reciprocity.

Christian people enter into many different relationships with one another and with all God's people. Fidelity to one's word is an important attitude for life in society. A commitment to truth and veracity is necessary if human relationships are to prosper. In addition to relations with individual neighbors there are also relationships within the church community and with society, including the state itself and the many voluntary associations and intermediate organizations and institutions to which people belong. The virtues and attitudes that should characterize the Christian person in such relationships once again heavily depend on the nature of the relationships and the institutions. Thus, for example, patriotism, or proper love of one's own country, has historically been recognized as a virtue, but the danger of excess in love of country is always a temptation. Respect and obedience toward lawful political authority are likewise important characteristics of the Christian, but blind obedience is not a virtue. There is a place for civil disobedience and some conscientious objection.

The Christian also lives in relationship with the world. Here there are two important attributes that should mark the disciple of Jesus' attitude toward the things of this world. Belief in creation as God's gracious gift moves the Christian to recognize that the goods of creation exist to serve the needs of all. No one has a right to arrogate to oneself an excessive amount of the goods of creation at the expense of the legitimate human needs of others. This basic attitude must color the Christian perspective on private property and on economic systems. Such an attitude does not necessarily rule out private property or certain economic systems, but these must be subordinate to and governed by the basic principle that the goods of creation exist to serve the needs of all.

Christians have frequently inculcated the attitude of stewardship to govern attitudes to the world and to the environment. Lately some Christians have been accused of using the command to subdue the earth as found in Genesis to justify a misuse of our natural resources and our physical world. Stewardship, however, should highlight both the creativity and the limitations human beings experience in dealing with the world of nature. We have a responsibility not only to the future generations who will come after us but also to the world of nature itself to preserve and enhance its existence.[31]

In a true sense one can even speak about the proper relationship to oneself. The Catholic Christian tradition has always been willing to recognize the proper love of self which is totally compatible with both love of God and love of neighbor. Being a disciple of Jesus ultimately should bring the individual to the fullest perfection of what it means to be human. A proper love of self is a disposition which avoids an excessive concern for oneself as well as a failure to properly appreciate and accept oneself. Pride and selfishness have traditionally been looked upon as the vices that give too much importance to the self and make self the center of everything. On the other hand the Christian tradition has perhaps not emphasized enough the dangers in a lack of self-esteem and a failure to appreciate truly oneself and one's gifts. The individual must have the attitude of using properly and creatively all the powers that are proper to a human being. In a true sense there is a great need for disciplining all our faculties and operations so that they serve the true good of the person and the person's relationships with others. The Thomistic tradition has talked about the concupiscible appetites which are above all directed and guided by the virtue of temperance and the irascible appetites which are governed by fortitude.

This study has not attempted a complete description of all the virtues and attitudes that should characterize the Christian person. The primary purpose has been to show that the moral person as agent and subject should be understood in relational terms. The dispositions and attitudes that characterize the person should be based on these relationships. This section has tried to illustrate, in skeleton form, the virtues that should characterize the follower of Jesus.

Moral growth and development have received much consideration in recent literature. Roman Catholic theology has been willing to talk about growth in the spiritual and moral life, although this was often discussed in somewhat extrinsic terms as an increase of grace. Some within the Protestant tradition have used the concept of sanctification to explain growth in discipleship, although other Protestants because of their position on justification have been unwilling to speak about a growth in the moral and spiritual life of Christians.

Bernard Häring explains growth in the Christian life in terms of the call to continual conversion.[32] The call to conversion is not a once-and-for-all event, but Christians must constantly grow in their discipleship. This need for continual growth is grounded in the eschatological tension between the already-present gift of redemption and the not-yet aspect of the fullness of resurrection-destiny. All Christians continue to fall short of the fullness of God's reign, but all are called to grow into a fuller Christian discipleship. The call to continuing conversion recognizes a basic truth in the phrase that the Christian is *simul justus et peccator* (simultaneously justified and sinner) and is called to strive to overcome the remnants of sin.

Deepening the relationships with God, neighbor, world, and self and the virtues which direct these relationships constitutes the growth and continual conversion of the person. The rhythm of growth can be seen in terms of the rhythm of dying and rising, for the Christian person lives out and shares in the paschal mystery of Jesus. Continual conversion involves a dying to sin and a rising in the newness of life. Continuing sinfulness can be seen as the lack of fullness in our relationships with others and the need to overcome selfishness and evil in order to enter more fully into relationships with God, neighbor, and the world.

A phenomenological understanding of growth also illustrates that growth in multiple relationships involves the rhythm of dying and rising. Think of some typical growth experiences such as going away to school or getting married. The first day in school for most children is a traumatic experience. One feels alone and abandoned in a very wide and unfamiliar universe which is so different from the comfortable and familiar surroundings of the family and the home. But it is necessary to leave the familiar but limiting environment of the home and family in order to grow by entering into broader relationships with others and with an expanding world itself. Marriage illustrates this rhythm of the growth process and requires a dying to the past to enter into a fuller and deeper relationship with another in the community of marriage and family. Growth involves pain and some loss, but it is necessary to die to the past in order to rise in the newness of life.

Birth is a good example of a very significant growth experience. In order to grow and to expand one's relationships it is necessary to leave the security and warmth of the womb. Is it any wonder that the first reaction of the baby on coming out of the womb is to cry! For the believer death can be understood in the same way. We as human beings experience the negative side of death—the break, the loss, the separation; the Christian understanding of death also sees it as a transformation. Just as the resurrection of Jesus transformed his death, so too for the follower of Jesus death can be transformed. The phenomenological understanding of growth can also provide a better understanding of what death involves for the Christian. Resurrected life in the fullness of the eschaton means a complete union of love with God, neighbor, world, and self—in other words the fullest and deepest relationships possible. Death is necessary in order to enter into the fullness of these relationships. This life of bodily existence, especially as weakened and debilitated by old age and sickness, ultimately prevents our entering into the fullest, broadest, and deepest relationships. The reality of death is necessary in order that we might die to the limitations of the present and be able to experience the fullest and deepest relationships of love. Thus for the believer death itself can also be seen in the light of an understanding of growth based on a dying to the present in order to rise into a more full existence.

The importance of the person as subject and agent of the moral life underlines the significance of the moral formation of the person with the requisite virtues and dispositions that should characterize such a person. In many different ways a primary function of the Christian community is that of moral formation. The liturgy is one very important school of moral formation because it is here that the community celebrates its own reality as a convenant people chosen by God and commits itself to live out the life of discipleship which it celebrates. In all that it does—in telling its story, in celebrating its reality, in living out its life—the Christian community forms disciples and inculcates the attitudes that should mark the members of the Christian community.

One aspect of the moral formation of the person which has received less emphasis in the Catholic life in the post-Vatican II church is the recognition of the importance of the saints. The lives of the saints were often used in the past to provide models of heroism for contemporary Christians. Telling and retelling the stories of the lives of the saints, like telling and retelling the Christian story itself, helps to form the true character of followers of Jesus. The whole process of the formation of the Christian person calls for a holistic approach. Formation is personal and communitarian in the broadest sense of the terms. It is not just intellectual or abstract but involves the head, the heart, the emotions, and the total person. Theory and practice, as well as celebration and life, work together in the Christian community's attempt to form its members.

In the light of the universal call to all to share in God's salvific life and love, a Christological soteriology does not mean that Christian persons will necessarily be that different from all other people. This is an "in principle" statement which also recognizes that all do not necessarily respond to God's gift. I have proposed that there is no unique moral content to Christian morality in the sense that many other people besides Christians can and do arrive at the same moral judgments and accept the same dispositions and values as Christians such as love, mercy, forgiveness, and even love of enemy. Christians cannot claim these attitudes or virtues as exclusively their own.[33] Such an understanding of soteriology and Christology has great repercussions not only on anthropology but also on ecclesiology. The church in the sociological language of Weber and Troeltsch is not a sect which is characterized as a small group of disciples who are separated from and often in opposition with most of the world. Just as the Christian person will share things with many other persons who have accepted the gift of redemption, so too the Christian Church will not necessarily be in opposition with the world or even with other religions. This is not to deny that there are distinctive things about being Christian persons and belonging to the discipleship of Jesus, but Christians cannot claim to have a unique moral content to their morality.

Theories such as mine which stress the universality of God's salvific gift must constantly remember that not all is grace, goodness, and the fullness of God's reign. Human finitude, sin, and the lack of eschatological fullness will always characterize human existence and our world. Sin is ever present, and the sin of the world at times is perceptibly present in the injustice, hunger, oppression, poverty, pride, and selfishness which are experienced in our lives and in our world. Moreover, the Church itself always remains a sinful Church whose members are affected by the same realities of finitude, sin, and the lack of eschatological fullness. There is a constant struggle against sin both as it exists in the world and in the community of the Church itself.

This section has tried to develop a basic understanding of the Christian person as moral agent and subject. The person must primarily be seen in terms of multiple relationships, for such an approach most adequately fits with the findings of contemporary Christology. The virtues or attitudes that should characterize the Christian person are those that affect the person both in respect to all the relationships in which one is involved and with respect to particular relationships. Growth and development in the Christian life involve the widening and deepening of these relationships and the virtues that affect these relationships. However, it is necessary to remember that Christian persons who have been redeemed by God's love through the Spirit in Jesus will not necessarily be that different from many other human beings, since God does call all human beings to the fullness of love.

III. Comparison with Other Approaches

The understanding of the person as moral agent and subject developed here can and should be compared with some other contemporary approaches proposed in moral theology. Three different approaches will be considered—the theory of

the fundamental option, Kohlberg's theory of moral development, and Stanley Hauerwas's approach to the virtues and
Christian ethics.

Many Catholic moral theologians have accepted the theory
of the fundamental option to explain the basic orientation of
the person and to distinguish this basic orientation from particular individual acts. There have been different ways of
understanding the fundamental option. Bernard Häring has
used both Scripture, philosophy, and psychology to provide
a basis for developing a theory of the fundamental option.
Häring rightly recognizes that the fundamental option then
must be embodied in fundamental attitudes or virtues, especially what he calls the eschatological virtues.[34] In my judgment Häring's recognition of these different levels of moral
reality is very important—the fundamental option, the virtues which embody it, and the particular acts which express it.

Timothy O'Connell has made the fundamental option an
important part of his contemporary manual of moral theology.[35] O'Connell's book still shares the primary purpose of
the manuals of moral theology in training ministers for the
sacrament of penance. Although the author does not explicitly
maintain that his book has this rather limited purpose, the
whole development of the book indicates such a somewhat
narrow approach. One chapter is entitled "Morality, Sin, and
Virtue," but for all practical purposes the entire chapter is
devoted to sin. Lacking is a development of the virtues as em-
bodiments of the fundamental option, while the main focus
of the book is to come to a better understanding of what is
sin and what actions are wrong.

O'Connell bases his approach to the fundamental option
on the thought of Karl Rahner. The person as subject is
distinguished from the person as agent; being is distinguished
from doing. Transcendental freedom involves the core freedom
of the person as subject, whereas categorical freedom refers
to the freedom of the person as agent to perform particular
categorical acts. In every categorical act there is not only the
particular act which is done by the agent, but there is also
the involvement of the subject who in the process may be determining oneself as subject. Since the fundamental option occurs on a level of transcendental freedom, human beings can-

not be reflexively conscious of it as they are of categorical acts. The fundamental option is a transcendental act of self-disposition occurring through and in the concrete categorical acts.

In general Rahner's transcendental anthropology has been criticized by some, as Johann Baptist Metz, for its failure to give enough importance to the social and political dimensions of human existence.[36] I believe this critique is even more applicable to O'Connell's description of the fundamental option. The fundamental option exists on the transcendental level and the level of the subject. The categorical level and the level of the agent are thus distinguished from the fundamental option. The Christology developed in the first section stresses that redemption involves more than simply the individual's relationship to God. The relational model of person tries to do greater justice to the multifaceted aspects of redemption involving not only our relationship with God on the spiritual level but also our relationships with others, the world, and self in terms of the historical, social, and political levels. The fundamental option as an acceptance of God's gracious gift must recognize all the constitutive dimensions of redemption.

Note that my objection has been centered especially on O'Connell's interpretation of the fundamental option. Part of the problem stems from the purpose and intended audience of O'Connell's book. *Principles for a Catholic Morality* was written primarily for seminarians. Although the book has creatively incorporated many contemporary developments into its approach to moral theology, it still continues to share the purpose of the older manuals of moral theology of preparing ministers for the sacrament of penance. In this connection O'Connell is rightly reacting against the concept of mortal sin found in the manuals of moral theology. Mortal sin was previously understood as a serious offense against the law of God and was a quite frequent occurrence in the Christian life. In contrast, O'Connell uses the concept of fundamental option primarily to obtain a better understanding of mortal sin. Mortal sin is on the level of transcendental or core freedom, not on the level of categorical freedom. The thrust of O'Connell's approach is to stress the distinction between the categorical and the transcendental, between the agent and the subject, between doing and being. Mortal sin cannot be equated with any categorical act as such since by definition it occurs on the level of the transcendental. Yet O'Connell does not emphasize enough the relationship between the transcendental and the categorical, nor does he develop the positive aspects of fundamental option as the loving response of the Christian to the gift of God in Christ Jesus which must continue to deepen and develop in one's life. Thus, O'Connell's orientation emphasizes the distinction between the categorical and the transcendental and neglects the positive aspect of fundamental option as being so significant in the life of the Christian person.

Rahner's concept of fundamental option can be developed in such a way that it does not necessarily involve a failure to appreciate the totality of relationships and does not unduly separate the transcendental from the categorical. Recall that one very important implication of fundamental option for Rahner is bringing together in a unity the love of God and the love of neighbor. This union is possible because in all of our categorical acts with regard to neighbor, world, and self there is also present our relationship as subject to God who is subject. The love of God is not a categorical act alongside other categorical acts. Rather the love of God is present in and with all our categorical acts.

Yes, there is a distinction between the categorical and the transcendental, but what is distinguished should not be separated. Transcendental freedom is the condition for the possibility of categorical freedom. Acts of categorical freedom are ultimately grounded in transcendental freedom.

A full discussion of fundamental option in moral theology should see not only its negative aspect in sin but also its positive aspect in love. The fundamental option or fundamental orientation is what gives meaning to the person as subject and influences what the agent does. The biblical concepts of discipleship, conversion, and love can all be explained in terms of the theory of the fundamental option. In this understanding, for example, continual conversion means the growth in our love of God on the transcendental level and the concomitant growth of our relationships with neighbor, world, and self on the categorical level.

Lawrence Kohlberg's theory of moral development has frequently been discussed in moral literature.[37] Again, the stress on moral growth and development is important, but I would view moral growth from a somewhat different perspective. Kohlberg has distinguished six stages within three levels of moral development going from the preconventional, through the conventional level, to the postconventional level. The postconventional, autonomous, or principled level in the sixth stage emphasizes universal principles and recognizes the rights of others and of society.

My understanding of moral growth and development differs from that proposed by Kohlberg. From my perspective there are two inherent limitations in Kohlberg's approach to the whole question. First, his entire theory is based on a cognitive structural theory which basically limits his approach only to decision-making. Second, he is attempting to propose a theory of moral development which is acceptable in a pluralistic society, and hence he tries to avoid questions of content and substance, because such questions raise insurmountable problems in a morally pluralistic society. Kohlberg's approach is primarily a formal understanding of morality based on justice. Such an approach also fits in well with his own Kantian philosophy, but moral theology should be interested in the content of Christian morality.

In my perspective moral development means growth in the relationships involved in being a person and in the attributes and virtues that should guide and direct these relationships. In this light Kohlberg limits growth merely to the decision-making level and lacks the broader development of the moral person as such. Not only does Kohlberg limit the area of development to the decision-making process itself, but there are further limitations. His primary concern seems to be that of formal justice, but other important moral areas such as love, mercy, forgiveness, reconciliation, etc. are not discussed. Others have criticized Kohlberg for not giving enough importance to affectivity. Carol Gilligan has objected to his approach because of its male bias.[38]

In general Kohlberg's approach to the question of moral development seems too limited and does not deal with the person as such who lives in a multiplicity of relationships. Kohlberg himself has dismissed the concept of virtue and its role in moral growth.[39] However, even in Kohlberg's limited theory there are some traces both of relationality and of virtue. The postconventional stage recognizes that the person lives in relationships with many other human beings who have their rights and dignity and with society. The postconventional moves beyond the self-centered level of reward and punishment and beyond the conventional level with its recognition of the expectations of the group. The postconventional stage recognizes that the social group with its common good and the rights and roles of other persons in the group or society must be respected. The emphasis on universality and impartiality indicates a recognition of one's existing in relationships with others and with society. Also, the sixth stage of universal, in-principled orientation can be understood as a virtue or attribute that characterizes the decision-making process of the person. In general Kohlberg's approach is too limited and fails to see moral development in terms of the growth of the person, the person's relationships, and the virtues which modify the person in these relationships. However, within the limited area of decision-making there are aspects of both relationality and virtue approaches in Kohlberg.

No contemporary Christian ethicist has written more on character and virtue than Stanley Hauerwas. Hauerwas's work has focused attention on this important question which has too often been neglected in contemporary Christian ethics and moral theology. From his doctoral dissertation to his present writing this prolific and creative thinker has been developing a narrative-based Christian ethics which highlights the importance of virtue, vision, and the character of the disciple living within the Christian community of the Church.[40] It is impossible to do justice to Hauerwas's work in a few pages, but I will point out the primary areas of my disagreement.

Hauerwas readily recognizes that his attempt to seek a foundation for morality in the historical, contingent Christian community is at odds with the mainstream of modern ethical theory. Christian ethics for Hauerwas is that ethics done within the Christian community which remembers and retells the story of Jesus, thus creating a people of character, vision, and virtue who will be faithful witnesses of that story. Christian social ethics according to Hauerwas stresses the partiality and distinctiveness of Jesus and of the Christian community or Church. The first social ethical task of the Church is to be the Church — not to make the world more peaceful or just. The Church is to be a faithful manifestation of God's reign in the world. Such an understanding stresses the uniqueness of Christianity and implies a strong distinction and even gulf between Christian ethics and other ethics.

In the light of the basic thrust of this study I will concentrate on my primary differences with Hauerwas in the area of Christology. The first difference is methodological, while the second concerns the substantive question of the relationship between redemption in Christ Jesus and the universal will of God to offer redemptive love to all people.

In the recent summary of his thought Hauerwas recognizes that the most significant chapter in developing his own ethical theory is the one on the ethical significance of Jesus.[41] Here the author insists on beginning not with Christology but with the Jesus portrayed in the Gospels, even though he realizes that this is not the "real Jesus." In this light the chapter includes sections on Jesus, Israel and the Imitation of God, Jesus and the Kingdom of God, the Resurrection: the Establishment of a Kingdom of Forgiveness and Peace. In this light the Church does not have but is a social ethics. The Church is a community of the followers of Jesus who are a people of virtue — not simply any virtue but the virtues necessary for remembering and retelling the story of a crucified savior.[42] In many of his writings Hauerwas has emphasized the role of the Church and of the Christian in remembering and retelling the story of Jesus.[43]

In his Christology (Hauerwas might not even want to use the word, however, because of his insistence on the importance of the Jesus of the Gospels) Hauerwas gives primary and almost exclusive emphasis to the Jesus of the Scriptures. As mentioned earlier, I would agree with the methodological approach proposed by O'Collins which respects the full range of Christian and Catholic experience, expectations, teachings, reflections, and activity which span the present, the future, and the past. Such a methodology would obviously include more than only the Jesus of the Scripture and thus be more inclusive than Hauerwas's Christology. At the same time such a method would insist on more than only remembering and retelling the past story but would also highlight the present Christian experience and the future Christian hope.

The important substantive question somewhat connected to the preceding methodological one is the relationship between redemption offered in Christ Jesus and the universal salvific will of God who wants to offer all people the fullness of redemptive love. Hauerwas does not give much explicit attention to this question. By recognizing that God does offer salvation and redemption to all human beings one must conclude that redemption exists beyond the sphere of the explicitly Christian and the Christian Church. In this light my position would not see the Christian person or the Church community as so unique and different from all others. Hauerwas accepts too great a distinction between the Church and the world for it to be compatible with my understanding of the universality of the offer of redemption. In keeping both with his methodology and with his emphasis on the distinctiveness of redemption in Jesus, Hauerwas insists that being Christian is not equivalent to being human. I have maintained that the material content of Christian morality in terms of acts, proximate dispositions, values, and goals (e.g., love, mercy, forgiveness, even willingness to sacrifice one's life for others) is not unique and that others can and do prize and arrive at the same moral content. Hauerwas's approach is nuanced because he admits that to be Christian is to fulfill the most profound human desires, but for Hauerwas Christian ethics knows what it knows only in and through the Christian story.[44] With Schillebeeckx I stress the need for Christians today, especially in the light of contemporary experience, to write their own fifth gospel.

Another great difference between my approach and that of Hauerwas involves his making narrative and story the only way of understanding not only the Gospel message but also the moral life of the Christian and of the Church. Christian ethics in its full reflection on Christian existence must in my judgment appeal to much more than narrative and story. It is this exclusively narrative emphasis that also governs his approach to particular moral questions. Hauerwas, for example, argues that the Christian moral arguments against abortion have failed primarily because they have dealt with the questions and answers proposed by a universal ethic.[45] There are other areas of disagreement which flow from these more fundamental differences. I see a much greater role for reason and experience in mediating the Christian faith experience to the questions of moral methodology, the meaning and understanding of the moral person, the process of decision-making, and the morality of acts. In addition, the Christian conclusions on questions such as abortion, peace, economic justice, and sexuality should be open to and, in principle, communicable to all other human beings.

Hauerwas has made many creative suggestions in the area of moral theology and has rightly stressed the importance of character and virtue. Here I have concentrated on the Christological differences between his approach and my own and on the consequent different understanding of how character and virtue relate to the Christian person. Hauerwas tends toward a somewhat sectarian understanding of Christianity, whereas I opt for a traditionally more Catholic type of methodology, Christology, and ecclesiology.

This chapter has attempted to understand the person as moral agent and subject especially in the light of considerations taken from contemporary Christology. After a schematic development of my understanding of the Christian person as moral agent and subject, the final section pointed out some differences with other contemporary approaches in moral theology to the person.

NOTES

I am grateful to my colleagues William Hill and Elizabeth Johnson for helping my study of contemporary Christology.

1. For an understanding of the virtues from a Thomistic perspective see George P. Klubertanz, *Habits and Virtues* (New York: Appleton-Century-Crofts, 1965).

2. As examples of attempts to renew moral theology by appealing to the Thomistic tradition of virtues see Thomas Deman, *Aux origines de la théologie morale* (Montréal: Inst. d'Études Médiévales, 1951); Gérard Gille-

man, *The Primacy of Charity in Moral Theology* (Westminster, MD: Newman Press, 1959); S. Pinckaers, *Le renouveau de la morale* (Paris: Casterman, 1964).

3. Alasdair MacIntyre, *After Virtue: A Study in Moral Theory* (Notre Dame, IN: University of Notre Dame Press, 1981).

4. The works of Stanley Hauerwas dealing with this approach are *Character and the Christian Life: A Study in Theological Ethics* (San Antonio, TX: Trinity University Press, 1975); *Vision and Virtue: Essays in Christian Ethical Reflection* (Notre Dame, IN: University of Notre Dame Press, 1974); *Truthfulness and Tragedy: Further Investigations in Christian Ethics* (Notre Dame, IN: University of Notre Dame Press, 1977); *A Community of Character: Toward a Constructive Christian Social Ethic* (Notre Dame, IN: University of Notre Dame Press, 1981); *The Peaceable Kingdom: A Primer in Christian Ethics* (Notre Dame, IN: University of Notre Dame Press, 1983).

5. For Häring's latest development of this theme see Bernard Häring, *Free and Faithful in Christ*, vol. I: *General Moral Theology* (New York: Seabury Press, 1978), pp. 378-470.

6. Walter E. Conn, *Conscience: Development and Self-Transcendence* (Birmingham, AL: Religious Education Press, 1981).

7. Hans Küng, *On Being a Christian* (New York: Doubleday, 1976).

8. Leo J. O'Donovan, "The Ethical Implications of Schillebeeckx's Christology," *Proceedings of the Catholic Theological Society of America* 37 (1983): 119-122.

9. Leonardo Boff, *Jesus Christ Liberator* (Maryknoll, NY: Orbis Books, 1979).

10. Enda McDonagh, *The Making of Disciples* (Wilmington, DE: Michael Glazier, Inc., 1982), pp. 11-21.

11. Hauerwas, *Character and the Christian Life*, pp 3ff., 179ff.

12. *Enchiridion Symbolorum Definitionum et Declarationum De Rebus Fidei et Morum*, 32nd ed., ed. H. Denzinger, A. Schönmetzer (Barcelona: Herder, 1963), nn. 301ff.

13. For overviews of contemporary Christologies, in addition to the works already cited, see Bernard Cooke, "Horizons on Christology in the Seventies," *Horizons* 6 (1979): 193-217; Francis Schüssler Fiorenza, "Christology after Vatican II: A Shift of Horizons," *The Ecumenist* 18 (1980): 81-89.

14. Raymond Brown, "Review of Edward Schillebeeckx, *Jesus: An Experiment in Christology*," *Catholic Biblical Quarterly* 42 (1980): 420-423.

15. In describing the different understandings of discipleship in the Gospels I am heavily dependent upon Francis Schüssler Fiorenza, *Foundational Theology: Jesus and the Church* (New York: Crossroad, 1984), pp. 133-154.

16. Häring, *Free and Faithful in Christ*, vol. 1, pp. 53-109.

17. Edward Schillebeeckx, *Jesus: An Experiment in Christology* (New York: Crossroad, 1981), pp. 573ff.

18. Elisabeth Schüssler Fiorenza, "Toward a Feminist Biblical Hermeneutics: Biblical Interpretation and Liberation Theology," in *The Challenge of Liberation Theology: A First World Response*, ed. Brian Mahan and

L. Dale Richesin (Maryknoll, NY: Orbis Books, 1981), pp. 91-112; also Schüssler Fiorenza, *In Memory of Her: A Feminist Theological Reconstruction of Christian Origins* (New York: Crossroad, 1983).

19. Gerald O'Collins, *Interpreting Jesus* (Ramsey, NJ: Paulist Press, 1983), pp. 5-13.

20. For a contemporary, somewhat revisionist approach to the Mennonite tradition see John Howard Yoder, *The Politics of Jesus* (Grand Rapids, MI: William B. Eerdmans, 1972).

21. Karl Rahner, *Foundations of Christian Faith: An Introduction to the Idea of Christianity* (New York: Seabury, 1978), especially chapters 5 and 6.

22. Raimundo Panikkar, *The Unknown Christ of Hinduism: Toward an Ecumenical Christophany*, rev. ed. (Maryknoll, NY: Orbis Books, 1981).

23. Teresa Mary DeFerrari, *The Problem of Charity for Self* (Boston: St. Paul Editions, 1962).

24. Justice in the World in *Renewing the Earth: Catholic Documents on Peace, Justice, and Liberation*, ed. David J. O'Brien and Thomas A. Shannon (Garden City, NY: Doubleday Image Books, 1977), p. 391.

25. Charles M. Murphy, "Action for Justice as Constitutive of the Preaching of the Gospel: What Did the 1971 Synod Mean?" *Theological Studies* 44 (1983): 298-311.

26. Schillebeeckx, *Jesus*, pp. 662ff.

27. Häring, *Free and Faithful*, vol. 1, pp. 105-163.

28. Francis P. Sammon, "The Expression 'Signs of the Times' in Recent Theology" (S.T.L. diss., The Catholic University of America, 1979).

29. Donal Dorr, *Option for the Poor: A Hundred Years of Vatican Social Teaching* (Maryknoll, NY: Orbis Books, 1983).

30. For an understanding of distributive justice as applied to the contemporary American scene see Daniel C. Maguire, *A New American Justice: Ending the White Male Monopolies* (Garden City, NY: Doubleday, 1980).

31. Charles Birch, "Nature, Humanity, and God in Ecological Perspective," and Vitaly Borovoy, "Christian Perspectives on Creation in a Time of Ecological Unsustainability," in *Faith and Science in an Unjust World: Report of the World Council of Churches' Conference on Faith, Science, and the Future*, vol. 1, ed. Roger L. Shinn (Philadelphia: Fortress Press, 1980), pp. 62-73; 80-86.

32. Häring, *Free and Faithful in Christ*, vol. 1, pp. 216ff.

33. For an overview of different positions on this subject see Charles E. Curran and Richard A. McCormick, eds., *Readings in Moral Theology No. 2: The Distinctiveness of Christian Ethics* (New York: Paulist Press, 1980).

34. Häring, *Free and Faithful in Christ*, vol. 1, pp. 164-222.

35. Timothy E. O'Connell, *Principles for a Catholic Morality* (New York: Seabury Press, 1978), especially pp. 57-82.

36. Johann Baptist Metz, *Faith in History and Society: Toward a Practical Fundamental Theology* (New York: Seabury, 1980).

37. For a very helpful collection of Kohlberg's essays on this subject see Lawrence Kohlberg, *Essays on Moral Development*, 2 vols. (San Francisco: Harper and Row, 1981, 1983).

38. Carol Gilligan, *In a Different Voice: Psychological Theory and Women's Development* (Cambridge, Mass.: Harvard University Press, 1982). For a

recent evaluation and critique of Kohlberg by a moral theologian see Philip S. Keane, *Christian Ethics and Imagination: A Theological Inquiry* (New York: Paulist Press, 1984).

39. Paul J. Philibert, "Kohlberg's Use of Virtue," *International Philosophical Quarterly* 15, 4 (1975): 455-479.

40. See note 4 for Hauerwas's principal publications beginning with his revised doctoral dissertation. His latest work, *The Peaceable Kingdom*, is the most systematic and serves as the basis for the summary given in the text.

41. Hauerwas, *The Peaceable Kingdom*, pp. 72-95.

42. Ibid., p. 103.

43. Hauerwas, *A Community of Character*, pp. 9-71.

44. For Hauerwas's position on these questions see *The Peaceable Kingdom*, pp. 50-71.

45. Hauerwas, *A Community of Character*, pp. 212-229.

4. Sin

Does sin have any meaning for modern people? Is sin a vital reality for the twentieth century Christian? Maybe the sense of sin was just a morbid concept from the Middle Ages which people come of age have rightly put behind themselves.

There is a reluctance on the part of all of us to admit our sinfulness, but it seems that sin still retains an importance in contemporary human experience. Technology and science have given us an awesome power over creation; knowledge has been increasing at an ever growing rate; we are continually finding out more about ourselves and our world. But sinfulness also marks the lives of individual human beings and of society. In times of great scientific strides and progress we human beings tend to forget our own limitations and sinfulness, but a meditative reflection on reality cannot help but uncover even in our modern world the existence and importance of sin.

Sin can simply be described for the present as a lack of love and an alienation from God and others. If we are honest with ourselves, we have to admit our own sinfulness. Our own selfishness and unwillingness to go out of our way to help others are factors we cannot forget as much as we might like to. Are we willing to share what we have with the poor? Are we willing to embrace the outcast and the forgotten? Are we primarily motivated by the demands of our neighbor in need or rather by our own selfish needs? Are we really willing to change the established structures of our society in which we hold privileged positions at the expense of others? If sin is the opposite of love, then there is quite a bit of sin in our lives, despite the fact that we become uncomfortable when we think about it.

But sin is not just an individual phenomenon. Sin shows its effects in our society as a whole and perhaps is most present in the fact that many of us are unwilling to admit our own sinfulness. A few years ago the death of God theology and the secular city theology tended to downplay the reality of sin. Charles West of Princeton Theological Seminary has described the two opposing viewpoints at the 1966 Conference on Church and Society sponsored by the World Council of Churches as the "theological technocrats" versus the "theological guerrillas."[1] The theological technocrats were those who celebrated the joys of the secular city in which human beings are becoming progressively more whole and more free. However, their opponents pointed out that while these people were finding salvation and freedom in the secular city, this same secular city society was imprisoning two-thirds of the world in hunger, misery and poverty. Today we can be thankful for the protest movements that have reminded us of the sins that are existing in our society. We must acknowledge that our sins both individually and collectively have been hurting many others.

How easy it is to forget our own sinfulness while at the same time condemning the sinfulness of others. A few years ago there was a television documentary on the Hitler regime in Germany. The final portion of the film showed the last days of the Third Reich and portrayed Hitler as a megalomaniac whose distorted pride and fury made him keep fighting to the bitter end despite all the human death and suffering caused by him. However, never once did the film even suggest that part of the responsibility might have been ours. What right did we as Christians have to demand an unconditional surrender? Perhaps we were just as responsible as Hitler in prolonging the carnage of war. Some years ago the Sunday Magazine section of the *New York Times* had an article on the end of the hippie movement which was called "The Death of Love." The hippie community was an attempt to have people live together in the bonds of love, but the experiment was unsuccessful precisely because people forgot the existence of sin. Sin ultimately entered the hippie community in the form of drugs, taking advantage of others, self-promotion and feuds. How often today many overly romantic people fail to realize the existence of sin in the world! On the surface it might seem that we have outgrown the reality of sin, but a moment's reflection reminds us of the existence of sin in our own lives and in our own world. Unfortunately, sin is alive and well in the twentieth century.

The Christian message has always realized the importance of sin; in fact, the Christian mystery does not make sense apart from the reality of sin. "It was a fundamental assertion of the kerygma that Jesus came into the world to save sinners, and that he in fact did so by his death."[2] According to the Matthean account (1:21) he was called Jesus precisely because he would save his people from their sins. The redemptive work of Jesus has meaning only in terms of sin; the Paschal Mystery is ultimately the triumph over sin and death. Although his death showed forth the power of sin and the separation between sin and Jesus, the resurrection was the sign and promise of victory. The gospel message clearly sees the mission of Jesus in terms of redemption and victory over sin. The early Church was aware of its call to continue this mission and free people from sin and bring them into the newness of life in Christ. Christian anthropology recognizes the limited and sinful nature of human beings; in fact, anthropology which does not give sufficient attention to sinfulness cannot claim to be Christian.[3]

Despite the importance of sin in the Christian message, Catholic theology has been negligent in developing an adequate understanding of sin. Too often sin has been considered only in terms of the model of law and obedience which emphasizes sin as a specific external action. These actions were then thoroughly categorized and catalogued in lists. Sin as an external action viewed in the light of obedience to the law of God is a very inadequate model for understanding the reality of sin. A mechanical, individualistic, and actualistic concept of sin robbed sin of its real existential meaning for the Christian. Perhaps it is true that the world has lost the sense of sin, but even more unfortunate is the fact that Catholic Christians have lost a true understanding of sin.

A renewed understanding of sin should find its basic inspiration in the Scriptures but also make use of the insights of contemporary understandings of anthropology.[4] Both Scripture and contemporary understandings argue for a view of sin that follows the model of relationality. The individual person is a creature living in a multiplicity of relationships, sin is that which destroys these relationships. Perhaps the best illustration of the meaning of sin in the Scriptures is the account given in the first chapters of the book of Genesis. Modern scripture studies remind us that the Genesis account is not an historical account of two people but rather a reflective meditation many years later on the reality of sin. The authors of Genesis faced the basic problem that confronts all who believe in a good and gracious God. If the good God made all things, why is there so much evil in the world? Their answer? Sin. The Judaeo-Christian message makes no sense without an understanding of sin, and the authors here narrate in a very fanciful way their understanding of sin. Contemporary theologians can only marvel at the insight of the authors of Genesis.[5]

The convenant relationship characterizes the whole of the scriptural understanding of the relationship between God and her people. The story of salvation is the story of God's loving choice of a people as her own. Sin is the refusal of creatures to accept the gift of God's love. Although creatures spurned this gift, God is so faithful in his commitment that he sent his Son to restore the relationship of love and offer all human beings an opportunity to enter into his covenant relationship. The Christian believes that all people receive this same invitation in one way or another from God. Thus in Genesis sin is viewed not primarily as a particular external act or even as a particular act of disobedience seen in itself (these are aspects of the reality of sin but not the primary aspect), but rather as the refusal of human beings to accept their relationship of loving dependence on God. Creatures wanted to be like God — this was the temptation which was proposed by the evil one.

The fact that sin is to be seen in terms of a relationship is more evident in other details of this story. The author implies that God came down and walked with Adam and Eve in the evening in the cool of the garden — a very fanciful way of picturing the relationship of love between them. As a consequence of sin, however, Adam and Eve hid themselves when Yahweh came to walk with them in the garden. As a result of their sin Adam and Eve were expelled from the garden, a sign they had truly broken their relationship of loving dependence on God. Death, according to Genesis, is the penalty of sin; but such a penalty cannot be conceived as merely an arbitrary punishment for wrongdoing. Since sin itself is separation from the author of life, then death is the natural consequence of sin and not just an extrinsic penalty or punishment.

But sin also affects one's relationship with fellow creatures. Genesis is lyrical in its description of the love union of Adam and Eve. Eve is the helpmate and companion that Adam was not able to find in the rest of creation; she is flesh of his flesh and bone of his bone. The love union of the two is described by the fact that they left all other persons and things to become one body. But sin deeply affected that union of love, as is portrayed in Adam's reaction to Yahweh after his sin. Adam, instead of defending and protecting his wife with whom he formed one body, now placed the blame on her — "It was the woman you put with me; she gave me the fruit, and I ate it" (Genesis 3:12). The very next chapter describes how the children of Adam and Eve killed one another. The author graphically makes his point: sin affects the relationships existing among human beings.

The Genesis narrative develops its meditative reflection on sin by illustrating that sin also affects our relationship with the world. Before the "fall," Adam is portrayed as the king of all creation which exists in perfect subordination to him as is evidenced by the fact that Adam gave a name to all the animals. Sin brings discord into this marvelous harmony of the world. In that which is most characteristically masculine, man's relationship with the cosmos is changed through sin. From henceforth he will know suffering, sweat, and fatigue as he tries to work the fields to provide for his needs and those of his family. The remarkable harmony in which the world would have been as putty in his hands is shattered so that man will now know pain and suffering in work as he tries to eke out his existence against the forces of the world rather than in harmony with them. Sin's effect on our relationship to the world is also graphically illustrated in the case of Eve, for she is affected in that which (in the mentality of the author) is most characteristically womanly — the bearing of children. As a result of sin she would now know the pains of childbirth and bring forth her children in pain and suffering. Thus the membranes of her own body would resist the process of childbirth and cause her pain rather than exist in perfect harmony with the birth process. One can only admire the theological acumen and literary genius which thus presents the reality of sin as affecting our relationship to God, neighbor and the total cosmos.

The opening eleven chapters of Genesis and much of the Old Testament underline the dynamic aspect of sin especially in its cosmic dimension. In the last few years Catholic theology and catechetics have emphasized the concept of salvation history, but the opening chapters of Genesis

are truly a history of sin. Human beings continue to fall
into sin which then by incarnating itself in society and
structures tends to grow and increase. The Old Testament
frequently recalls the many saving interventions of God
(e.g., Noah, Abraham, Moses, etc.); but despite all these
saving interventions, the people fall back into the condition of sin. The Old Testament was very conscious of the
cosmic aspect of sin which has been emphasized in the
concept of the sin of the world developed by some contemporary theologians.[6] Sin affects the individual and
incarnates itself in the structures, customs and institutions
of our environment, and thus the reign of sin grows and
increases. In such an environment other individuals easily
become contaminated by sin. There are many ways in
which one can view the reality of sin, e.g., disobedience
to the divine commands; but the model of multiple relationships from the viewpoint of the Scriptures and the
best insights of contemporary anthropology appears to be
the most adequate.

In the Christian understanding, salvation or redemption
is the gracious act of God freeing human beings from sin
and restoring them to the relationship of love. Catholic
theology has always required the free acceptance of this
gift of God's love which involves a change of heart and
entrance into a relationship of love with the Father
through Christ Jesus, which affects all the relationships
which constitute the person. This gift of salvation, which
some theologians today call wholeness, is offered in one
form or another to all persons; but for the Christian it is
made explicit in the gospel message preached by the
Church, which continues the mission of Jesus in time and
space. Does the Christian ever overcome the sinful condition? The answer is yes and no. Traditional Catholic theology understands that when the individual accepts the
gracious gift of salvation he or she has now overcome
the radical separation from God and neighbor, but every
human being in this world falls short of the fullness of
love in relationships with God and neighbor. In this sense

the Christian is at the same time justified and a sinner (*simul justus et peccator*). Thus conversion, justification, or salvation (whatever term is chosen to describe this reality) is never perfect but always striving for a greater wholeness. Also there is the possibility that one might entirely break off that relationship of love with God and neighbor and thus again separate oneself in sinful isolation. Human sinfulness and sin occupy an important place in the Christian understanding of reality, so that if one does not know or experience the reality of sin and sinfulness then the concept of conversion or penance is meaningless.

The above description corresponds to the traditional concept of mortal and venial sin, but the distinction is not viewed primarily in terms of a particular action. Mortal sin from the scriptural viewpoint is better interpreted in terms of a relationship which affects not only the individual's relationship with God but also the relationship with one's neighbors and the whole world, thus affecting the very core of the person. According to the Scriptures conversion is the process of passing from death to life, from darkness to light, from the old to the new, from flesh to the spirit, a change of heart animated by the gift of the life-giving Spirit.[7] Mortal sin is the opposite of this process and is described in the older categories as the passing from the state of grace to the state of sin.

Contemporary theologians with this scriptural basis and borrowing insights from various philosophical viewpoints have lately described sin in terms of a fundamental option.[8] From a Thomistic viewpoint mortal sin is seen as the orientation of the person away from God as one's last end with the substitution of another ultimate end, which in the last analysis is oneself. From an existentialist perspective, mortal sin is the project of existence which overturns the foundational orientation and tendency of the life of the person. From a personalist understanding, sin is the breaking of the relationship of love with God and neighbor. All these different viewpoints emphasize the fact that mortal sin is not just an external action viewed in itself but rather a fundamental orientation of the person, a notion which corresponds with the biblical concept of a change of heart.

In the past moral theology distorted the concept of mortal sin by understanding sin primarily in terms of an external act, thereby viewing sin more as a thing than as a relationship. Catechisms and textbooks frequently classified the catalogues of actions which were mortal sins. Thus sin lost its intensely personal meaning, to say nothing of its social and cosmic dimension. If mortal sin is viewed as just an external act, then the existence of mortal sin appears to be much more frequent than in the concept of a relationship.

A more relational understanding of sin especially as specified in the theory of the fundamental option gives less importance to the external action itself. The external act in such a theory is essentially ambiguous, for it has meaning only insofar as it is revelatory of the human person and the person's relationships with others. Common sense and prudence have always accepted the reality that you cannot judge a person on the basis of just one short meeting or in the light of one particular action. One cannot judge the ability of an athlete by just seeing the results of one particular action. The sharp word that a person utters may have a variety of meanings. It could very well indicate an intense dislike for the person with whom one is talking, or it might only be indicative of impatience, a migraine headache or the failure to have had a second cup of coffee. Modern psychology also emphasizes the ambiguity of the external act. The full personal meaning of a particular act very often can never be truly known, for even the individual is not always that conscious of her personal motives. A particular act would involve mortal sin only if the act were expressive of this breaking of a fundamental relationship of love with God and neighbor.

Catholic theology has long recognized that the individual goes from "sin" to "grace" not by one action but by a long series of actions which form one process. Mortal sin must now be viewed in the same way. One does not change so fundamental a relationship just in one particular action, but ordinarily there is a process taking place over a period of time in which this relationship gradually becomes weakened and then is finally broken. This process must ultimately culminate in an action which involves the very existential core of the person and such actions are not frequent in our lives. In such an understanding it is impossible for a person to be in and out of mortal sin two or three times a week. The poor approach of the past has cheapened the very notion and concept of mortal sin which as a consequence has lost real meaning for many Catholics today. Mortal sin is not a common occurrence, and is generally the culmination of a development lasting over a period of time. Again, personal experience reminds us how difficult and hard it is for us to change some of our basic human orientations. This experience in our relationships with others and with ourselves should reveal some understanding of the reality of our relationship with God.

The stress on the external act in the past definitely distorted the concept of mortal sin. In fairness even to the catechism requirements for mortal sin, it must be pointed out that they included other criteria in addition to the act itself. The threefold criteria for the existence of mortal sin included: grave matter, full knowledge, and full consent of the will. These three conditions if properly understood call for an almost total reaction from the depth of the person, a truly fundamental option or orientation. Unfortunately, theology and catechetics gave primary importance to the matter itself as the ultimate determining criterion of the existence of mortal sin. Such a concept even led to the conclusion that certain actions always involve grave matter.[9] The theory behind this insistence on the matter of the external action itself in its best possible interpretation was the presumption that grave or important matter will ordinarily involve the person in the very core of his or her existence, whereas light matter will ordinarily not evoke a total response on the part of the person. Today our knowledge of human beings and human relationships is such that it is difficult to place much importance on such presumptions especially because we now appreciate the difficulty involved in saying that any one action expresses the very depths of the person. Once sin is viewed in terms of the fundamental relationship between the person and God which consists primarily in a basic orientation and not in individual actions, then even the presumptive nature of the older approach no longer retains great value or usefulness.

What then are the criteria for establishing the existence of mortal sin? In actuality there are no certain criteria by which one can establish the existence of mortal sin. Perhaps the best approach remains that found in the Scriptures. Our relationship with God is known and manifested in our relationship with our neighbors. This is the gist of the so-called judgment scene in Matthew. "Lord, when did we see you hungry or thirsty, a stranger or naked, sick or in prison, and did not come to your help?" (Matt. 25:44). John reminds us that we cannot love the God we do not see if we do not love our neighbor whom we do see. The Christian commandment joins together love of God and love of neighbor into a unity so that the best criterion of our love for God is precisely our love for our neighbor, but even this criterion fails to be very specific and remains difficult to apply accurately, again because of the essential ambiguity of the external act. It always remains difficult to tell if one has broken this multiple relationship of love. Even the individual person in many cases cannot be aware of it in any reflexive way because of the very nature of this relationship and because of the difficulties of totally understanding one's own motives.

Some theologians conscious of the ambiguity of the external action viewed apart from the orientation of the person have tended to introduce other distinctions in the understanding of sin. For example, a threefold distinction is made: Mortal sin, serious sin, venial sin. Mortal sin is reserved for that which really separates us from love;

whereas serious sin is an action viewed in itself which is of serious nature but by itself cannot indicate whether the relationship of love is broken or not.[10] Another theologian introduces such distinctions as sin, mortal sin, serious sin, subjectively non-serious sin, venial sin, light sin, subjectively no imputation of sin.[11] I do not believe that such distinctions are necessary or ultimately even that helpful from a theological or catechetical viewpoint. At best they tend to be only presumptions, and the danger always exists of making them into rigid categories. While such elaborate distinctions serve as a salutary reminder of the complexity and ambiguity of the reality of sin, they remain only approximations which tend in a somewhat simplistic way to analyze the relationship between God and her creatures. It seems to be better to retain just the concepts of mortal sin and venial sin with the realization that mortal sin is the breaking of this multiple love relationship and thus involves a core decision of the whole person, whereas venial sin refers to the lessening of the relationship without involving a total break in that relationship. Naturally there are many degrees involved in the way in which this relationship can be affected without being severed.

However, there is a possible danger of dualism in the approach which sees sin primarily in terms of this fundamental relationship or option which involves one in the very core of one's being. In the past there was an overemphasis on the external act itself, but in the newer perspective there is the danger of not giving enough importance to the external act itself. Mortal sin should be viewed primarily in terms of intentionality, subjective involvement, and personalist categories; but there remains the danger of forgetting about the external act itself. Catholic theology in the last decade has embraced the more personalist categories of thought, but there is an inherent danger that such thought patterns will not pay enough attention to the social, political, and cosmic aspects of reality. The problems facing the world today are of such social complexity that a narrowly personalist approach will not be able to cope with them.[12] The human act remains a very complex entity. In theology most problems arise not from positive error but from a failure to give the proper weight to all the elements involved.

The notion of mortal sin described above views the individual act insofar as it is an expression of the whole person existing in his fundamental relationships with God and neighbor. However, the complex external act can be viewed from other aspects; for example, one can consider the external act insofar as it affects the persons and the world itself independently of the personal intentionality and involvement of the person placing the act. When a deranged person maims another, there is very little subjective involvement of the core of personhood in such an act, but such an action does have very drastic consequences on the unfortunate victim and on society itself. A highly scientific and technological society (which, however, is not to be canonized) appreciates the importance of the external act, as does a theology which sees the Christian as called to help create the new heaven and the new earth by one's own actions. If one is going to reserve the word sin for the fundamental option of love, then perhaps it would be helpful to speak of the external act viewed in relationship to self, others and the cosmos apart from the intentionality of the person in terms of right or wrong. Thus one could say that certain actions (cruelty, indiscriminate warfare, etc.) are wrong without necessarily involving grave sin on the part of the person.

An older Catholic theology did appreciate the problem by making the distinction between formal and material sin. Formal sin was precisely the external act insofar as it proceeded from the knowledge and will of the subject, whereas material sin was the act viewed in itself apart from the subjective involvement of the person in the act. One could even employ the term sin in a true but analogous way to describe the external act viewed in terms of its "objective" relationships, but perhaps the need to emphasize the reality of sin as the deeply per-

sonal orientation of one's life in terms of the primary relationships which constitute that existence would argue
against using the term sin to describe this other aspect of
the external act. No matter what terminology is chosen,
an understanding of sin in terms of relationality and the
fundamental option must avoid the danger of not paying
sufficient attention to the external action viewed in its
relationships to self, others, and the world apart from the
intentionality of the agent. This problem in the understanding of sin points to the deeper philosophical problem involving a proper understanding of the relationship
between subjective and objective. Theology today is
striving to overcome a false dichotomy, but at times some
distinctions such as those made above will be necessary.

Thus a better approach views mortal sin in terms of personal relationships, the involvement of the subject in one's
own orientation, and a process which gradually develops
over the course of time. Such an understanding of sin has
important practical and pastoral consequences. In practice
one cannot speak of the act viewed in itself as mortal sin.
There is no possible answer to the question: Is killing or
lying or adultery or blasphemy a mortal sin? (It would be
a legitimate question to ask if such an action were right or
wrong.) In fact one cannot even have mortal sins. The
plural form indicates that sin would be a thing, but if
mortal sin is properly understood in terms of a broken
relationship of love then it does not admit the plural usage.
There are no definite criteria for determining the existence
of mortal sin precisely because of the essential ambiguity
of the external act. Mortal sin seen as the culmination of a
gradual process resulting in the breaking of these fundamental relationships is obviously a rare occurrence in com-
parison with an older understanding of mortal sin.

The reality behind the concept of venial sin must also
be viewed in terms of a condition of the person and that
person's fundamental relationships with God, neighbor,
and the world. Catholic teaching has maintained that the
ordinary Christian cannot avoid the reality of venial sin in

one's life. This is another way of saying that the Christian always remains, *simul justus et peccator* (justified and a sinner at the same time), for the relationship of love with God, neighbor, and the world is never perfect. The individual act of venial sin refers to an action which does not come from a core personal involvement in an orientation away from God but rather is expressive of a coolness or lack of full dedication in this relationship of love. In the theory of the fundamental option venial sin remains a peripheral action which does not involve the core decision of the person. In the Thomistic perspective venial sin involves an illogical act because while the person in the core of her being is still united to God as ultimate end, this particular act is contrary to that orientation. However, the act remains on the periphery of the self and does not change the reality of one's orientation to God as ultimate end. Venial sin illustrates the condition of the Christian who constantly falls short of the total love union with God, neighbor and the world to which all are called. An emphasis in the past on particular acts has tended to see venial sin primarily in terms of particular acts of commission, whereas the realization of the sinful condition of the person opens up the wider horizons of the human condition itself and also acts of omission as well as commission.

New approaches in moral theology have been criticized by some for doing away with the concept of sin; in fact, people have applied to some contemporary theologians the scriptural words: "Behold the one who takes away the sins of the world." There is no doubt that an older theology and catechetics tended to develop a very warped notion of sin in the minds of many. The danger remains that in rejecting such inadequate notions the contemporary Catholic is at times tempted to forget the whole concept of sin. But the Christian message is robbed of its true meaning if one does not appreciate the reality of human sinfulness.

The loving gift of God in Christ to all of us presupposes the sinful condition of all in which we would be imprisoned without the gracious gift of God's redeeming love. No one can appreciate the great gift of God's love without an understanding of the reality of sin from which we have been freed by her gracious mercy and forgiveness. Mortal sin is a comparatively very rare occurrence in the Christian life, but this should only emphasize its importance and its true meaning as the breaking of our multiple relationships of love with God, neighbor and the world. The contemporary Christian also needs to be more conscious of our enduring, sinful condition — the fact that even though we are united in love with God and neighbor, nevertheless, we constantly fall short of the love that is asked of us. Superficial thinking at times does tend to forget the reality of sin. The history of theology furnishes many examples of theologies which have forgotten the existence of sin and its impact on our existence. The naive hopes of utopian dreams have been dashed against the reality of human sinfulness. Despite all the progress of science and technology we have not been able to overcome the basic human problems of selfishness, exploitation, self-interest, and the failure to accept responsibility for the neighbor in need. Many Catholics today have passed from a triumphalism of the Church to a triumphalism of the world. We are now very much aware of the sinfulness of the Church and the fact that a pilgrim Church is constantly in need of reform and renewal, but frequently we forget the reality of sin existing in the world itself with the suffering, hardship and frustration which that will entail. The perennial danger is to be lulled into forgetting the existence of sin. Then one's whole life and one's Christianity can become very comfortable. Is this not the problem with much of what passes for Christianity today?

The contemporary Christian needs to become more aware of the reality of sin — not in a morbid and scrupulous way, but in a manner that enables one to appreciate more the reality of God's loving gift, to understand the continuing failure to respond totally to that gift, and to encourage the individual Christian to join with the Risen

Lord in the struggle against sin. Catholic theology has explained the sacramental system in terms of the extension of the Incarnation in time and space. The love of God for us and our response become visible in the sacramental celebration. The reality of sin also becomes incarnated in time and space through the actions of human beings in the world, so that there are truly "sacraments of sin" — signs which make present the reality of sin in our human existence. Poverty, war, discrimination, alienation, sexism, institutional violence — these are all among the many sacraments of sin existing in our world.

How easy it remains for the contemporary Christian to forget the existence of sin, but a thoughtful reflection on human existence today in the light of the scriptural message of love of God and neighbor, especially the neighbor in need, reveals the continuing presence of sin in our life and world. Since Christianity so joins together the love of God and neighbor that the love for neighbor becomes the sign and criterion for our love for God, so too our sinful condition is manifested 'above all in our relationships with our neighbor and the world. The inequities of our world, the fact that the rich people and nations exploit poor people and nations, the will for power and the subjection of the weak and the failure of people to accept their responsibilities for the world and others are all signs of the reality of sin. The social, political, cultural, economic, and even religious aspects of our human existence all contain elements that show forth the failure of Christians to live the gospel message of love of God and neighbor. Through the eyes of faith the conscientious Christian sees the sacraments of sin in our world. Just as the sacraments celebrate the loving gift of God to us so too the sacraments of sin constantly remind us of the reality of our failures to love. How can the Christian be complacent and uninvolved in the presence of sin in our lives and our world?

In the neo-Orthodox phase of Protestantism, sin was emphasized as reminding the individual Christian of

boundaries and limitations so that one became more conscious of the need for God's merciful love. In the last
few years, as exemplified to an extreme in the "death of
God" theology, Protestant theology has stressed not the
imperfections and the limitations of human beings but
especially human power and responsibility. People come
of age now must take responsibility for the shaping of
their earthy existence. Today there seems to be a tendency to realize that the thinking of the last few years
might have been too naively optimistic. A balanced theological perspective should keep in view both the aspect
of sin as it points up our continuing need for God's loving
mercy and also our redeemed vocation to take responsibility and struggle against the forces of sin in our lives
and in the world. (Remember that this gift of redemption
is offered to all human beings.) A proper understanding
of sin is necessary for the contemporary Christian to
appreciate the gift of God in Christ by which we have
been saved from sin and death, for redemption is meaningless unless we can appreciate the gratuitous, loving gift of
our redemption. The Christian message sees the reality of
sin as manifesting itself primarily in the very death of
Jesus who died because of the power of sin and death. Sin
is so important an aspect of human existence and so strong
that it brought about the death of Jesus, but his death and
resurrection also marked the triumph and victory over sin
and death.

The Christian now allied through baptism with the
Paschal Mystery of Jesus is called to overcome sin and
death in daily life and in the world through the same life-
giving love whose greatest sacrament remains the Paschal
Mystery of Jesus. Sin still exists in our world and always
will exist until the end of time, but the Christian cannot
merely sit back and be content in the presence of sin. The
Christian is called to cooperate in the redemptive work of
Jesus in overcoming the forces of sin and death in one's
life and in the world. This will be a continual struggle
which will never completely be successful and which will

end in death, but a death which is also a share in the victory of Jesus over sin and death itself. To forget the reality of sinfulness is to forget a very indispensable part of the Christian mystery. Only one who is conscious of sin and sinfulness can appreciate the greatness of the gift of redemption and the Christian vocation to struggle against and ultimately triumph over the reality of sin through a self-giving love which gives even unto death.

NOTES

1. Charles West employed this description in a paper read at the 1967 meeting of the American Society of Christian ethics.

2. Jerome Murphy-O'Connor, O.P., "Sin and Community in the New Testament," in *Sin and Repentance,* ed. Denis O'Callaghan (Staten Island: Alba House, 1967), p. 18.

3. Roger Lincoln Shinn, *Man: The New Humanism* (Philadelphia: Westminster Press, 1968), pp. 145-164.

4. Ph. Delhaye et al., *Théologie du péché* (Tournai: Desclée et Cie, 1960), which has been published in English by Desclée in a number of small volumes, the most important of which is Albert Gelin and Albert Descamps, *Sin in the Bible* (New York: Desclée, 1965). *Il Peccato,* ed. Pietro Palazzini (Rome: Edizioni Ares, 1959), a 928-page volume which has appeared in English in three smaller volumes published by Scepter.

5. Stanislaus Lyonnet, S.J., *De Peccato et Redemptione,* vol. 1 (Rome: Pontifical Biblical Institute, 1957).

6. Piet Schoonenberg, S.J., *Man and Sin* (Notre Dame, Ind.: University of Notre Dame Press, 1965), pp. 98-123.

7. Bernard Häring, C.SS.R., "Conversion," in *Pastoral Treatment of Sin* (New York: Desclée, 1968), pp. 87-176.

8. John W. Glazer, S.J., "Transition Between Grace and Sin: Fresh Perspectives," *Theological Studies* 29 (1968), 260-274, summarizes some of the recent literature on the fundamental option especially from a more existentialist viewpoint. Other articles on the subject with appropriate bibliographies include: M. Flick, S.J., and Z. Alszeghy, S.J., "L'opzione fondamentale della vita morale e la grazia," *Gregorianum* 41 (1960), 593-619; Pierre Fransen, S.J., "Toward a Psychology of Divine Grace," *Lumen Vitae* 12 (1957), 203-232. The approach adopted in this study tries to do justice

at one and the same time to the subjectivity of the individual person and one's relationships with God, neighbor, and the world. The core decision or option of the human person is seen primarily in terms of these multiple relationships. The denial or lack of emphasis on transcendence in some contemporary theological writing tends to over-emphasize the relationship to neighbor and the world at the expense of the person's relationship to God. It is true that an older theology pretended to know too much about this relationship, but a theological vision of the human must always consider this most important aspect of human existence and unceasingly try to give a better understanding and appreciation of it. For a somewhat "updated traditional Thomistic" approach to the question, see F. Bourassa, S.I., "Le Péché Offense de Dieu," *Gregorianum* 49 (1968), 563-574.

9. Anton Meinrad Meier, *Das Peccatum Mortale ex Toto Genere Suo: Entstehung und Interpretation des Begriffes* (Regensburg: Verlag Friedrich Pustet, 1966).

10. F. J. Heggen, *Confession and the Service of Penance* (Notre Dame, Ind.: University of Notre Dame Press, 1968), pp. 70-77.

11. Kevin F. O'Shea, "The Reality of Sin: A Theological and Pastoral Critique," *Theological Studies* 29 (1968), 241-259.

12. Johannes B. Metz, "The Church's Social Function in the Light of a Political Theology," *Concilium* 36 (June 1968), 2-18. Metz incorporates this article and others developing the same theme in his book *Theology of the World* (New York: Herder and Herder, 1969).

5. Natural Law

Catholic ethical theory and its application have traditionally embraced a natural law methodology in their approach to moral questions. The manuals of moral theology, which were the textbooks of this discipline until a few years ago, and official Catholic moral teaching were based on natural law. This chapter will study the natural law methodology employed in the Catholic tradition and will primarily use as an illustration of that methodology the teaching found in the 1968 encyclical of Pope Paul VI, *Humanae Vitae*, which condemned artificial contraception in marriage. Many Catholic theologians have recently questioned both the traditional natural law methodology and the conclusions drawn from it in *Humanae Vitae* and elsewhere.[1] This chapter situates natural law in the light of my stance (developed in chapter 2 above), offers a critique of natural law in general, applies this criticism to *Humanae Vitae*, indicates how other methodologies arrive at different conclusions, and in the light of the problem of physicalism explains the reason for questioning some of the other moral teachings which have been proposed in Catholicism.

I. Natural Law in the Total Christian Perspective

The recent papal pronouncement realizes that natural law forms only a part of the total horizon of moral theology. The Apostles and their successors have been consti-

119

tuted "as guardians and authentic interpreters of all the moral law, not only, that is, of the law of the Gospel, but also of the natural law, which is also an expression of the will of God" / (*H.V.* n. 4). The encyclical admits there is a source of ethical wisdom and knowledge for the Christian apart from the explicit revelation of the Scriptures, so that Christians and the Church do learn ethical wisdom from non-Christians and the world.

There have been many theologians especially in the more strict Protestant tradition who would tend to deny any source of ethical wisdom and knowledge which Christians share with humankind.[2] Such theologians based their position on the uniqueness and self-sufficiency of the scriptural revelation, the doctrine of justification, and an emphasis on sin as corrupting whatever exists outside the unique revelation of Jesus Christ.[3] However, contemporary Protestant theologians generally maintain the existence of some ethical wisdom apart from the explicit revelation of God in the Scriptures and in Christ Jesus, even though they may avoid the term natural law.[4] Protestant theologians in the last few decades have employed such concepts as the orders of creation (Brunner), the divine mandates (Bonhoeffer), love and justice (Reinhold Niebuhr), love transforming justice (Ramsey), common ground morality (Bennett), and other similar approaches.

The natural law theory as implied in the encyclical has the theological merit of recognizing a source of ethical wisdom for the Christian apart from the explicit revelation of God in Christ Jesus. This recognition remains a most important and lasting contribution of Catholic thought in the area of theological ethics. The difficult question for Christian theology centers on the relationship between the natural law and the distinctively Christian element in the understanding of the moral life of the Christian. The same basic question has been proposed in other terms. H. Richard Niebuhr describes five different models of the relationship between Christ and culture.[5] An older Catholic theology spoke about the relationship between nature and grace, be-

tween the natural and the supernatural. Niebuhr has described the typical Catholic solution to the question of
Christ and culture in terms of "both-and" — both culture
and Christ.[6] Such an approach corresponds with an un-
nuanced understanding of the relationship between nature
and grace. The two are neither opposed nor identical; but
they exist side by side. Grace adds something to nature
without in any way destroying it. A simplistic view of the
supernatural sees it as something added to the natural. But
the natural retains its own finality and integrity as the substratum to which the supernatural is added.[7]

In such a perspective the natural tends to be seen as
something absolute and sufficient in itself to which the
supernatural is added. The natural law thus exists as a self-
contained entity to which the law of the gospel or revelation is then added. *Humanae Vitae* seems to accept such a
"both-and" understanding of the relationship between natural law and the gospel or revelation. "All the moral law"
is explained as "not only, that is, of the law of the Gospel,
but also of the natural law, which is also an expression of
the will of God . . ." (*H.V.* n. 4). The papal letter calls for
an anthropology based on "an integral vision of man and
his vocation, not only of his earthly and natural, but also
his supernatural and eternal, vocation" (*H.V.* n. 7). The
"both-and" relationship appears again in paragraph 8
which refers to "the entire moral law, both natural and
evangelical."

Not only the wording of the encyclical but the methodology presupposed in the argumentation employs a "both-
and" understanding of the relationship of natural law and
evangelical law. Msgr. Lambruschini, who explained the
encyclical at a press conference, said that purposely no
mention was made of scriptural arguments, but the entire
reasoning was based on natural law.[8] Bernard Häring has
criticized the encyclical because it does not even mention
the admonition of St. Paul that husband and wife should
"not refuse each other except by mutual consent, and then
only for an agreed time, to leave yourselves free for prayer;

then come together again in case Satan should take advantage of your weakness to tempt you" (1 Cor. 7:5).[9] The
Pastoral Constitution on the Church in the Modern World
did take heed of Paul's admonition. "But where the inti-
macy of married life is broken off, it is not rare for its
faithfulness to be imperiled and its quality of fruitfulness
ruined" (n. 51). However, the primary criticism is not the
fact that there is no reference to any particular scriptural
text, but the underlying understanding that the natural law
is something totally integral in itself to which the evangelical or supernatural law is added.

Christian ethics cannot absolutize the realm of the natural as something completely self-contained and unaffected
by any relationships to the evangelical or supernatural.
Christian theology derives its perspective from the Christian faith commitment. The Christian views reality in the
light of the total horizon of the Christian faith commitment — creation, sin, incarnation, redemption, and parousia. Natural law itself is thus Christocentric.[10] The doctrine
of creation forms the theological basis for natural law, and
Christ as logos is the one in whom all things are created
and through whom all things are to be returned to the
Father. Natural law theory has taken seriously the implications of the incarnation through which God has joined
himself to the human, the worldly, and the historical.
However, nature and creation form only a part of the total
Christian view. The reality of "the natural" must always be
seen in the light of sin, redemption, and the parousia. Nature and creation are relativized by the transforming Christian themes of redemption and final resurrection destiny
of all creation. The natural law theory is theologically
based on the Christian truths of creation and incarnation,
but these aspects are not independent and unrelated to the
full horizon of the Christian view of reality. The Christian
situates natural law in the context of the total history of
salvation which transforms and criticizes what is only "the
natural." Thus in the total Christian perspective there is a
place for the "natural," but the natural remains provisional

and relativized by the entire history of salvation.

The full Christian view of reality also takes account of the existence of sin and its effects on human existence. However, the natural law theory as illustrated in *Humanae Vitae* does not seem to give sufficient importance to the reality and effect of human sinfulness. In section III under "Pastoral Directives" the papal letter speaks about the compassion of Christ and the Church for sinners. "But she [the Church] cannot renounce the teaching of the law which is, in reality, that law proper to a human life restored to its original truth and conducted by the Spirit of God" (*H. V.* n. 19). The implication remains that the disruptive force of sin has already been overcome by the grace of God. Such an approach has definite affinities with a simplistic view of sin as depriving the Christian of the supernatural gift of grace, but not affecting the substratum of nature. However, in the total Christian horizon the disrupting influence of sin colors all human reality.

Humanae Vitae does recognize some effects of sin in human beings. Sin affects the will, but the help of God will strengthen our good will (*H. V.* n. 20). Sin affects the instincts, but ascetical practices will enable the reason and will to achieve self-mastery (*H. V.* n. 21). Sinfulness also makes itself felt in some aspects of the social environment, "which leads to sense excitation and unbridled customs, as well as every form of pornography and licentious performances" (*H. V.* n. 22). But no mention is made of the fact that sin affects reason itself and the very nature on which natural law theory is based. Sin relativizes and affects all reality. How often has reason been used to justify human prejudice and arrogance! Natural law has been appealed to in the denials of human dignity and of religious liberty. The just war theory has been employed to justify wars in which one's own nation was involved.[11] History shows the effect of sin in the very abuses which have accompanied natural law thinking.

Recently, I have proposed the need for a theory of compromise in moral theology precisely because of the exis-

tence of sin in the world.[12] The surd brought about by
human sinfulness is so oppressive that occasionally we cannot overcome it immediately. The presence of sin may
force a person to do something one would not do if there
were no sin present. Thus in sin-filled situations (notice all
the examples of such situations in the current literature)
the Christian may be forced to adopt a line of action
which one would abhor if sin were not present. A theory
of compromise does not give us a blank check to shirk our
Christian responsibilities. However, there are situations in
which the value sacrificed is not proportionate to the demand asked of the Christian. Protestant theology has often
adopted a similar approach by saying that in some circumstances the Christian is forced to do something sinful. The
sinner reluctantly performs the deed and asks God for
mercy and forgiveness.[13] At times Protestant theology has
overemphasized the reality of sin, but Catholic theology at
times has not paid enough attention to the reality of sin.

The recent papal encyclical presupposes a natural law
concept that fails 'to indicate the relative and provisional
character of natural law in the total Christian perspective.
Critics have rightly objected to a theory which tends to
absolutize what is only relative and provisional. Take, for
example, the teaching in Catholic theology on the right of
private property. The modern popes have approached the
question of private property in a much more absolute way
than Thomas Aquinas. The differences of approach are instructive for the moral theologian. The popes, especially
Leo XIII, stressed private property as the right of every
individual stemming from the dignity of the human person,
the person's rational nature, labor, the need to provide for
self and family, and the need to overcome the uncertainties
of life.[14] Thomas gave greater importance to the social
function of all property and the reality of human sinfulness. Perhaps Thomas was influenced by the often-cited
opinion of Isidore of Seville that according to the natural
law all things should be held in common.[15] Thomas ultimately sees the sin of human beings as the reason for the
existence of private property. Society would not have

peace and order unless everyone possessed his or her own goods. Likewise, Thomas pointed out that earthly goods are not properly cared for if they are held in common.[16] Thomas maintained there would be no need for private property in the world of original justice.

There are other indications that private property is not as absolute a human right as proposed in some papal encyclicals. With his understanding of a more absolute right of private property, Leo XIII spoke of the obligation of the rich to share their goods with the poor as an obligation of charity and not justice.[17] However, a very respectable and long tradition in the medieval Church maintained that the rich had an obligation in justice to share their goods with the poor.[18] Even in our own day one can ask if private property is the best way to protect the dignity and freedom of the human person. The great inequalities existing in society today at the very least must modify and limit the concept of the right of private property. In our historical circumstances we are much more conscious of the social aspect of property than was Leo XIII.[19] The teaching on private property well illustrates the dangers of a natural law approach that is not relativized by the whole reality of salvation history.

The natural law theory suggested in, and employed by, the encyclical *Humanae Vitae* has the advantage of affirming the existence of a source of ethical wisdom apart from the explicit revelation of God in Christ in the Scriptures. However, such a concept of natural law tends to absolutize what the full Christian vision sees as relative and provisional in the light of the entire history of salvation. The "natural" does not and never has existed as such. All of creation must be seen and understood in the light of redemption and resurrection destiny.

II. A Critique of Natural Law

The debate over the condemnation of artificial contraception in *Humanae Vitae* indicates a basic dissatisfaction

with the natural law methodology employed in the encyclical. The encyclical uses a notion of natural law which
has generally been found in the classical textbooks and
manuals of moral theology, but precisely this concept of
natural law is subject to severe negative criticism. This section will point out three major weaknesses in that concept
of natural law: (1) a tendency to accept natural law as a
monolithic philosophical system with an agreed upon body
of ethical content which is the source for most, if not all,
of Catholic moral teaching; (2) the danger of physicalism
which identifies the human act with the physical or biological structure of the act; (3) a classicist worldview and
methodology.

Not a Monolithic Philosophical System

The first defect will only be summarized here, since it is
treated at greater length elsewhere. Natural law remains a
very ambiguous term.[20] The first section of this study used
the concept of natural as distinguished from supernatural;
in addition, it has been pointed out that the word nature
had over twenty different meanings in Catholic thinking
before Thomas Aquinas. The word law is also ambiguous,
since it tends to have a very legalistic meaning for most
people today; whereas for Thomas law was an ordering of
reason. Natural law ethics has often been described as a
legalistic ethic, that is, an ethic based on norms and laws;
but in reality for Thomas natural law is a deliberative ethic
which arrives at decision not primarily by the application
of laws, but by the deliberation of reason. Many thinkers
in the course of history have employed the term natural
law, but frequently they defined natural law in different
ways. Thinkers employing different natural law approaches
have arrived at different conclusions on particular moral
topics. Natural law in the history of thought does not refer
to a monolithic theory, but tends to be a more generic
term which includes a number of different approaches to
moral problems. There is no such thing as *the* natural law

as a monolithic philosophical system with an agreed upon body of ethical content existing from the beginning of time.

Many erroneously believe that Catholic theology is committed to a particular natural law approach to moral problems. In practice, however, the vast majority of Catholic teaching on particular moral questions came into existence even before Thomas Aquinas enunciated his theory. Likewise, contemporary Catholic theology recognizes the need for a pluralism of philosophical approaches in the Christian's quest for a better understanding of man and his reality. There is no longer "one Catholic philosophy."

The Danger of Physicalism

Ethical theory constantly vacillates between two polarities — naturalism and idealism. Naturalism sees the human being in perfect continuity with the nature about her. Nature shapes and even determines the individual. Idealism views the human being completely apart from nature and as completely surpassing nature. Even Thomistic philosophy, the main Catholic proponent of natural law theory, knows an ambivalence between nature and reason.

The Thomistic natural law concept vacillates at times between the order of nature and the order of reason.[21] The general Thomistic thrust is towards the predominance of reason in natural law theory. However, there is in Thomas a definite tendency to identify the demands of natural law with physical and biological processes. Thomas, too, is a historical person conditioned by the circumstances and influences of his own time. These influences help explain the tendency (but not the predominant tendency) in Thomas to identify the human action with the physical and biological structure of the human act. A major influence is Ulpian, a Roman lawyer who died in 228.

Ulpian and Thomas. Ulpian defined the natural law as that which nature teaches all the animals. Ulpian distinguished the natural law from the *ius gentium*. The *ius naturale* is that which is common to all animals, whereas the *ius gentium* is that which is proper to humans.[22] Albert the Great rejected Ulpian's definition of the natural law, but Thomas accepted it, and even showed a preference for such a definition.[23] In the *Commentary on the Sentences*, for example, Thomas maintains that the most strict definition of natural law is the one proposed by Ulpian: *ius naturae est quod natura omnia animalia docuit.*[24]

In his *Commentary on the Nichomachean Ethics*, Thomas again shows a preference for Ulpian's definition. Aristotle has proposed a twofold division of *iustum naturale* and *iustum legale*, but Ulpian proposed the threefold distinction of *ius naturale, ius gentium* and *ius civile*. Thomas solves the apparent dilemma by saying that the Roman law concepts of *ius naturale* and *ius gentium* both belong under the Aristotelian category of *iustum naturale*. The human being has a double nature. The *ius naturale* rules that which is proper to both humans and the animals, such as the union of the sexes and the education of offspring; whereas the *ius gentium* governs the rational part of human beings which is proper to humans alone and embraces such things as fidelity to contracts.[25]

In the *Summa Theologiae* Thomas cites Ulpian's definition on a number of occasions.[26] In the classification of natural law again Thomas shows a preference for Ulpian's definition. Thomas accepts the division proposed by Isidore of Seville, according to which the *ius gentium* belongs to the category of human law and not the category of divine law. Thomas uses Ulpian's definition to explain Isidore's division. The natural law pertains to the divine law because it is common to humans and to all the animals.[27] In a sense, the *ius gentium* does pertain to the category of human law because humans use reason to deduce the conclusions of the *ius gentium*.

Thomas thus employs Ulpian's definition of natural law as opposed to what reason deduces (the *ius gentium*) to defend the division of law proposed by Isidore. The same question receives somewhat the same treatment later in the *Summa.*[28] The texts definitely show that Thomas knew and even accepted the definition of natural law proposed by Ulpian.

Ulpian's Concept of Natural Law. Ulpian is important for the understanding of natural law morality. The natural law for Ulpian is defined in terms of those actions which are common to humans and all the animals. There results from this the definite danger of identifying the human action with a mere animal or biological process. "Nature" and "natural" in Ulpian's meaning are distinguished from that which is specifically human and derived by reason. Traditional theology has in the past definitely employed the words "natural" and "nature" as synonymous with animal or biological processes and not as denoting human actions in accord with the rational, human nature.

Moral theology textbooks even speak of sins according to nature. The manuals generally divide the sins against the sixth commandment into two categories — the sins against nature (*peccata contra naturam*) and sins in accord with nature (*peccata secundum naturam*). "Nature" is thus used in Ulpian's sense, as that which is common to humans and all the animals. In matters of sexuality (and Ulpian himself uses the example of the sexual union as an illustration of the natural law), humans share with the animal world the fact of the sexual union whereby male seed is deposited in the vas of the female. Sins against nature, therefore, are those acts in which the animal or biological process is not observed — pollution, sodomy, bestiality, and contraception. Sins according to nature are those acts in which the proper biological process is observed but something is lacking in the sphere which belongs only to rational beings. These include fornication, adultery, incest, rape, and sacrilege.[29]

The classification of sins against chastity furnishes concrete proof that "nature" has been used in Catholic theology to refer to animal processes without any intervention of human reason. Many theologians have rightly criticized the approach to marriage and sexuality used by Catholic natural law theoreticians because such an approach concentrated primarily on the biological components of the act of intercourse. The personal aspects of the sexual union received comparatively scant attention in many of the manuals of moral theology. Ulpian's influence has made it easier for Catholic natural law thinking to identify the human act simply with the physical structure of the act.

Ulpian's Anthropology. Ulpian's understanding of the natural law logically leads to disastrous consequences in anthropology. The distinction between two parts in humans — that which is common to humans and all the animals, and that which is proper to humans — results in a two-layer version of human beings. A top layer of rationality is merely added to an already constituted bottom layer of animality. The union between the two layers is merely extrinsic — the one lies on top of the other. The animal layer retains its own finalities and tendencies, independent of the demands of rationality. Thus the individual may not interfere in the animal processes and finalities. Note that the results of such an anthropology are most evident in the area of sexuality.

A proper understanding of the human should start with that which is proper to humans. Rationality does not just lie on top of animality, but rationality characterizes and guides the whole person. Animal processes and finalities are not untouchable. Our whole vocation, we have come to see, is to bring order and intelligence into the world, and to shape animal and biological finalities toward a truly human purpose. Ulpian's concept of natural law logically falsifies the understanding of the human and tends to canonize the finalities and processes which humans share with the animal world.

A better anthropology would see the distinctive in human beings as guiding and directing the totality of one's being. For Thomas rationality constituted what is distinctive and characteristic in humans. Modern philosophers differ from Thomas on what is distinctively human. Phenomenologists tend to view the individual being as a symbolic person; while personalists look upon the human as an incarnate spirit, a "thou" in relation to other "you's." However, all would agree in rejecting an anthropology that absolutizes animal finalities and tendencies without allowing any intervention of the specifically human rational aspect of human beings.

I am not asserting that Thomas always identified human actions with animal processes or the physical structure of the act. In fact, the general outlines of the hylomorphic theory, by speaking of material and formal components of reality, try to avoid any physicalism or biologism. Nevertheless, the adoption of Ulpian's understanding of "nature" and "natural" logically leads to the identification of the human act itself with animal processes and with the mere physical structure of the act. Such a distorted view of the human act becomes especially prevalent in the area of medical morals, for in medical morality one can more easily conceive a moral human action solely in terms of the physical structure of that action.

Likewise, Ulpian's notion of nature easily leads to a morality based on the finality of a faculty independent of any considerations of the total human person or the total human community. One must, of course, avoid the opposite danger of paying no attention to the physical structure of the act or to external actions in themselves. However, Catholic theology in its natural law approach has suffered from an oversimple identification of the human action with an animal process or finality.

Marriage and Sexuality. Ulpian's understanding of natural law logically has had another deleterious effect on Catholic moral theology. Until the last decade magisterial pronouncements frequently spoke of the primary and secondary ends of marriage.[30] The latest statements of

popes as well as the Pastoral Constitution on the Church in
the Modern World (*Gaudium et Spes*) happily avoid this
terminology.[31] However, such a distinction has obviously
influenced Catholic teaching on marriage and sexuality.
Many people have questioned the distinction as being con-
tradicted by the experience of married couples.

The distinction logically follows from Ulpian's concept
of the natural law and the human, although I do not claim
that Ulpian is the source of such a distinction. "Primary"
is that which is common to humans and all the animals.
Ulpian, and Thomas in citing Ulpian, use the union of the
sexes and the procreation and education of offspring as
examples of that which is common to humans and all the
animals. "Secondary" is that which is proper to humans.
Since only humans and not animals have sexual intercourse
as a sign and expression of love, the love union aspect of
sexuality remains proper to humans and therefore secondary. The former teaching on the ends of marriage is logically connected with Ulpian's understanding of the human
being and natural law. Thus the teaching of Ulpian on natural law has a logical connection with the inadequate
understanding of a human action as identified with an animal process.

A More Primitive Attitude. Another historical factor
based on the conditions of a primitive culture has also influenced the tendency to make the processes of nature in-
violable. Stoic philosophy well illustrates a more general
historical factor that tends to identify the human action
with its physical or natural structure. One should avoid too
many generalizations about the Stoics because Stoic philosophy included a number of different thinkers who covered
a comparatively long span of years. In addition, Stoic philosophers invoked the natural law to justify practices that
contemporary natural law theoreticians brand as immoral.[32] However, there is a common thrust to the ethical
doctrine proposed by the Stoics.

Ethics considers human beings and their actions. We

humans want to find happiness. What actions should we perform to find happiness and fulfillment? A more primitive and less technical society will come to conclusions different from those reached by a more technically and scientifically developed society. Primitive people soon realize that they find happiness in conforming to the patterns of nature.

Primitive people remain almost helpless when confronted with the forces of nature. The forces of nature are so strong that the human individual is even tempted to bow down and adore. One realizes the futility in trying to fight them. Happiness will come only by adjusting oneself to nature.

Nature divides the day into light and dark. When darkness descends, there is little or nothing that humans can do except sleep. When the hot sun is beating down near the equator, one will find happiness only by avoiding work and overexposure in the sun. In colder climates, one will be happy only when using clothing and shelter as protection against nature. If one wants to be happy, one will stay under some form of shelter and avoid the rain and snow. If there is a mountain in one's path, the wise person will walk around the mountain rather than suffer the ardors of trying to scale the peak. For people living in a primitive society (in the sense of nonscientific and nontechnical), happiness is found in conforming self to nature.

Stoic philosophy built on this understanding of life in a nontechnical society. As Greeks, the Stoics believed in an intelligible world. They made the universe as a whole — the cosmos — their principle of intelligibility. Stoic philosophy held that reason governed the order of nature. Human happiness consisted in conforming to reason, that is, in conforming to the order of nature. Reason rather easily became identified with the order of nature. The primary norm of morality, therefore, was conformity to nature.[33]

We who live in a scientific and technological society will have a different view of human life and happiness. Modern people do not find happiness in conforming to nature. The whole ethos and genius of modern society is different. Contemporary humans make nature conform to them rather than vice-versa. Through electricity we can change night into day. There are very few things that moderns cannot do at night now that it is illuminated by electricity.

We contemporary people use artificial heat in the winter and air conditioning in the summer to bring nature into conformity with our needs and desires. Nature did not provide us with wings to fly; in fact, the law of gravity seems to forbid flying. However, science has produced the jet plane and the rocket, which propel us at great speeds around the globe and even into the vast universe. When a mountain looms up as an obstacle, we either level the mountain with bulldozers or tunnel under the terrain. We could never tolerate a theory which equates human happiness with conformity to nature. We interfere with the processes of nature to make nature conform to us.

But a word of caution is in order. In the last few years the ecological crisis has made us aware of the danger of not giving enough importance and value to the physical aspects of worldly existence. We are not free to interfere with nature any way we see fit. Just as it is wrong to absolutize the natural and the physical, so too it is wrong to give no meaning or importance to the natural and the physical.

These few paragraphs have not attempted to prove the influence of Stoic philosophy on St. Thomas. Rather, Stoic philosophy was used to illustrate how the conditions existing in a nontechnological society will influence the philosophical understanding of anthropology and ethics. Thomas too lived in an agrarian, nonscientific world. The nontechnological worldview would be more prone to identify the human act with the physical process of nature itself.

Reality or Facticity. A more primitive society also tends to view reality in terms of the physical and the sensible. The child, unlike the adult, sees reality primarily in terms of externals. The tendency to identify the human action with the physical structure would definitely be greater in a more primitive society. For example, the importance that Catholic theology has attached to masturbatory activity, especially the overemphasis since the sixteenth century, seems to come from viewing it purely in terms of the physiological and biological aspects of the act. Modern psychology, however, does not place that great importance on such activity.

Theologians must incorporate the findings of modern science in trying to evaluate the human act of masturbation. To view it solely in terms of the physical structure of the act distorts the total reality of this human action. Contemporary theologians cannot merely repeat what older theologians have said. Today we know much more about the reality of the human act of masturbation than, say, St. Alphonsus or any other moral theologian living before the present century.[34]

It would be erroneous to say that Catholic theology has identified the human act with the brute facticity of natural processes or just the physical structure of the act itself. In the vast majority of cases, moral theology has always distinguished between the physical structure of the action and the morality of the action. The moral act of murder differs from the physical act of killing. The physical act of taking another's property does not always involve the moral act of stealing. However, in some areas of morality (for example, contraception, sterilization, direct effect) the moral act has been considered the same as the physical structure of the act itself.

The Morality of Lying. Another area in which Catholic theologians are moving away from a description of the human act in purely physical or natural terms is lying. The contemporary theological understanding of lying serves as a salutary warning to the natural law concept found in the manuals of theology because the morality of lying cannot be determined merely by examining the faculty of speech and its finality, apart from the totality of the human person speaking and the community in which one speaks.

The manuals of moral theology traditionally define lying as *locutio contra mentem*. The faculty of speech exists to express what is in the mind. When human speech does not reflect what is in the mind there is a perversion of the faculty. The perverted faculty argument is based on the finality of the faculty of speech looked at in itself. Accordingly, a lie exists when the verbal utterance does not correspond with what is in the mind. Theologians then had to face the problem created by the fact that at times the speaker simply could not speak the truth to his hearer or questioner (for example, in the case of a committed secret). A casuistry of mental reservations arose to deal with such situations.[35]

Today most contemporary Catholic theologians accept the distinction between a lie and a falsehood. A falsehood involves an untruth in the sense that the external word contradicts what is in the mind. However, the malice of lying does not consist in the perversion of the faculty of speech or the lack of conformity between the word spoken and what is in the mind. The malice of lying consists in the harm done to society and the human community through the breakdown of mutual trust and honesty. Thus, some theologians distinguish between a lie as the denial of truth which is due to the other and falsehood which is a spoken word not in conformity with what is in the mind.

The distinction between lying and falsehood obviates the rather contrived casuistry associated with broad and strict mental reservations.[36] But what does the more contemporary understanding of lying indicate? The new definition denies the validity of the perverted faculty argument. It is not sufficient merely to examine the faculty of speech and determine morality solely from the purpose of the faculty in itself. Likewise, the malice of lying does not reside in the lack of "physical" conformity between word and thought.

To view the faculty of speech apart from the total human situation of the person in society seems to give a distorted view of lying. The faculty of speech must be seen and judged in a human context. One can interfere with the physical purpose of the faculty for a higher human need and good. Perhaps in a similar vein, the notion of "direct" in the principle of the double effect cannot be judged merely from the sole immediate effect of the physical action itself, apart from the whole human context in which the act is placed. The morality must be viewed in a total human context, and not merely judged according to the physical act itself and the natural effect of the act seen in itself apart from the whole context.

The influence of Ulpian and the view of primitive society tend to identify the total human action with the natural or biological process. A better understanding of such historically and culturally limited views should help the ethician in evaluating the theory of natural law as understood in *Humanae Vitae*. I have not proved that the human act never corresponds with the physical structure of the act. However, I think it is clear that ethicians must be very cautious that older and inadequate views of reality do not influence their contemporary moral judgments. It does seem that the definition of Ulpian and the general views of a more primitive society have a logical connection with what seem to be erroneous conclusions of the natural law theory of the manuals.

→ *A Changed Worldview*

A third major weakness with the theory of natural law presupposed in the Encyclical stems from the classicist worldview which is behind such a theory of natural law. Bernard Lonergan maintains that the classicist worldview has been replaced by a more historically conscious worldview.[37] In the same vein, John Courtney Murray claimed that the two different theories on Church and State represent two different methodologies and worldviews.[38] And today, other more radical Catholic thinkers are calling for a change from a substantive to a process metaphysics.[39] At the least, all these indications point to an admission by respected Catholic scholars that the so-called classicist worldview has ceased to exist.

The following paragraphs will briefly sketch the differences in the two approaches to viewing reality. There are many dangers inherent in doing this. There is really no such thing as *the* classical worldview or *the* historically conscious worldview — there are many different types of historical mindedness. By arguing in favor of an historically conscious worldview, I by no means intend to endorse all the theories and opinions that might be included under such a heading.

Since this section of the chapter will argue against a classical worldview, a reader might conclude that I am denying to past thinkers the possibility of any valid insights into the meaning of reality. Such a conclusion is far from true. There are even those (for example, Lonergan and Murray) who would argue that a moderate historically conscious methodology is in continuity with the best of Thomistic thought. We must never forget that some of the inadequacies in the classical worldview stem from the poor interpretation of St. Thomas by many of his so-called followers.

Two Views of Reality. The classicist worldview emphasizes the static, the immutable, the eternal, and the unchanging. The Greek column symbolizes this very well. There is no movement or dynamism about a Doric or Ionic column; the simple Greek column avoids all frills and baroque trimmings. The stately Greek column gives the impression of solidity, eternity, and immutability. Its majestic and sober lines emphasize an order and harmony which appear to last forever. This classical worldview speaks in terms of substances and essences. Time and history are "accidents" which do not really change the constitution of reality itself. Essences remain unchangeable and can only go through accidental changes in the course of time. Growth, dynamism, and progress therefore receive little attention.

The Platonic world of ideas well illustrates this classical

worldview. Everything is essentially spelled out from all eternity, for the immutable essences, the universals, exist in the world of ideas. Everything in this world of ours is a participation or an accidental modification of the subsistent ideas. We come to know truth and reality by abstracting from the accidents of time and place, and arriving at immutable and unchangeable essences. Such knowledge based on immutable essences is bound to attain the ultimate in certitude.

The more historically conscious worldview emphasizes the changing, developing, evolving, and historical. Time and history are more than mere accidents that do not really change essential reality. Individual and particular differences receive much more attention from a correspondingly more historically conscious methodology. The classical worldview is interested in the essence of human beings, which is true at all times in history and in all civilizations and circumstances. A historically minded worldview emphasizes the individual traits that characterize the individual. Moderns differ quite a bit from primitives precisely because of the historical and individual traits that an individual has acquired today.

In the more historical worldview the world is not static but evolving. Progress, growth, and change mark the world and all reality. Cold, chaste, objective order and harmony are not characteristic of this view. Blurring, motion, and subjective feeling are its corresponding features, as in the difference between modern art and classical art. Modern art emphasizes feeling and motion rather than harmony and balance. It is not as "objective" as classical art. The artists impose themselves and their emotions on the object.

Perhaps modern art is telling the theologian that the older distinction between the objective and the subjective is no longer completely adequate. Music also illustrates the change that has occurred in our understanding of the world and reality. Classical measure and rhythm are gone; free rhythm and feeling mean very much to the modern ear. What is meaningful music to the ear of the modern is only cacophony for the classicist. Changes in art and music illustrate the meaning of the different worldviews and also show graphically that the classical worldview is gone.

Two Methodologies. The two worldviews created two different theological methodologies. The classicist methodology tends to be abstract, *a priori*, and deductive. It wants to cut through the concrete circumstances to arrive at the abstract essence which is always true, and then works with these abstract and universal essences. In the area of moral theology, for example, the first principles of morality are established, and then other universal norms of conduct are deduced from these.

The more historical methodology tends to be concrete, *a posteriori*, and inductive. The historical approach does not brush by the accidental circumstances to arrive at the immutable essences. The concrete, the particular, and the individual are important for telling us something about reality itself. Principles are not deduced from other principles. Rather, the modern person observes and experiences and then tentatively proceeds to conclusions in a more inductive manner. Note that the historical consciousness as a methodology is an abstraction, but an abstraction or theory that tries to give more importance to particular, concrete, historical reality.

As we have noted above, John Courtney Murray claims that the different views on Church and State flow from the two different methodologies employed.[40] The older theory of the union of Church and State flows from a classicist methodology. It begins with the notion of a society. The definition of a society comes from an abstract and somewhat *a priori* notion of what such a society should be. The older theory then maintains that there are two perfect societies, and deduces their mutual duties and responsibilities, including their duties and obligations vis-à-vis one another. The theory concludes that the *cura religionis*, as it was then understood, belongs to the State. The State has the obligation of promoting the true faith.

What happens when the older theory runs headlong into

a *de facto* situation in which the separation of Church and State is a historical fact? The older solution lies in a distinction between thesis and hypothesis, which roughly corresponds to the ideal order which should exist and the actual order which can be tolerated because of the presence of certain accidental historical circumstances. Notice the abstract and ahistorical characteristics of such a theory.

The newer theory of Church and State as proposed by Murray employs a more historically conscious methodology. Murray does not begin with an abstract definition of society and then deduce the obligations and rights of Church and State. Rather, Murray begins from a notion of the State derived from his observations of states in contemporary society. The modern State is a limited, constitutional form of government.

Its limited role contrasts with the more absolute and all-embracing role of the State in an earlier society. It does not interfere in matters that belong to the private life of individuals, such as the worship of God. Murray's theory has no need for a distinction between thesis and hypothesis, since he begins with the concrete historical reality. His conclusions then will be in harmony with the present historical situation.[41] Using a historical methodology, he can even admit that in the nineteenth century the older opinion might have been true, but in the present historical circumstances separation of Church and State is required.[42]

A classicist mentality is horrified at the thought that something could be right in one century and wrong in another. Note, however, that the historical methodology employed by Murray and Lonergan insists on a continuity in history and rejects any atomistic existentialism which sees only the uniqueness of the present situation without any connection with what has gone before or with what will follow in history.

A New Catholic Perspective. Theologians and philosophers are not alone in speaking of the changed perspective. In the documents of Vatican II the bishops do not officially adopt any worldview or methodology. But Vatican II definitely portrays reality in terms of a more historical worldview, and also employs a historically conscious methodology. The fact that the council has chosen to call itself a "pastoral" council is most significant; but "pastoral" must not be understood in opposition to "doctrinal." Rather, pastoral indicates a concern for the Christian faith not as truths to be learned but as a life to be lived.

The pastoral orientation of the council reflects a historical worldview. The bishops at the council also acknowledged that the Church has profited by the history and development of humanity. History reveals more about human beings and opens new roads to truth. The Catholic Church must constantly engage in an exchange with the contemporary world.[43]

Gaudium et Spes frequently speaks of the need to know the signs of the times. The introductory statement of this constitution asserts the need for the Church to know them and interpret them in the light of the Gospel (n. 4). The five chapters of the second section of the constitution begin with an attempt to read the signs of the times. The attention given to what was often in the past dismissed as accidental differences of time and history shows a more historical approach to reality. The constitution does not begin with abstract and universal ideas of Church, society, state, community, and common good, but rather by scrutinizing the signs of the times. *Gaudium et Spes* thus serves as an excellent illustration of the change in emphasis in Church documents from a classicist methodology to a more historically conscious approach.

The teachings on the Church as contained in the Constitution on the Church (*Lumen Gentium*) and the other documents of Vatican II also reflect a more historical approach and understanding. Previously Catholics pictured the Church as a perfect society having all the answers, and as the one bulwark of security in a changing world. However, *Lumen Gentium* speaks often and eloquently of the pilgrim Church. The charge of triumphalism rang true in the conciliar halls of Vatican II. A pilgrim Church, however, does not pretend to have all the answers.

A pilgrim Church is ever on the march towards its goal of perfect union with Christ the spouse. A pilgrim Church is constantly striving, probing, falling, rising, and trying again. A pilgrim is one who is constantly on the road and does not know there the security of one's own home. So too the pilgrim Church is a church always in need of reform (*ecclesia semper reformanda*). Change, development, growth, struggle and tension mark the Church of Christ in this world. The notion of the pilgrim Church, even in language, differs very much from the perfect society of the theological manuals.

The conciliar documents underscore the need for the Catholic Church to engage in dialogue — dialogue with other Christians, dialogue with Jews, dialogue with other non-Christians, dialogue with the world. Dialogue is not monologue. Dialogue presupposes that Catholics can learn from all these others. The call for dialogue supposes the historical and pilgrim nature of the Church, which does not possess all the answers but is open in the search for truth. The need for ongoing dialogue and ongoing search for truth contrasts sharply with the classicist view of reality and truth.

Lumen Gentium rebuilds ecclesiology on the notion of the Church as the people of God and points out the various functions and services which exist in the Church (chapter 2). Hierarchy is one form of service which exists in it. Another office is prophecy. The prophetic function exists independently of the hierarchy (n. 12). The hierarchical Church can learn, and has learned, from the prophetic voice in the Church. History reminds us that in the Church change usually occurs from underneath. Vatican Council II brought to fruition the work of the prophets in the biblical, liturgical, catechetical and ecumenical movements.

Thank God for Pope John and the bishops at Vatican II, we can say, but there never would have been a Vatican II if it were not for the prophets who went before. Many of them were rejected when they first proposed their teaching, but such has always been the lot of the prophet. The pilgrim Church, with the prophetic office, will always know the tension of trying to do the truth in love. The Church sorely needs to develop an older notion of the discernment of the Spirit, so that the individual and the total Church will be more open and ready to hear its true voice while rejecting the utterances of false prophets.[44]

The Church portrayed in Vatican II is a pilgrim Church which does not have all the answers but is constantly striving to grow in wisdom and age and grace. Thus the conciliar documents reflect a more historical view of the Church, and even employ a historically conscious methodology.

Theological Consequences

A historical worldview and a more historically conscious methodology will have important consequences when applied to the field of moral theology, for the manuals of moral theology today definitely reflect the classicist approach. In fact, there is a crisis in moral theology today precisely because such theology seems out of touch with the contemporary understanding of reality. Of course I do not claim that every modern view about reality is correct, but then not everything in the classicist worldview was correct.

Sin infects the reality we know, and the Christian thinker can never simply accept as is whatever happens to be in vogue. However, the God of creation and redemption has called us to carry on his mission in time and space. The Christian, then, is always called upon to view all things in the light of the gospel message, but whatever insights we may gain into reality and the world of creation can help us in our life.

Change and Development. The first important consequence of this new worldview and methodology affects our attitude towards change and development. The classical worldview, as we have seen, had little room for change. Only accidental changes could occur in a reality that was already constituted and known in its essence. Naturally such a view rejected any form of evolutionary theory because it was most difficult to explain evolution in such a system. On the other hand, the new worldview emphasizes the need for change. Change and growth do not affect merely the accidental constitution and knowledge of reality.

Human beings thirst for truth and constantly try to find it. The human person is never satisfied with the knowledge one has at any given moment. The contemporary person is continually probing to find out more about reality. The growth and progress of modern society demonstrate that development is absolutely necessary. The classicist methodology, on the other hand, claims a comparatively absolute and complete knowledge. Change naturally becomes a threat to the person who thinks that she or he already possesses truth. Of course, we recognize that not all change is good and salutary. There will be mistakes on the way, but the greatest error would be not to try at all.

Let us take as an example the dogmatic truth about the nature of Christ. The early christological councils proposed the formula of one person and two natures in Christ, a formula that is not present in the Scriptures. At the time there was an agonizing decision to go beyond the language of the Scriptures. But why does change have to stop in the fifth century? Might there not be an even better understanding of the natures and person of Christ today? Modern people might have different — and better — insights into the reality of Christ. Who can say that the fifth century was the final point in the development of our understanding?

When the classical worldview does speak of development, it places much emphasis on the fact that the truth always remains the same but it is expressed in different ways at different times. The same essential truth wears different clothing in different settings. However, does not the truth itself change and develop? There is more involved than just a different way of stating the same essential reality. Even in such sacrosanct dogmatic teachings there is room for real change and development.

The historical worldview realizes the constant need for growth and development, and also accepts the fact that mistakes and errors will always accompany such growth. But the attitude existing towards theology on the part of many Catholic priests in this country epitomizes the older worldview. As seminarians, they learned all the truths of the Christian faith. There was no need, in this view, to continue study after ordination, since the priest already possessed a certain knowledge of all the truths of the Christian faith.

Such an attitude also characterized the way in which theology was taught. Very little outside reading was done. The student simply memorized the notes of the professor which contained this certain knowledge. But the new methodology will bring with it a greater appreciation of the need for change and development in all aspects of the life and teaching of the Church.

Theology and Induction. Theology must adopt a more inductive methodology. Note that I am not advocating a unilaterally inductive and *a posteriori* approach for theology. However, in the past theology has attached too much importance to a deductive and somewhat *a priori* methodology. (Of course, as we shall see, with a more inductive approach moral theology can never again claim the kind of certitude it once did. At best, in some areas of conduct the ethician will be able to say that something clearly appears to be such and such at the present time.)

The classical methodology was a closed system, whereas a more historically conscious methodology proposes an open and heuristic approach. It will always remain open to new data and experience. Nothing is ever completely solved and closed, for an inductive methodology is more tentative and probing.

An inductive approach recognizes the existence of mistakes and errors, and even incorporates the necessary mechanism to overcome them. The building and manufacture of the Edsel automobile illustrates the possibility of error in a more inductive approach. Obviously, elaborate and expensive tests were run beforehand to see if there was a market for a car in the class of the projected Edsel. The decision to market the car was made on the best possible evidence. However, experience proved that the Edsel was a failure. A few years later, after similar exhaustive testing, the same company produced the Mustang, which has been a great success.

Theology, of course, is not the same as the other sciences. Progress and growth are much more evident in the area of the empirical sciences. However, the historicity of the gospel message and the historicity of human beings and the world demand a more historical approach in theology and the integration of a more inductive methodology. A more inductive approach in theology, especially in moral theology, will have to depend more on the experience of Christian people and all people of good will. The morality of particular actions cannot be judged apart from human experience. History seems to show that the changes which have occurred in Catholic morality have come about through the experience of all the people of the community. The fact that older norms did not come to grips with reality was first noticed in the experience of people.

Changes have occurred in the areas of usury, religious liberty, the right to silence, the role of love as a motive for marital relations, and other areas.[45] Certainly the rigorism of the earlier theologians on the place of procreation in marriage and marital intercourse has been modified by the experience of Christian people — for example, they held that marriage relations without the express purpose of procreation was at least venially sinful. And when the older theory of Church and State did not fit in with the historical circumstances of our day, John Courtney Murray showed that the living experience of people in the United States was more than just a toleration of an imperfect reality. In each case, experience showed the inadequacy of the older theory.

The older casuistry of mental reservation never set well with the experience of Christian people. The dissatisfaction with such casuistry played an important part in the understanding of lying now accepted by most contemporary theologians. Of course, just as theological methodology can never become totally inductive (the theologian always begins with the revelation of God in Christ), so too experience can never become the only factor in the formation of the Christian ethic. However, experience has a very important role to play. Since the experience of Christian people and all people of good will is a source of moral knowledge, an ethician cannot simply spell out in advance everything that must be done by the individual. Contemporary theology should enlarge upon and develop the concept of prudence which was an important experiential factor in the thought of Aquinas.

The Empirical Approach. Since a more historical methodology emphasizes the individual and the particular and employs a more inductive approach to knowing reality, Catholic theology will have to work much closer with the empirical and social sciences. It is these sciences that help human beings to pursue their goals and guide their development. A classicist approach which emphasized universals and essences was content with an almost exclusively deductive approach.

The Catholic Church in America today still reflects the fact that an older worldview did not appreciate or understand the need for the empirical and social sciences. The Catholic Church is probably the only very large corporation in America — I am here using "church" in the sense of a sociological entity and its administration — which does not have a research and development arm. How long could other corporations stay in existence without devoting huge sums to research and development? Heretofore, the Catholic Church has not realized the importance of change and growth.

Perhaps the crisis the Church faces today stems from a clinging to older forms of life when newer forms are required. However, without research and experimentation, who can determine which new forms are needed? The answers are not all spelled out in the nature of things.

Certitude. As we have already seen, a changed theological methodology must necessarily result in a different attitude towards certitude. The classicist methodology aimed at absolute certitude. It was more easily come by in the classical approach, for this method cut through and disregarded individual, particular differences to arrive at immutable, abstract essences. In a deductive approach the conclusion follows by a logical connection from the premise. Provided the logic is correct, the conclusion is just as certain as the premise. Since circumstances cannot change the essences or universals, one can assert that the conclusion is now and always will be absolutely certain. There is no room for any change. A deductive methodology can be much more certain than an inductive approach.

The penchant for absolute certitude characterized the philosophical system which supports the concept of natural law as found in theology manuals. Science, in this view, was defined as certain knowledge of the thing in its causes. Science, therefore, was opposed to opinion and theory. However, modern science does not aim at such certitude. Science today sees no opposition between science and the hypothetical; in fact, scientific opinion and scientific theory form an essential part of the scientific vocabulary.

Absolute certitude actually would be the great enemy of progress and growth. Once absolute certitude is reached, there is no sense in continuing research except to clear up a few peripheral matters.[46] In the Thomistic framework there was really no room for progress in scientific fields.

And there was little or no room for development within the sciences, so conceived, because the first principles of the science itself were already known. The revolutionary approaches within the modern sciences show the fallacy in the Thomistic understanding of science.[47]

A more historically conscious methodology does not pretend to have or even to aim at absolute certitude. Since time, history, and individual differences are important, they cannot be dismissed as mere accidents which do not affect essential truth. This approach does not emphasize abstract essences, but concrete phenomena. Conclusions are based on the observations and experience gleaned in a more inductive approach. Such an approach can never strive for absolute certitude.

Modern science views reality in this more historical manner and consequently employs this more inductive approach. Scientific progress demands a continuing search for an even better way. An inductive methodology can never cease its working. It constantly runs new experiments and observations, for modern science aims at the best for the present time, but realizes that new progress must be made for the future.

Positive Law. A more historically conscious approach and a greater emphasis on the person attribute a much changed and reduced role to positive law. Canon law exists primarily to preserve order and harmony in the society of the people of God, and not to serve as a guide for the life of the individual Christian.[48] Nor are civil laws primarily a guide for moral conduct. Civil law as such is not primarily interested in the true, the good, and the beautiful. Civil law has the limited aim of preserving the public order.[49]

Society functions better not when law dictates to everyone what is to be done, but rather when law tries to create the climate in which individuals and smaller groups within the society can exercise their creativity and development for the good of the total community.[50] No longer is society under a master plan minutely controlled by the rules of the society. Rather, modern society's progress and growth come from the initiative of people within the society. Thus, the more historically minded worldview has a different perspective on the meaning and role of law in human life. Natural and human laws are no longer seen as detailed plans which guide and direct all human activity.

The Nature of Reality. A classicist worldview tends to see reality in terms of substances and natures which exist in themselves apart from any relations with other substances and natures. Every substance has its own nature or principle of operation. Within every acorn, for example, there is a nature which directs the acorn into becoming an oak tree. The acorn will not become a maple tree or an elm tree because it has the nature of an oak tree. The growth and "activity" of the thing is determined by the nature inscribed in it. Growth is the intrinsic unfolding of the nature within the substance.

Notice how such a view of reality affects morality. Human action depends upon the human nature. Human action is its intrinsic unfolding in the person. Nature, therefore, tells what actions are to be done and what actions are to be avoided. To determine the morality of an action, one must study its nature. The above description, although a caricature of Thomas' teaching, does represent the approach to morality of the kind of unilaterally substantialist view of reality generally assumed in the manuals.

The contemporary view sees reality more in terms of relations than of substances and natures. The individual is not thought of as a being totally constituted in the self, whose life is the unfolding of the nature already possessed. There seemingly can be no real human growth and history when future development is already determined by what is present here and now. This is the point of difference between a naturalist view and a historicist view.[51]

According to a more contemporary, relational view, reality does not consist of separate substances existing completely independent of each other. Reality can be

understood only in terms of the relations that exist among
the individual beings. A particular being can never be adequately considered in itself, apart from its relations with
other beings and the fullness of being. An emphasis on relations rather than substances surely cannot be foreign to
Catholic thinking, since theologians have spoken of the
persons of the Trinity as relations.

Human experience also reminds us of the importance of
relationship even in constituting ourselves as human persons. A relational understanding of reality will never see
morality solely in terms of the individual substance or nature. Morality depends primarily not on the substance
viewed in itself but on the individual seen in relationship
to other beings. Unfortunately, the so-called traditional
natural law approach frequently derives its conclusions
from the nature of a faculty or the physical causality of an
action seen only in itself and not in relationship with the
total person and the entire community.

A brief defense of Aristotle is necessary here to avoid
false impressions. Aristotle did not have a static view of
reality. Nature itself was a principle of operation that
tended toward a goal, but the goal was specific rather than
individual. The emphasis was on the species of oak tree,
that is, and not on the individual oak as such. But Aristotle
did not conceive of the human person as he did of lesser
life.

As an acute observer of the human scene, he realized
that most individuals do not achieve their goal of happiness and self-fulfillment. The person, he thought, does not
possess an intrinsic dynamism which necessarily achieves
its goal. The human being's happiness, consequently, depends not on an intrinsic tending to perfection according
to the demand of nature, but rather one's happiness depends on extrinsic circumstances.

The individual person has no intrinsic orientation (a nature) necessarily bringing about personal perfection; rather,
according to Aristotle, one depends more on the contin-

gent and the accidental. The person needs freedom, health, wealth, friends, and luck to find fulfillment.[52] Notice that Aristotle himself constructed an anthropology that answers some of the strictures made against textbook natural law theories today.

The classicist worldview of the manuals tends to arrange the world in a very detailed pattern. The function of the individual is to correspond to this structure (the "natural law") as minutely outlined. One puts together the different pieces of human behavior much like one puts together the pieces of a jigsaw puzzle. The individual finds the objective pieces already existing and just fits them together. The more historical-minded worldview, on the other hand, sees the human being as creating and shaping the plan of the world. The person does not merely respect the intrinsic nature and finalities of the individual pieces of the pattern. Rather, one interferes to form new pieces and new patterns.

A different worldview, as we have seen, affects our understanding of reality. The older stressed the objectivity of reality. In this view truth consists in the mind's grasp of the reality itself. A clear distinction exists between the object and the subject. Meaning exists in the objective reality, and the subject perceives the meaning already present in reality. Modern thought and culture stress more the creative aspects (both intellectual and affective) of the subject. Modern art reveals the feelings and emotions of the subject rather than portraying an objective picture of reality. The modern cinema confronts the viewer with a very subjective view of reality that calls for imagination and perceptivity on the part of the viewer. Catholic theologians are now speaking in somewhat similar terms of a transcendental methodology in theology.

Karl Rahner has observed that natural law should be approached in this way.[53] A transcendental methodology talks about the conditions and structure in the subject necessary for it to come to know reality, for this very structure is part of the knowing process. Bernard Lonergan speaks about meaning in much the same way.[54] Human meaning can change such basic realities as community, family, state, etc. Meaning involves more than just the apprehension of the objective reality as something "out there."

A note of caution is necessary. Although Lonergan, for example, espouses a more historical consciousness and a transcendental method, at the same time he strongly proclaims a critical realism in epistemology. Lonergan definitely holds for propositions and objective truth, and truth as a correspondence. However, for Lonergan human knowing is a dynamic structure; intentionality and meaning pertain to that objectivity. He reacts against a "naive realism" or a "picture book" type of objectivity.

The problem in the past was that the objectivity of knowledge was identified with the analogy of the objectivity of the sense of sight. "Objective" is that which I see out there. Such a concept of objectivity is false because it identifies objectivity with just one of the properties of one of the operations involved in human knowing. Lonergan rejects both a naive realism and idealism.[55] It seems, however, that the objectivity talked about in manuals of moral theology is often a naive, picture-book objectivity.

The concept of natural law presupposed in Catholic theology manuals definitely reflects a classicist worldview, which sees a very precise and well-defined pattern existing for the world and human moral behavior. This ordering and pattern is called the natural law. Natural law reigns in the area of the necessary.

Within the area marked out by the pattern showing the absolute and the necessary is the contingent and the changing. Just as natural law governs the human life in the area of the principles common to all, so positive law, both civil and ecclesiastical, governs the human life in the contingent and the changing circumstances of life. The plan for the world is thus worked out in great detail in the mind of the creator, and the individual's whole purpose is to conform to the divine plan as made known in the natural and positive laws. (Despite the classical worldview of his day, in his system Thomas did leave room for the virtue of prudence and the creativity of the individual. However, the place later assigned to prudence in textbooks was drastically reduced, and thus Thomas' teaching was distorted.)

But a more historical-minded worldview does not look upon reality as a plan whose features are sketched in quite particular detail according to an unchanging pattern. Human moral life does not primarily call for conformity to such a detailed and unchanging plan. One looks upon existence as a vocation to find the meaning of human existence creatively in one's own life and experience. The meaning of human life is not already given in some pre-existing pattern or plan.

A historically conscious methodology must avoid the pitfall of a total relativism which occasionally creeps into Christianity in various forms of cultural Christianity. One needs to understand the ontological foundations of historical development; the Christian needs to understand all things in the light of the uniqueness of the once-for-all event of Christ Jesus. Both contemporary Protestant (for example, Macquarrie, Ogden) and Catholic (Rahner, Lonergan) scholars are addressing themselves to this problem.

Perhaps the characterization of the two worldviews in this chapter tends to be oversimplified. For one thing, the points of difference between them have been delineated without any attempt to show the similarities. The differences in many areas of morality — for example, the understanding and living of the evangelical norm of love and forgiveness — would be minimal. The reasoning developed in this section has prescinded, as well, from the question of growth and development in human values and morals. However, in the modern world, characterized by instant communication, rapid transportation, and changing sociological patterns, it is clear that the individual needs a more historical worldview and a more historically conscious methodology than the person who lived in a comparatively static and closed society.

III. Physicalism and a Classicist
Methodology in the Encyclical

The encyclical on the regulation of birth employs a natural law methodology which tends to identify the moral action with the physical and biological structure of the act. The core practical conclusion of the letter states: "We must once again declare that the direct interruption of the generative process already begun, and above all directly willed and procured abortion, even if for therapeutic reasons, are to be absolutely excluded as licit means of regulating birth" (*H. V.* n. 14). "Equally to be excluded . . . is direct sterilization. . . . Similarly excluded is every action which, either in anticipation of the conjugal act, or in its accomplishment, or in the development of its natural consequences, proposes, whether as an end or as a means, to render procreation impossible" (*H. V.* n. 14). The footnotes in this particular paragraph refer to the Roman Catechism and the utterances of more recent popes. Reference is made to the Address of Pius XII to the Italian Catholic Union of Midwives in which direct sterilization is defined as "that which aims at making procreation impossible as both means and end" (n. 13, *AAS* 43 [1951], 838). The concept of direct is thus described in terms of the physical structure and causality of the act itself.

The moral conclusion of the encyclical forbidding any interference with the conjugal act is based on the "intimate structure of the conjugal act" (*H. V.* n. 12). The "design of God" is written into the very nature of the conjugal act; the person is merely "the minister of the design established by the Creator" (*H. V.* n. 13). The encyclical acknowledges that "it is licit to take into account the natural rhythms immanent in the generative functions." Recourse to the infecund periods is licit, whereas artificial contraception "as the use of means directly contrary to fecundation is condemned as being always illicit" (*H. V.* n. 16). "In reality there are essential differences between the two cases; in the former, the married couple make legitimate use of a natural disposition; in the latter, they impede the development of natural processes" (*H. V.* n. 16). The natural law theory employed in the encyclical thus identifies the moral and human action with the physical structure of the conjugal act itself.

Humanae Vitae in its methodology well illustrates a classicist approach. The papal letter admits that "changes which have taken place are in fact noteworthy and of varied kinds" (*H. V.* n. 2). These changes give rise to new questions. However, the changing historical circumstances have not affected the answer or the method employed in arriving at concrete conclusions on implementing responsible parenthood. The primary reason for rejecting the majority report of the Papal Commission was "because certain criteria of solutions had emerged which departed from the moral teaching on marriage proposed with constant firmness by the teaching authority of the Church" (*H. V.* n. 6).

The encyclical specifically acknowledges the fact that there are new signs of the times, but one wonders if sufficient attention has really been paid to such changes. The footnotes to the encyclical are significant even if the footnote references alone do not constitute a conclusive argument. The references are only to random scriptural texts, one citation of Thomas Aquinas, and references to earlier pronouncements of the hierarchical magisterium. A more inductive approach would be inclined to give more importance and documentation to the signs of the times. The footnote references contain no indication of any type of dialogue with other Christians, non-Christians and the modern sciences. When the letter does mention social consequences of the use of contraception, no documentation is given for what appear to be unproven assumptions. Since the methodology describes the human act in physical terms, the practical moral conclusion is the absolute condemnation of means of artificial birth control. The encyclical thus betrays an epistemology that has been rejected by many Catholic theologians and philosophers today.

IV. Different Approaches with Different Conclusions

Natural law theory has traditionally upheld two values that are of great importance for moral theology: (1) the existence of a source of ethical wisdom and knowledge which the Christian shares with all humanity; (2) the fact that morality cannot be merely the subjective whim of an individual or group of individuals. However, one can defend these important values for moral theology without necessarily endorsing the particular understanding of natural law presupposed in the encyclical. In the last few years Catholic thinkers have been developing and employing different philosophical approaches to an understanding of morality. One could claim that such approaches are modifications of natural law theory because they retain the two important values mentioned above. Others would prefer to abandon the term natural law since such a concept is very ambiguous. There is no monolithic philosophical system called the natural law, and also the term has been somewhat discredited because of the tendency among some to understand natural in terms of the physical structure of acts. We can briefly describe three of the alternative approaches which have been advanced in the last few years — personalism, a relational and communitarian approach, a transcendental methodology. As mentioned above, these three approaches emerge within the context of a more historically conscious worldview and understand anthropology and moral reality in a way that differs from the concept of anthropology and moral reality proposed by the classical methodology. All these approaches would deny the absolute conclusion of the papal encyclical in condemning all means of artificial birth control.

A more personalist approach has characterized much of contemporary ethics. For the Christian, the biblical revelation contributes to such an understanding of reality. A personalist approach cannot be something merely added on to another theory. A personalist perspective will definitely affect moral conclusions, especially when such conclusions have been based on the physical structure of the act itself. Personalism always sees the act in terms of the person placing the act. The Pastoral Constitution on the Church in the Modern World realized that objective standards in the matter of sexual morality are "based on the nature of the human person and his acts" (n. 51). An essay by Bernard Häring shows how a personalist perspective would not condemn artificial contraception as being always immoral.[56]

Classical ethical theory embraces two types or models of ethical method: the teleological and the deontological. H. Richard Niebuhr has added a third ethical model — the model of responsibility. The moral agent is not primarily a maker or a citizen but a responder. There are various relationships within which the responsible self exists. "The responsible self is driven as it were by the movement of the social process to respond and be accountable in nothing less than a universal community."[57] Robert Johann in developing his understanding of anthropology acknowledges a great debt to Niebuhr.[58]

In the particular question of contraception, a more relational approach would not view the person or a particular faculty as something existing in itself. Each faculty exists in relationship with the total person and other persons within a universal community. Morality cannot merely be determined by examining a particular faculty and its physical structure or a particular act in itself. The changed ethical evaluation of lying well illustrates the point. Both Johann and William H. van der Marck (who embraces a more phenomenological starting point) have employed a more relational approach to argue for the licitness of contraception in certain circumstances.[59]

A third philosophical approach espoused by a growing number of Catholic thinkers today is a theory of transcendental method. Transcendental methodology owes much to the neo-Thomist Joseph Marechal and is espoused today in different forms by Bernard Lonergan, Karl Rahner, and Emerich Coreth.[60] In general, transcendental method goes beyond the object known to the structures of the human

knowing process itself. According to Lonergan, "the intrinsic objectivity of human cognitional activity is its intentionality."[61] Lonergan's ethics is an extension of his theory
of knowing. Moral value is not an intrinsic property of external acts or objects; it is an aspect of certain consciously
free acts in relation to my knowledge of the world. The
moral subject must come to examine the structures of the
knowing and deciding process.[62]

Lonergan uses as a tool the notion of horizon analysis.
Basic horizon is the maximum field of vision from a determined standpoint. This basic horizon is open to development and even conversion. Lonergan posits four conversions which should transpire from the understanding of the
structures of human knowing and deciding — the intellectual, the moral, the religious, and the Christian. Ethics
must bring people to this Christian conversion so that they
can become aware of their knowing and doing and flee
from inauthenticity, unreasonableness, and the surd of sin.
Thus Christian ethics is primarily concerned with the manner in which an authentic Christian person makes ethical
decisions and carries them out. However, such a meta-
ethics must then enter into the realm of the normative, all
the time realizing the provisional value of its precepts
which are limited by the data at hand.[63] One commentator
has said of Lonergan's ethic as applied to moral theology:
"The distinct contribution of the moral theologian to philosophical ethics would consist in clarifying the attitudes
which are involved in man's responding in faith to the initiative of a loving God who has redeemed man in Christ."[64]
Thus a transcendental method would put greater stress on
the knowing and deciding structures of the authentic
Christian subject. Such a theory would also tend to reject
the encyclical's view of anthropology and of human generative faculties.

There has been even among Catholic theologians a sharp
negative response to the practical conclusions of the papal
encyclical on the regulation of birth. This essay has tried
to explain the reason for the negative response. The con-

cept of natural law employed in the encyclical tends to define the moral act merely in terms of the physical structure of the act. In contemporary theology such an understanding of natural law has been severely criticized. Newer philosophical approaches have been accepted by many Catholic thinkers. Such approaches logically lead to the conclusion that artificial contraception can be a permissible and even necessary means for the regulation of birth within the context of responsible parenthood.

V. Application to the Situation Ethics Debate

In the last few years moral theology and Christian ethics have been immersed in a controversy over situation ethics. The controversy tends to polarize opinions and fails to show the huge areas of agreement existing among Christian moralists. There are, nevertheless, many real differences in approaches and in some practical conclusions. The principal areas of practical differences between some situationists and the teaching found in the manuals of moral theology are the following: medical ethics, particularly in the area of reproduction; conflict situations solved by the principle of the indirect voluntary, especially conflicts involving life and death, e.g., killing, abortion; sexuality; euthanasia; and divorce.

These major points of disagreement have one thing in common. In these cases, the manuals of Catholic moral theology have tended to define the moral action in terms of the physical structure of the act considered in itself apart from the person placing the act and the community of persons within which she lives. A certain action defined in terms of its physical structure or consequences (e.g., euthanasia as the positive interference in the life of the person; male masturbation as the ejaculation of semen) is considered to be always wrong. I have used the term "negative, moral absolutes" to refer to such actions described in their physical structure which are always wrong from a moral viewpoint. Thus the central point of disagreement in moral theology today centers on these prohibited actions which are described primarily in terms of their physical structure.

In the area of medical ethics certain actions described in terms of the physical structure of the act are never permitted or other such actions are always required. Artificial insemination with the husband's semen is never permitted because insemination cannot occur except through the act of sexual intercourse.[65] Contraception as direct interference with the act of sexual intercourse is wrong. Direct sterilization is always wrong. Masturbation as the ejaculation of semen is always wrong even as a way of procuring semen for semen analysis.[66] Frequently in such literature the axiom is cited that the end does not justify the means. However, in all these cases the means is defined in terms of the physical structure of the act. I believe in all the areas mentioned above there are circumstances in which such actions would be morally permissible and even necessary.

Catholic moral theology decides most conflict situations by an application of the principle of the indirect voluntary. Direct killing, direct taking of one's life, direct abortion, direct sterilization are always wrong. However, the manuals of theology usually define direct in terms of the physical structure of the act itself. Direct killing according to one author "may be defined as the performance (or the omission of) an act, the primary and natural result of which is to bring about death."[67] According to the same author "direct abortion is the performance of an act, the primary and natural effect of which is to expel a nonviable fetus from its mother's womb." In these cases direct refers to the physical structure and consequences of the act itself. One exception in the manuals of theology to the solution of conflict situations in terms of the principle of the indirect voluntary is the case of unjust aggression. The physical structure of the act is not the determining factor in such a conflict situation.

In general a Christian ethicist might be somewhat suspicious of conflict situations solved in terms of the physical structure of the act itself. Such a solution seems too facile and too easily does away with the agonizing problems raised by the conflict. Likewise, such an approach has tended to minimalize what is only an indirect effect, but the Christian can never have an easy conscience about taking the life of another even if it is only an indirect effect.

The case of "assisted abortion" seems to illustrate the inherent difficulties in the manualistic concept of direct and indirect. For example, the best available medical knowledge indicates that the woman cannot bring a living child to term. If the doctor can abort the fetus now, he or she can avert very probable physical and psychological harm to the mother from the pregnancy which cannot eventually come to term. The manuals indicate that such an abortion would be direct and therefore immoral. However, in the total context of the situation, it does not seem that such an abortion would be immoral. The example of assisted abortion illustrates the impossibility of establishing an absolute moral norm based on the physical description of the action considered only in itself apart from the person placing the action and the entire community. It seems that the older notion of direct enshrines a prescientific worldview which is somewhat inadequate in our technological age. Why should the doctor sit back and wait for nature to take its course when by interfering now she can avoid great harm to the mother? In general, I do not think that conflict situations can be solved merely in terms of the physical structure and consequences of the act.

Perhaps the approach used in conflict situations of unjust aggression would serve as a better model for the solution of other conflict situations. In unjust aggression the various values at stake are weighed, and the person is permitted to kill an unjust aggressor not only to save one's life but also to protect other goods of comparable value, such as a serious threat to health, honor, chastity, or even material goods of great importance.[68] (I believe that in some cases the older theologians went too far in equating the defense of these values and the life of the aggressor.) Thus in the question of abortion there seem to be cases when it is moral to abort to save the life of the mother or to preserve other very important values. I am not proposing that the fetus is an unjust aggressor but rather that the ethical model employed in solving problems of unjust aggression avoids some of the problems created by the model of direct and indirect effects when the direct effect is determined by the physical structure of the act itself.

The present discussion about the beginning of human life centers on the criteria for identifying human life. Are the physical criteria of genetics and embryology sufficient? Or must other criteria of a more psychological and personalistic nature be employed for discerning the existence of human life? What then would be the difference between the fetus in the womb and the newborn babe who is now existing outside her mother's womb? There are many complicated problems in such a discussion. For many, the biological and genetic criteria are the only practical way of resolving the problem.[69] I am merely pointing out that the problem exists precisely because some people will not accept the biological and genetic considerations as establishing an adequate criterion for determining the beginning of human life.

Many theologians maintain the meaning of sexuality has been distorted in the Catholic theological tradition for many reasons including an overemphasis on the physical structure of sexual actuation. In the question of euthanasia, Catholic and other theistic ethicists generally approach the problem in terms of the limited dominion which the individual has over his or her own life. Today even Christians claim a greater power over their own existence both because of scientific advances and because of better understanding of participation in the Lordship of Jesus. However, in one important aspect in the area of euthanasia the question of dominion over one's life is not primary. Catholic thinking has maintained that the patient does not have to use extraordinary means to preserve life. In more positive terms, there is a right to die. Many Catholic theologians remind doctors they have no obligation to give intravenous feeding to a dying cancer patient. Likewise, a doctor may discontinue such feeding with the intent that the person will thus die. But the manuals of theology would condemn any positive action on the part of the doctor — e.g., injection of air into the bloodstream — under the same circumstances.[70]

At the particular time when death is fast approaching, the primary moral question does not seem to revolve explicitly around the notion of one's dominion over life. The problem centers on the difference between not giving something or the withdrawal of something necessary for life and the positive giving of something to bring about death. Is the difference between the two types of action enough to warrant the total condemnation of positively interfering? I do not think so; Catholic theologians should explore the possibility of interfering to hasten the dying process, a notion similar to the concept of assisted abortion mentioned above. But the theologian would also have to consider the possibility of a general prohibition based on the societal effects of such interference.

The problem of describing moral reality in terms of the physical description of an act viewed in itself apart from the person also manifests itself in the question of divorce. According to Catholic teaching a consummated marriage between two baptized persons is indissoluble. But consummation is defined in solely physical terms. Thus the notion of consummation as found in the present law of the Church is inadequate.[71] Moreover, divorce in general qualifies as a negative moral absolute in the sense described above. A particular action described in nonmoral terms (remarriage after a valid first marriage) is always wrong. The entire question of divorce is too complex to be considered adequately in the present context since it involves biblical, historical, conciliar, and magisterial aspects. But the concept of "the bond of marriage" adds weight to the arguments against divorce. The bond becomes objectivized as a reality existing apart from the relationship of the persons which is brought into being by their marriage vows. All Christians, I believe, should hold some element transcending the two persons and their union here and now. But can this bond always be considered totally apart from the ongoing relationship between the two who exchanged the marital promises?

Thus a quick overview shows that the critical, practical areas of discussion in contemporary moral theology and Christian ethics center on the absolute moral prohibition of certain actions which are defined primarily in terms of the physical structure of the act. Moral meaning is not necessarily identical with the physical description of an act. Modern anthropology is in a much better position than medieval anthropology to realize that fact. The underlying problem is common to every human science — the need to clearly differentiate the category of meaning as the specific data of any science involving human reality. Historians of ideas would be familiar with this problem from the nineteenth century differentiation of Dilthey between the *Geisteswissenchaften* and *Naturwissenchaften*.[72] In the Anglo-American context, Matson has recently published an informative survey of the present status of this same differentiation involving the notion of human behavior.[73]

A word of caution is in order. It appears that some proponents of situation ethics have not given enough importance to the bodily, the material, the external, and the physical aspects of reality. On the other hand, contemporary theory is less prone to accept the physical and the biological aspects of reality as morally normative. An analysis of the current scene in moral theology and Christian ethics in a broad ecumenical view indicates that the primary point of dispute centers on the existence of negative moral absolutes in which the moral action is described in physical terms. It would be unwarranted to conclude that the moral act is never identified with the physical structure and description of the act. However, one can conclude that an ethical theory which begins with the assumption that the moral act is identified with the physical structure and consequences of the act will find little acceptance by contemporary theologians.

NOTES

1. E.g., *Light on the Natural Law,* ed. Illtud Evans, O.P. (Baltimore: Helicon Press, 1965); *Das Naturrecht im Disput,* ed. Franz Böckle (Dusseldorf: Patmos, 1966); "La Nature fondement de la morale? " *Supplément de la Vie Spirituelle* 81 (May 1967), 187-324; *Absolutes in Moral Theology?* ed. Charles E. Curran (Washington: Corpus Books, 1968).

2. Edward LeRoy Long Jr., *A Survey of Christian Ethics* (New York: Oxford University Press, 1967); Thomas G. Sanders, *Protestant Concepts of Church and State* (Garden City, N.Y.: Doubleday Anchor Books, 1965).

3. Such emphases can still be found, although not in an absolute sense, in the writings of Niels H. Söe. See Söe, "Natural Law and Social Ethics," in *Christian Social Ethics in a Changing World,* ed. John C. Bennett (New York: Association Press, 1966), pp. 289-309. The same article with a response by Paul Ramsey appeared in *Zeitschrift für Evangelische Ethik,* 12 (March 1968), 65-98.

4. John C. Bennett, "Issues for the Ecumenical Dialogue," in *Christian Social Ethics in a Changing World,* pp. 377, 378.

5. H. Richard Niebuhr, *Christ and Culture* (New York: Harper Torchbook, 1956).

6. Niebuhr actually describes the Thomistic approach as "Christ above culture." He goes on to explain that "Thomas also answers the question about Christ and culture with a 'both-and'; yet his Christ is far above culture, and he does not try to disguise the gulf that lies between them" (p. 129).

7. One cannot simplistically condemn the nature-grace and natural-supernatural distinctions. In their original historical contexts such distinctions tried with considerable success to describe and synthesize this complex reality. Although such distinctions do have some meaning today; nevertheless, many Catholic theologians realize the need to reinterpret such distinctions in the light of different metaphysical approaches. See the three articles by Bernard Lonergan, S.J., which appeared in *Theological Studies* 2 (1941), 307-324; 3 (1942), 69-88, 375-402. For an exposition of the thought of Karl Rahner on this subject, see Carl J. Peter, "The Position of Karl

Rahner Regarding the Supernatural," *Proceedings of the Catholic Theological Society of America* 20 (1965), 81-94.

8. A wire release of N. C. News Service with a Vatican City dateline published in Catholic papers in this country during the week of August 4, 1968.

9. Bernard Häring, C.SS.R., "The Encyclical Crisis," *Commonweal* 88 (September 6, 1968), 588-594.

10. Joseph Fuchs, S.J., *Natural Law*, trans. Helmut Reckter, S.J., and John Dowling (New York: Sheed and Ward, 1965).

11. Christian Duquoc, O.P., *L'Eglise et le progrès* (Paris: Editions du Cerf, 1964), pp. 68-117. The author considers the past teaching in the Church on slavery, the freedom of nations, the dignity of women, Church and State, torture, and questions of war and peace.

12. "Dialogue with Joseph Fletcher," *Homiletic and Pastoral Review*, 67 (1967), 828, 829.

13. Helmut Thielicke, *Theological Ethics I: Foundations*, ed. William Lazareth (Philadelphia: Fortress Press, 1966), 622ff.

14. Pope Leo XIII, *Rerum Novarum*, n. 7-14; Pope Pius XI, *Quadregesimo Anno*, n. 44-52.

15. Thomas explicitly cites Isidore in *I-II*, q. 94, a. 2, ob. 1. In *II-II*, q. 66, a. 2, Thomas gives the opinion proposed by Isidore without a direct reference. Thomas explains that reason has called for the right of private property not as something against natural law, but as something added to natural law.

16. The reasons adduced by Thomas in *II-II*, q. 66, a. 2, indicate that human sinfulness is a very important factor in the argument for the right of private property.

17. *Rerum Novarum*, n. 22.

18. Hermenegildus Lio, O.F.M., "Estne obligatio justitiae subvenire pauperibus?" *Apollinaris* 29 (1956), 124-231; 30 (1957), 99-201.

19. Leo XIII was conscious of the social aspect of property (*Rerum Novarum*, n. 22), but he did not emphasize it. The subsequent Popes down to Paul VI have put increasingly more emphasis on the social aspects of property. The concentration on such social aspects explains the many discussions about the notion of socialization in the encyclicals of Pope John XXIII.

20. See note 1; also my treatment of this precise question in *A New Look at Christian Morality* (Notre Dame, Ind.: Fides Publishers, 1968), pp. 74-89.

21. Jean Marie Aubert, "Le Droit Naturel: ses avatars historiques et son avenir," *Supplément de la Vie Spirituelle* 81 (1967), especially 298 ff.

22. *The Digest* or *Pandects of Justinian*, Book 1, t. 1, nn. 1-4.

23. Odon Lottin, *Le Droit Naturel chez Saint Thomas d'Aquin et ses prédécesseurs*, 2nd ed. (Bruges: Charles Beyaert, 1931), p. 62.

24. *In IV Sent.* d. 33, q. 1, a. 1, ad 4.

25. *In V Ethic.*, lect. 12.

26. *I-II*, q. 90, a. 1, ob. 3; q. 96, a. 5, ob. 3; q. 97, a. 2; *II-II*, q. 57, a. 3, ob. 1, and *in corp.*

27. *I-II*, q. 95, a. 4.

28. *II-II*, q. 57, a. 3. For a detailed analysis of Thomas's teaching that comes to the same conclusion, see Michael Bertram Crowe, "St. Thomas Aquinas and Ulpian's Natural Law," in *St. Thomas Aquinas, 1274-1974: Commemorative Studies,* vol. 1 (Toronto, Canada: Pontifical Institute of Medieval Studies, 1974), pp. 261-282.

29. E.g., H. Noldin et al., *Summa Theologiae Moralis: De Castitate,* 36th ed. (Oeniponte: F. Rauch, 1958), pp. 21-43.

30. Decree of the Holy Office on the ends of marriage, April 1, 1944, *AAS,* 36 (1944), 103. Also various addresses of Pius XII: *AAS,* 33 (1941), 422; 43 (1951), 835-854.

31. Regis Araud, S.J., "Évolution de la théologie du marriage," *Cahiers Laënnec,* 27 (1967), 56-71; W. van der Marck, O.P., "De recente ontwikkelingen in de theologie van het huwelijk," *Tijdschrift voor Theologie* 7 (1967), 127-140. English summary on page 140.

32. Gerard Watson, "The Early History of Natural Law," *The Irish Theological Quarterly* 33 (1966), 65-74.

33. John L. Russell, S.J., "The Concept of Natural Law," *The Heythrop Journal* 6 (1965), 434-438; Pierre Colin, "Ambiguités du mot nature," *Supplément de la Vie Spirituelle* 81 (1967), 253-255.

34. Charles E. Curran, "Masturbation and Objectively Grave Matter: An Exploratory Discussion," *Proceedings of the Catholic Theological Society of America* 21 (1966), 95-109; also chapter 7.

35. H. Noldin et al., *Summa Theologiae Moralis,* vol. 2: *De Praeceptis* (Oeniponte: F. Rauch, 1959), pp. 553-560; E. F. Regatillo, S.J., and M. Zalba, S. J., *Theologiae Moralis Summa,* vol. 2 (Matriti: Biblioteca de Autores Cristianos, 1953), 1000-1018.

36. J. A. Dorszynski, *Catholic Teaching about the Morality of Falsehood* (Washington: Catholic University of America Press, 1949); Francis J. Connell, C.SS.R., *More Answers to Today's Moral Problems,* ed. Eugene J. Weitzel, C.S.V. (Washington: Catholic University of America Press, 1965), p. 123, 124. Augustine had at one time accepted the distinction between falsehood and lying, but he later changed his opinion.

37. Bernard Lonergan, S.J., *Collection* (New York: Herder and Herder, 1967), pp. 252-267; Lonergan, "A Transition from a Classicist Worldview to Historical Mindedness," in *Law for Liberty: The Role of Law in the Church Today,* ed. James E. Biecher (Baltimore: Helicon Press, 1967). Lonergan along with other theologians such as Marechal, Rahner, and Metz maintains that although Thomas Aquinas reflected a classical worldview, the followers of Thomas distorted his teaching especially in such areas as the emphasis on a

deductive methodology and a nonrelational understanding of being.

38. John Courtney Murray, S.J., "The Declaration on Religious Freedom," *Concilium* 15 (May 1966), 3-16.

39. Eulalio R. Baltazar, *Teilhard and the Supernatural* (Baltimore: Helicon Press, 1966); Leslie Dewart, *The Future of Belief* (New York: Herder and Herder, 1966). Lonergan espouses historical mindedness but strenuously opposes the approach of Dewart. See Lonergan, "The Dehellenization of Dogma," *Theological Studies* 28 (1967), 336-351.

40. Murray, Declaration of Religious Freedom," pp. 11-16.

41. John Courtney Murray, S.J., *The Problem of Religious Freedom* (Westminster, Md.: Newman, 1965).

42. John Courtney Murray, S.J., "Freedom, Authority, Community," *America* (December 3, 1966), 735.

43. *Gaudium et Spes* (The Pastoral Constitution on the Church in the Modern World), n. 44. For a competent one-volume translation of the documents of Vatican II, see *The Documents of Vatican II,* ed. Walter M. Abbot, S.J. (New York: America Press and Association Press, 1966).

44. Karl Rahner, S.J., *The Dynamic Element in the Church* (New York: Herder and Herder, 1964).

45. Daniel C. Maguire, "Moral Absolutes and the Magisterium," *Absolutes in Moral Theology?*, pp. 57-107.

46. Herbert Butterfield, *The Origins of Modern Science, 1300-1800* (New York: Macmillan, 1951); Lonergan, *Collection*, p. 259 ff.

47. Andreas van Melsen, "Natural Law and Evolution," *Concilium* 26 (June, 1967), 49-59.

48. *Law for Liberty: The Role of Law in the Church Today*, passim.

49. *Documents of Vatican II*, p. 686, n. 20. The footnote on the role of civil law was written by John Courtney Murray.

50. Thomas B. McDonough, "Distribution of Contraceptives by the Welfare Department: A Catholic Response," in *The Problem of Population*, vol. 2 (Notre Dame: University of Notre Dame Press, 1964), pp. 94-118.

51. Douglas Sturm, "Naturalism, Historicism, and Christian Ethics: Toward a Christian Doctrine of Natural Law," *The Journal of Religion* 44 (1964), 40-51. Note again that some Catholic thinkers see in the excessive emphasis on *res in se* apart from any relational consideration a distortion of the understanding of St. Thomas.

52. Russell, "Concept of Natural Law," pp. 434-438.

53. Karl Rahner, S.J., "Theology and Anthropology," in *The Word in History*, ed. T. Patrick Burke (New York: Sheed and Ward, 1966), pp. 1-23; Rahner, "Naturrecht," *Lexikon für Theologie und Kirche,* vol. 7, pp. 827-828.

54. Lonergan, "Dimensions of Meaning," *Collection*, pp. 252-267.

55. Lonergan, *Collection*, pp. 221-239; *Theological Studies* 28 (1967), 337-351.

56. Bernard Häring, "The Inseparability of the Unitive-Procreative Functions of the Marital Act," *Contraception: Authority and Dissent*, ed. Charles E. Curran (New York: Herder and Herder, 1969), pp. 176-192.

57. H. Richard Niebuhr, *The Responsible Self* (New York: Harper and Row, 1963), p. 88.

58. Robert O. Johann, S.J., *Building the Human* (New York: Herder and Herder, 1968), pp. 7-10.

59. Robert O. Johann, S.J., "Responsible Parenthood: A Philosophical View," *Proceedings of the Catholic Theological Society of America* 20 (1965), 115-128; William H. van der Marck, O.P., *Toward a Christian Ethic* (Westminster, Md.: Newman Press, 1967), pp. 48-60. Note that Germain G. Grisez in his *Contraception and the Natural Law* (Milwaukee: Bruce, 1964), argues against artificial contraception although he explicitly denies the "perverted faculty" argument. However, Grisez seems to accept too uncritically his basic premise that the malice of contraception "is in the will's direct violation of the procreative good as a value in itself, as an ideal which never may be submerged."

60. For a succinct exposition of transcendental philosophy, see Kenneth Baker, S.J., *A Synopsis of the Transcendental Philosophy of Emerich Coreth and Karl Rahner* (Spokane: Gonzaga University, 1965).

61. Lonergan, *Collection*, p. 228.

62. In addition to the bibliography of Lonergan's which has already been mentioned, see Bernard J. F. Lonergan, S.J., *Insight* (New York and London: Longmans, Green, and Co., 1964); Donald H. Johnson, S.J., "Lonergan and the Redoing of Ethics," *Continuum* 5 (1967), 211-220; and John P. Boyle, "Lonergan's *Method in Theology* and Objectivity in Moral Theology," *The Thomist* 37 (1973), 589-601.

63. David W. Tracy, "Horizon Analysis and Eschatology," *Continuum* 6 (1968), 166-179.

64. Johnson, "Lonergan and the Redoing of Ethics," 219, 220.

65. Pope Pius XII, Address to the Fourth World Congress of Catholic Doctors, Rome, September 29, 1949, *A.A.S.* 41 (1949), 560; Pope Pius XII, Address to the Italian Catholic Union of Midwives, October 29, 1951, *A.A.S.* 43 (1951), 850; Pope Pius XII, Address to the Second World Congress of Fertility and Sterility, May 19, 1956, *A.A.S.* 48 (1956), 472.

66. Pope Pius XII, *A.A.S.* 48 (1956), 472; Pope Pius XII, Address to the Italian Urologists, October 8, 1953, *A.A.S.* 45 (1953), 678; Decree of the Holy Office, August 2, 1929, *A.A.S.* 21 (1929), 490.

67. John McCarthy, *Problems in Theology II: The Commandments* (Westminster, Md.: Newman Press, 1960), pp. 159, 160. The author mentions other current definitions of direct killing (e.g., an act which aims, *ex fine operis*, at the destruction of life) earlier on pp. 119-122.

68. Marcellinus Zalba, S.J., *Theologia Moralis Summa II; Theologia Moralis Specialis* (Madrid: Biblioteca de Autores Cristianos, 1953), pp. 275-279.

69. Such an approach is adopted by Paul Ramsey who claims that at least from blastocyst the fetus must be considered as a human being. For further developments in Ramsey's thought and my own critique, see Charles E. Curran, *Politics, Medicine and Christian Ethics: A Dialogue with Paul Ramsey* (Philadelphia: Fortress Press, 1973), pp. 110-131.

70. Gerald Kelly, S.J., *Medico-Moral Problems* (St. Louis: Catholic Hospital Association, 1957), pp. 128-141.

71. For a fuller critique of the notion of consummation, see Dennis Doherty, "Consummation and the Indissolubility of Marriage," *Absolutes in Moral Theology?*, pp. 211-231.

72. Wilhelm Dilthey, *Pattern and Meaning in History* (New York: Harper Torchbook, 1967).

73. Floyd W. Matson, *The Broken Image* (Garden City, N.Y.: Doubleday Anchor Books, 1966).

6. Utilitarianism, Consequentialism, and Moral Theology

The last few chapters have indicated that within the last decade in Roman Catholicism there has been a growing theological literature questioning the existence of absolute behavioral norms in moral theology. More specifically, many theologians have objected to exceptionless moral norms in which the moral action is described in terms of the physical aspect of the act. At the same time there has been a growing debate in philosophical ethics about the adequacy of a utilitarian approach. Often these debates have been taking place in isolation. The purpose of this chapter is to compare the different debates that have taken place within utilitarian thought, to examine the arguments proposed against a utilitarian position in order to clarify the terms of the discussion, to situate the debate which has taken place in Roman Catholic ethics in the light of the discussion about utilitarianism, and to suggest approaches for Roman Catholic ethics.

Debates within Utilitarianism

Utilitarianism is described as the ethical attitude which seeks to produce the greatest good for the greatest number. Since the morality of an action depends in some way on producing good and/or avoiding evil, utilitarianism is generally understood as a form of teleological ethics or consequentalism. Teleological theories are generally contrasted with deontological theories which maintain that it is possible to have a moral obligation to do an act which does not produce the most good or avoid the most evil in the manner suggested by teleologists. Utilitarianism is a form of consequentialism because moral obligation is determined by the good or bad consequences produced. J. J. C. Smart, a contemporary defender of utilitarianism, describes it as the view that the rightness or wrongness of an act depends only on the total goodness or badness of the consequences.[1]

Calculating Consequences

Utilitarians themselves as well as their opponents have frequently recognized some difficulty in calculating consequences. Bentham attempted a calculus of pleasure and pain by indicating seven different dimensions which had to be taken into account. John Stuart Mill, reacting to Bentham's calculus based on quantity, introduced a qualitative distinction between higher and lower pleasures.[2] But the problem of calculating the consequences is even more complex. Whatever utility means, the theory of utilitarianism calls for it to be maximized. Since our actions very often affect more than one person and many societal institutions, it must be possible to calculate the total net utility to all affected by the various alternative actions which are open to the subject. Different theories of calculation are still being proposed by various contemporary thinkers (e.g., Braybrooke, Rescher, and Brandt).[3] Most philosophers recognize the difficulty in constructing such a calculation of the consequences of acts.

Two points deserve mention in response to the problem of calculating consequences. Utilitarians do not believe that human beings should always attempt to make such exhaustive calculations before acting. They readily accept rules of thumb often called summary rules. Such summary

rules are not absolute and should be violated if the violation brings about better consequences, but ordinarily one
can follow such rules of thumb as the distillation of experience about what usually produces the most utility.

Secondly, one must admit there is no universal agreement even among utilitarians on how consequences of acts
should be calculated. The difficulty or lack of agreement
does not constitute a totally convincing argument against
utilitarianism or any consequentialist theory. Calculating
consequences is a problem for all other types of ethics as
well. Roman Catholic manualistic moral theology has
often appealed to consequences to justify the morality of
particular actions. The principle of proportionality in war
maintains that the good to be achieved by the war must
outweigh the evils involved. Here one is asked to consider
the consequences of alternative actions involving many
different human values including the taking of human lives
and the very existence of peoples and nations. Traditional
Catholic moral theology thus has to face the same difficulty as utilitarians although not all the time.

Act-utilitarianism and Rule-utilitarianism

A very significant and important debate among utilitarians concerns the difference between act- and rule-
utilitarianism. Until the last two or three decades utilitarianism was understood in terms of act-utilitarianism —
the rightness or wrongness of the action is determined by
the consequences of the act itself. Antiutilitarians brought
up a number of objections to utilitarianism because by
making the consequences of the individual act morally
determinative one goes against many accepted moral
teachings, e.g., punishment of the innocent, judicial murder, not voting in an election, not keeping secrets, not
telling the truth, etc. Michael Bayles has collected an
anthology of essays to show the development of rule-
utilitarianism as a refinement of the basic utilitarian
approach which was proposed in the intervening years to
overcome some of the above objections.[4] According to

rule-utilitarianism acts are to be regarded as right only if they conform to rules which can be supported on utilitarian grounds. Urmson maintains that John Stuart Mill himself was really a rule-utilitarian and not an act-utilitarian.[5]

In the 1960s David Lyons and others maintained that rule-utilitarianism and act-utilitarianism, if properly understood as including all the circumstances, especially threshold phenomena, are equivalent so that there is no real difference between them.[6] Lyons' thesis of equivalence has been attacked,[7] but it is safe to describe the present state of the debate by indicating that there is a growing consensus among utilitarians themselves that rule-utilitarianism very frequently if not always collapses into act-utilitarianism.[8]

The debate within utilitarianism about act- and rule-utilitarianism does not have any immediate parallels in the current debates in Roman Catholic moral theology. However, it seems that Roman Catholic moral theology might profit from this discussion with its emphasis on the principle of universalizability. Richard A. McCormick has recently proposed that some norms (e.g., direct taking of innocent life, direct killing of noncombatants, difference between commission and omission as seen in so-called passive and active euthanasia) are "teleologically established and yet are virtually exceptionless." In weighing all the consequences of actions one comes to the conclusion that the actions are wrong and that the dangers and risks that might result from any exceptions are so great that the norm is virtually exceptionless. The establishment of such a norm is based on an analogy with the establishment of a positive law on the basis of a presumption of a common and universal danger.[9]

McCormick's argument for exceptionless norms consists in a wedge argument that any possible exceptions would ultimately lead to greater evils than the good that might possibly be achieved in the one exception. The debate about act- and rule-utilitarianism has frequently made use of the principle of universalizability or generalizability which might be employed here to allow certain exceptions without necessarily involving all the evils that McCormick fears might come from any exceptions.

McCormick himself maintains that the existing laws or norms accepted in Catholic moral theology have ultimately come about by refining the principle that killing is wrong except where there is a proportionate reason. Exceptions have been made in this general norm for proportionate reasons (self-defense, killing in war, etc.) without endangering the value to be preserved by the norm itself.[10] Now one might attempt to push the question one step further — can exceptions be made in the now accepted norms of no direct killing of the innocent and no active euthanasia which could allow for some exceptions without entailing all the evil consequences that McCormick fears if one no longer accepts the existing distinctions?

In the case of directly killing noncombatants in war I am in basic agreement with McCormick's fears, but in the case of directly killing the innocent, it might be possible to make some very limited exceptions. Consider a case which was proposed by Williams. A foreigner comes across a scene where a tyrannical military captain is prepared to shoot a group of villagers taken at random to discourage other protesters in the village and bring about loyalty to the existing government. The captain offers the foreigner the privilege of killing one of the villagers with the promise that he himself will then let the others go free. The presuppositions are that the captain will do as he threatens and there is absolutely no other way to save the villagers or any number of them.[11] Is it not possible to acknowledge some exception clause for hard cases like this without necessarily involving the many long-range consequences feared by McCormick? Could one not accept the rule — directly killing the innocent is wrong except in those cases where one is forced into a situation in which there is certitude that this is the only way a far greater number of innocent persons can be saved? Such a restricted exception clause could allow such killing in a few cases and still maintain the general principle of not killing innocent people in almost all situations. Here it is necessary to insist on the sin-filled aspects of the situation and on the certitude that one has that this is the only way in which a far greater number of innocent persons can be saved. Such a condition is rarely present and impossible in the complex situation of warfare and the direct killing of noncombatants.

In the case of the difference between killing and letting die as acts of commission and omission, is it not possible to make some nuanced distinction which acknowledges there is not always an absolute difference between the two but still avoids some of the bad consequences that McCormick fears? I have proposed that once the dying process begins the distinction between omission and commission ceases to be of decisive importance. More practically, the dying process can be identified as the time that extraordinary means could be discontinued as now being useless, since there is no hope of success in thus treating the patient. Is there that great a difference between turning off the respirator with the intention of allowing the person to die and positively interferring at the same time to bring about the same effect? The presumption is that in both cases the death of the person will follow certainly, inevitably, and with about the same degree of immediacy from either the act of omission or commission. In the vast majority of cases the two acts of omission and commission would not be the same regarding certainty, inevitability, and immediacy of the effect of death, and thus one avoids most of the dangers mentioned by McCormick. However, there is the difference that in the case of shutting off the respirator I am not the cause of the death in exactly the same way as in an act of commission, but the difference does not seem to constitute the basis for a different moral judgment where the conditions mentioned above are the same.

Utilitarianism, Teleology, and Consequentialism

Clarifications and Rejection of Utilitarianism

In the recent literature there has been a general tendency to point out the insufficiency of utilitarianism as a moral theory and to advocate other approaches as at least modifications of the utilitarian approach. The terms involved have been defined in different ways, but in the context of the utilitarian debate, utilitarianism, teleology, and consequentialism are generally understood as ethical theories which determine the moral rightness or wrongness of the act (or rule) solely on the basis of the consequences of the act (or rule). J. J. C. Smart maintains that the rightness or wrongness of an action depends only on the total goodness or badness of the consequences; i.e., on the effect of the action on the welfare of all human beings.[12]

In a critique of utilitarianism especially with the theory of Smart in mind, Bernard Williams devotes a large section of his monograph to the structure of consequentialism and emphasizes that the alternative to consequentialism does not involve the acceptance of the position that there are certain actions which one should do or never do whatever the consequences. Williams himself admits some circumstances in which direct killing of the innocent would be morally good. The denial of consequentialism only involves the admission that there would be some situations in which acts would be good even though the state of affairs produced by doing these acts would be worse than some other state of affairs accessible to the actor. In other words to oppose consequentialism it is necessary to hold that consequences are not the only morally relevant considerations; one does not have to affirm that it is always wrong to do acts no matter what the consequences.[13]

In the more recent debate authors who modify or reject utilitarianism such as Rawls and Lyons employ the word teleological in this same sense. Lyons states in the very beginning of his book that teleologists claim that the rightness of acts depends solely on their utility; whereas deontologists claim that rightness is not simply a function of utility.[14] Rawls insists that in teleological theory the good is defined independently of the right. In accord with this description Rawls maintains that if the distribution of the good is also counted as a good and perhaps a higher order one, we no longer have a teleological view in the classical sense.[15] Such an understanding of teleological is in accord with the position of William Frankena who defines teleology as the system in which the moral quality or value depends on the comparative nonmoral value of what is produced or brought about. Deontological theories, as opposed to teleological theories, affirm that there are at least other considerations which make an action or rule right or obligatory besides the goodness or badness of consequences. Frankena recognizes that deontologists can be of two types: either those for whom the principle of maximizing the balance of good over evil is not a moral criterion or those for whom such a principle is not the only basis or ultimate one.[16]

Objections to the theory of utilitarianism or teleology or consequentialism as proposed by Rawls, Frankena, Williams, and others in the contemporary debate are not based on the fact that these authors necessarily maintain that some actions are always right or wrong whatever the consequences. Rather, their objections to utilitarianism, teleology, or consequentialism may be summarized as follows: (1) Aspects other than consequences must be taken into account; (2) the good cannot be determined independently of the morally right; (3) not only the consequences of the action but also the way in which the actor brings about the consequences has moral significance. To refute utilitarianism, teleology, or consequentialism, these authors do not have to maintain that certain actions are right or wrong whatever the consequences, but they must accept that acts can be the right thing to do even though the state of affairs produced by acts would be worse than other states of affairs accessible to the actor.

A consideration of promise keeping which is often mentioned in the literature about the adequacy of utilitarian ethics illustrates well the differences between utilitarians and their opponents. The case is often proposed about a promise to a dying person on a desert isle to give this person's money to a jockey club. When the survivor comes back to civilization should he say the dying man wanted his money given to the jockey club or to a hospital which could do much more good for people? The utilitarian or consequentialist would judge only upon what would have the best consequences — giving the money to the jockey club or to a needy hospital. The consequentialist recognizes the importance of promise keeping in society and must consider this aspect, but in this case the presupposition is that no one knows about the promise. Since no one else knows about the promise, there would be no harm done to society if the maker of the promise did not keep it. Working on the supposition that the promisor is a good utilitarian, such a person would never feel guilty about now giving the money to the hospital.

The antiutilitarian argues that in addition to consequences there is an obligation of fidelity on the part of the promisor which must be taken into account. The antiutilitarian, together with the traditional textbooks of Catholic moral theology, acknowledges that promises are not always to be kept, for a change in the matter or the person might make the promise no longer obliging. The antiutilitarian argues here that the good consequences cannot be considered apart from the criterion of the right and something other than consequences (namely, the obligation of fidelity) must be taken into account. Likewise, the integrity of the person who made the promise is involved.

In the light of this understanding of utilitarianism, consequentialism, and teleology, the antiutilitarians attempt to show the inadequacy of utilitarianism in the following areas: questions of fidelity, gratitude, and punishment; questions of distribution involving justice and fairness; intentionality and integrity of the person. The antiutilitarian appeals to questions of fidelity, gratitude, and punishment because here there are sources of moral obligation other than the future consequences. In fidelity, moral obligation arises from the promise made in the past. In gratitude, moral obligation arises from the past act of generosity or beneficence. In punishment, moral obligation arises from the wrong act which the person did in the past. It is not necessary to assert that an absolute moral norm can be derived from these other sources of obligation, but at least it must be asserted that these sources of moral obligation must be considered as well as the future consequences. However, very often the utilitarian and the antiutilitarian conclusions will coincide.

Questions of distribution, justice, and fairness have frequently been proposed as problems for a utilitarian ethic. The only controlling moral criterion cannot be the net aggregate of good over evil achieved by the act, for one must also consider the distribution of the good. Rawls first proposed a form of rule-utilitarianism in his famous essay, "Two Concepts of Rules," as a means of strengthening the utilitarian view especially in matters of justice and promises. On the basis of that article Rawls was often wrongly called a rule-utilitarian, but he himself expressly indicted he was not proposing the rule-utilitarian position as completely defensible.[17] Later, in his *Theory of Justice,* Rawls indicates that utilitarianism needs to be modified by considerations of justice and fairness which call for a proper distribution of benefits and burdens, rights and duties. Rawls develops these principles of justice relating to the basic equality of all and to the way in which all inequalities in societies are to be arranged.

In this connection of justice, one can consider the frequently debated example of the sheriff who, to avoid a race riot in which many blacks would be killed in a southern town in the United States, frames and executes one innocent black person. Philosophers have been arguing about this case and now Catholic moral theologians, e.g., Connery and Schüller, have taken different sides of the argument. However, both in the philosophical literature and now in the theological literature it seems as if the exact force of the particular case is often overlooked by both sides. Some argue that if all the consequences are properly taken into account, then one could never accept judicial execution. However, a staunch act-utilitarian such as Smart recognizes the bite of this particular case. If no one knows an innocent person was framed, and the presupposition is that no one can find out about it, then there would be no harmful effects on the role of justice and criminal law in society if the innocent person were executed. Smart admits that it is logically possible for such a situation to exist and that the utilitarian must logically opt for the judicial murder in this case, but existentially he hopes the case would never happen.[18] Again the importance of the illustration shows what are the differences between the two approaches.

Another series of objections proposed against utilitarianism emphasizes the intentionality of the agent. The bottom-line consideration of the net good over the net evil is not the only factor to be considered — one must also consider how the good and evil were accomplished. There is a difference between effects or consequences that are merely foreseen by the agent and those that are intended by the agent. The way in which the agent brings about the effects is also important. The case of judicial murder also illustrates this problem as exemplified in the already-mentioned case of a foreigner who in a South American country comes upon a military captain who is about to kill innocent villagers. The point is that the foreigner is not the cause of the death of the others in the same way he would be the cause of the death of the one. An individual's actions and decisions flow from one's projects, but in this case the foreigner's action is determined by the project of the captain. It is absurd to demand that the foreigner leave aside his own deepest projects and decisions and base his actions only on the utilitarian calculus of the number of lives ultimately lost when this has been greatly determined by the project of another. Williams who proposes such a case leans toward doing the deed, but considerations other than consequences enter into the moral decision.[19]

Another Antiutilitarian Position

Within the body of recent literature specifically discussing utilitarianism, the antiutilitarian approach generally agrees with the position just expounded and does not directly appeal to or accept the principle that certain actions are right or wrong no matter what the consequences.[20] However, within the philosophical literature in general, if not in the utilitarian literature specifically, there is another form of the antiutilitarian approach which is based primarily on accepting such a principle.

G. E. M. Anscombe includes all modern moral philosophy under indictment for leaving open to debate whether such a procedure as judicial murder might not be the right one to adopt. Although some of the present Oxford moral philosophers think it permissible to make a principle never to do such a thing as judicial murder, Anscombe condemns them for proposing a philosophy according to which the consequences of such an action could morally be taken into account to determine if one should do such an action. Anscombe opposes such a theory because it is willing even to consider the possibility of exceptions based on consequences. She thus places all modern moral philosophy under the indictment of what she calls consequentalism. (One can thus see the terminological problem which exists in the philosophical literature.) Anscombe and her followers accept the principle that there are actions which are right or wrong whatever the consequences.[21] In subsequent literature the position defended by Anscombe and others has been called absolutist,[22] conservative,[23] and Catholic.[24] This position can properly be called Catholic (even though authors like Bennett reject the term) because it describes the position generally taken in the manuals of moral theology that certain actions are intrinsically wrong, e.g., contraception, sterilization, direct killing of the innocent, and can never be justified no matter how much good might result. Likewise, Catholic philosophers such as Anscombe and John Finnis defend this position.[25]

Concluding Clarifications

In conclusion, an overview of the philosophical literature indicates that there are three different positions, but terminology differs in describing these different opinions. The following descriptions will not agree with the terminology employed by many of the authors themselves, but it seems to be necessary to bring about needed clarifications. The first position is properly described as utilitarianism, strict teleology, or strict consequentialism. The third position, Anscombe et al., may be described as nonconsequentialism or even deontology — some actions are wrong no matter what the consequences. I will call the middle position a mixed consequentialism or mixed teleology. This middle position differs from strict teleology or strict consequentialism because it maintains the following three points: (1) moral obligation arises from elements other than consequences, (2) the good is not separate from the right; (3) the way in which the good or evil is achieved by the agent is a moral consideration. Since such an opinion does not necessarily hold that certain actions are always wrong no matter what the consequences, it has been called consequentialist by Anscombe. The good consequences are able to be determinative of the right and wrong of actions. The terminological confusion increases when one realizes that some proponents of this middle position can also properly be identified as deontologists; e.g., W. D. Ross who speaks about *prima facie* obligations. Ross acknowledges morality consists in such *prima facie* obligations but also recognizes the existence of conflicts in which the consideration of good consequences can be equally determinative of which obligations one must follow.[26]

Situating Catholic Moral Theology

Where does Catholic moral theology fit into such a schema? The moral theology of the manuals definitely belongs under the third position — the nonconsequentialist position which maintains that some actions are intrinsically wrong no matter what the consequences. (I realize that some contemporary theologians are trying to reinterpret what this meant, but at least there is no doubt that as generally understood the teaching of the manuals belongs under this category.)

In the 1960s some Roman Catholic moral theologians reacted in general and especially in the context of the debate over artifical contraception against what I have called physicalism — the tendency to indentify the moral act with the physical structure of the act. The physical is only one aspect of the human and the totality of the human cannot be identical with just this one aspect. Many authors refer to physical or premoral or ontic evil as distinguished from moral evil. In this light these theologians (rightly in my judgment) rejected the traditional teaching that contraception, sterilization, masturbation for seminal analysis, artificial insemination even with the husband's seed and the killing of the fetus to save the mother were always wrong. Beginning with Knauer an appeal was made to commensurate reason or proportionate reason to justify some of the actions which the manuals described as intrinsically wrong.[27] Schüller and others spoke of a teleological justification and a consequentialist calculus to determine if such actions were right or wrong.[28] Reforming Catholic theologians thus appealed to commensurate reason, proportionate reason, or the calculation of consequences to indicate that premoral evil could on some occasions be justified. Knauer also argued that one should not speak of the evil as being an effect with the act as its cause but rather spoke of the effects as an aspect of the act so that one might see here some similarity with the position maintaining there is no difference between effects which are foreseen and effects which are intended. In the light of the terminology and of some of the reasoning, the question arises if these Catholic authors are utilitarians or consequentialists in the strict sense.

Notice that early in the discussion within Roman Catholicism the debate centered almost exclusively on problems present in the Catholic theological tradition such as contraception and sterilization. The questions that were being discussed in the debate about utilitarianism such as promise keeping, fidelity, gratitude, justice, punishment, and integrity were not even discussed by the Catholic moral theologians. Once some of these questions such as the prohibition of direct killing of noncombatants or questions of judicial murder began to be discussed by the reforming Catholic ethicists, their understanding of consequentialism and teleology became clear. McCormick rightly insists on a difference between an intending and a permitting will.[29] Schüller recognizes that the consequences alone are not the only considerations and that consequences are always considered in the light of what is right.[30] Thus as the debate progressed it became quite evident that the reforming Catholic theologians generally speaking do not embrace utilitarianism or what Rawls, Frankena, Williams, and others have called teleology or consequentialism. In the schema proposed above, they fit into the middle category which can be described as mixed consequentialism.

Even in the general statement of their theories, it is clear that the reforming Catholic theologians do not belong to the first position of strict consequentialism or utilitarianism. Knauer himself insists on commensurate reason, and thus attributes some value to the physical act in relationship to the end which is sought. Fuchs gives attention to all three aspects of the human act — object, end, and circumstances.[31] Janssens sees a reciprocal causality existing between the material and the formal element of the human act so that the consequences alone are not determinative.[32] Milhaven requires an objective evaluation of the consequences in light of moral criteria.[33] Yes, there is a problem in terminology, but as the debate continued it became more evident that these Catholic authors do not embrace utilitarianism or strict consequentialism or strict teleology. Thus I disagree with the contention of John Connery that many of these Catholic authors are tending to consequentialism, which he understands in the strict sense.[34] In light of the three different positions explained above, most of the reforming authors in the Catholic tradition fit into the second position called mixed consequentialism, but perhaps this position should be described differently.

Clarifications and Relationality

Problems exist both in the philosophical literature and in the literature of Catholic moral theology about the exact meaning of the terms teleology and consequentialism. Teleology is generally contrasted with deontology, yet the second position described above as mixed consequentialism also includes people like Ross who are often classified as deontologists.

In my judgment at least part of the confusion arises from the fact that the difference between teleology and deontology can refer to two different realities in ethical discussion — the general model of the moral life and the more particular question of the establishment of moral norms or the criterion for decision making in concrete cases. When referring to the model of the ethical life, teleology refers to an approach which sees the moral life primarily in terms of goals and ends. In this view Aristotle and the manualists of moral theology are teleologists, as well as all utilitarians. Deontology understands the moral life primarily in terms of duties, obligations, and laws. Kant serves as an example of deontology, but Ross with his emphasis on *prima facie* obligations also fits under this category. From the viewpoint of theological ethics, Rudolf

Bultmann's insistence on morality as radical obedience also makes him a deontologist.[35] However, in terms of the more limited aspect of determining moral norms or the criterion of concrete obligations one could characterize these ethicists differently. Certainly Aristotle and some manualists of theology would not be characterized as determining moral norms on the basis of consequences and strict teleology. Ross has been classified as a consequentialist (at least by Anscombe). Bultmann is often described as a situationist. There is a difference between the level of ethical model and the level of the formulation of the ethical norms.

One of the unfortunate aspects of the debate about situation ethics and norms in the last decade has been that moral theology is often reduced to the one question of whether or not there is a law. Questions of attitudes, dispositions, ideals, values, goals, perspectives, and intentionalities have not received the attention they deserve in a complete consideration of moral theology. The ultimate model of the ethical life therefore should be broad enough to consider all the more specific questions and topics that form part of ethics and moral theology. Therefore both in practice and in theory one can legitimately distinguish between the level of the ethical model and the level of establishing norms or the criterion for decision making in specific cases.

On the level of ethical model I prefer to accept an ethical model of relationality and responsibility as a third model distinguished from both teleology and deontology. Such a model seems to be more in keeping with both theological and ethical data. Theology views the life of grace and the reality of sin primarily in terms of relationships as is evident in the concepts of covenant and love. In the perspective of Christian eschatology the individual does not have that much power and control over one's end and destiny. The cross and the paschal mystery remind us that our end or goal is not completely in our hands. We as Christians live in the hope that the evils and problems of the present can be transformed somewhat even now by the power of God and ultimately transformed into the fullness of life.

A phenomonological reflection on all human existence also seems to indicate that our lives are more understandable in terms of responding to the many happenings of human existence rather than adhering to a prearranged plan in search of our goal. Teleological and consequential models emphasizing only the goal or consequences obviously laid the foundation for a technological model of human existence, but technological progress can never be identified with truly human progress. Likewise an emphasis on consequences, goals, and ends very readily places all value in terms of what one does, makes, or accomplishes. The Christian approach does not seem to react in the same way, for there will always be a Christian bias in favor of those who do not accomplish or are not successful — the poor, weak, and the outcast. One might retort that the teleological model does not necessarily involve the kind of problems that I have described here, but even at its most refined understanding, the teleological model seems less apt than the relationality responsibility model of the ethical life of the Christian.[36]

On the level of the formulation of moral norms and the criteria for concrete decision-making I would opt for the second position described above as mixed consequentialism. The problem of terminology has already been pointed out since strict teleology is different from this position, and both teleologists and deontologists rightly fall into this category. Here again I am trying to develop a relationality approach as a third type distinct from both teleology and deontology, but this needs much greater development in my thought at the present time. At the very least it solves the terminological problem which now exists. Such a relational type has the advantage of including all the elements that should be considered and not reducing reality only to consequences or to duties. One might also argue that the relationality approach is not merely a middle approach between the other two but in a sense also opts for a somewhat different understanding of the moral decision-making process. Certainly it is not as rationalistic as the consequentialist approach. Likewise, it avoids the inflexibility that might often be associated with various aspects of the nonconsequentialist approach. By seeing all reality in terms of relationships one is less willing to absolutize any one aspect or one individual, since the individual by definition exists in multiple relationship with others; but the theory can still insist on the fundamental importance of the individual person. However, this approach obviously needs much further development.

Conflict Situations

In general one might say that the entire discussion deals with conflict situations — a point which is even more true when it is limited to the discussion of philosophical literature but which can also be verified in the literature of Catholic moral theology. In my judgment it is important to recognize that there are different sources of conflict situations. Specifically I propose four sources of conflict situations which Christian ethics can and should distinguish: (1) conflicts arising from the difference between the subjective and the objective aspects of human acts; (2) conflicts arising from creaturely finitude and limitation; (3) conflicts arising from eschatological tension; (4) conflicts arising from the presence of sin. In concluding this essay it is not possible to develop these different sources of conflicts at length, but a brief description will suffice. However, since my theory about the source of conflicts resulting from sin has often been misunderstood, some further clarification is necessary.[37]

Catholic moral theology traditionally recognized the distinction between the objective and the subjective aspects of the human act. An act might be objectively wrong but the individual is not subjectively guilty or responsible for it because of various impediments to a voluntary act. The manuals traditionally referred to the question of invincible ignorance of the obligation, but many contemporary authors rightly insist that the notion of invincible ignorance today must be seen in the perspective which emphasizes the existential totality of the human person so that invincible ignorance is a matter of the inability of the person to realize a moral obligation because of the situation in which one finds oneself. Moral philosophers recognize the same reality in the distinction between reasons which justify an act and reasons which excuse an act. Here the objective evaluation of the act is not changed, whereas in the other three types of conflict situations the objective evaluation of the act is changed.

The second source of conflict situations is human finitude and limitation. Here one finds most of the problems in which the physical aspect of the act has become absolutized, for different premoral values will often exist in conflict with one another so that one cannot be absolutized. Here too the principle of double effect has been employed to solve some conflict situations such as the birth room dilemma of mother or child. The third source of conflict situation arises from the tension between the eschatological fullness and the present. Since Catholic moral theology in the past was so heavily based on natural law and did not appeal to grace and eschatological realities as being morally obligatory for all, this type of conflict seldom arose. However, it is quite present in the situation of divorce which in my judgment cannot be an absolute prohibition. The fourth source of conflict situation is the presence of sinfulness. In response to the presence of sin I have developed a theory of compromise which in the light of subsequent debate needs to be properly understood.

The theory of compromise was never meant to apply to all conflict situations but only to those conflict situations in which sinfulness predominates. The problem of physicalism or what others call physical evil as distinguished from moral evil constitutes a distinct question. The conflict here most often arises from finitude and limitation either of time or space. As chapter 5 clearly shows, I do not appeal to compromise to solve the questions of contraception, sterilization, artificial insemination, many cases solved by double effect, etc. However, it was a mistake to use the term the "theory" of compromise as if it were primarily an ethical term, for it refers primarily to a theological reality — the source and the cause of the ethical conflict. The ultimate ethical solution of the conflict requires an ethical approach such as those discussed earlier. I would apply in these situations the second or mixed approach which I prefer to call a relational approach which involves weighing all the values involved.

From a theological perspective it is more accurate to distinguish the various sources of conflict even though in particular cases it might be difficult to discern if the conflict is due primarily to one or the other sources; e.g., finitude, sin, or the eschaton. Even in the ethical order there are important ramifications in distinguishing the conflicts arising from sinfulness. Sinfulness as the origin of conflict situations might be understood in three different ways — the universal sinfulness existing in the world which was the basis for Thomas Aquinas' teaching on the ownership of private property; the sinfulness incarnate in the human situation which in my judgment affects the person who is an irreversible homosexual; and the sinful actions of another person affecting my action as illustrated in the case of the captain threatening to shoot a large number of innocent villagers unless I shoot one of them myself.

Some philosophers claim that many of the examples proposed in the debate about consequentialism are rather bizarre.[38] To a certain extent this is true, but the bizarre character of the examples often comes from the fact that personal human sinfulness is present as in the South American example. The exceptions will be less and severely limited when it is a case of the personal sinfulness of another. Likewise the sinfulness of the social situation affects a limited number of people. Finitude affects all in a more comprehensive way than sin when it is not the universal sin of the world. The Christian must try to limit all evil, but evil resulting from finitude and limitation will always exist together with the human. Evil resulting from sin is somewhat different. Its presence does not come from the human condition as such, and the Christian has an obligation to try to overcome the effects of sin. However, in the imperfect world in which we live it is never possible to overcome all the effects of sin this side of the eschaton — sometimes one must accept the limitations of the sinful situation. This explains the theological concept of compromise because of which an act which in ordinary circumstances would be wrong for this person in the sinful situation is not wrong. But the exact determination weighing all the values involved depends upon ethical criteria.

This chapter has not attempted a complete discussion of the philosophical debates about utilitarianism but has considered only those aspects most instructive for the current considerations of Roman Catholic moral theologians. In the process it has been possible to clarify and perhaps advance the discussions within Roman Catholic ethics.

NOTES

1. J. J. C. Smart in J. J. C. Smart and Bernard Williams, *Utilitarianism: For and Against* (Cambridge: Cambridge University Press, 1973), p. 4.

2. J. B. Schneewind, "Introduction," in *Mill's Ethical Writings*, ed. J. B. Schneewind (New York, Collier Books, 1965), pp. 19, 20.

3. For an analysis of the present debate on the measurement of utility and for a comprehensive view of recent debates in utilitarianism, see Dan W. Brock, "Recent Work in Utilitarianism," *American Philosophical Quarterly* 10 (1973), 245-249.

4. *Contemporary Utilitarianism*, ed. Michael D. Bayles (Garden City, N.Y.: Doubleday Anchor Books, 1968).

5. J. O. Urmson, "The Interpretation of the Moral Philosophy of J. S. Mill," *The Philosophical Quarterly* 3 (1953), 33-39.

6. David Lyons, *Forms and Limits of Utilitarianism* (Oxford: Clarendon Press, 1965).

7. J. H. Sobel, "Rule-Utilitarianism," *Australasian Journal of Philosophy* 46 (1968), 146-165.

8. Brock, *American Philosophical Quarterly* 10 (1973), 261.

9. Richard A. McCormick, *Ambiguity in Moral Choice*, the 1973 Père Marquette Theology Lecture, Marquette University, 91ff.; McCormick, "The New Medicine and Morality," *Theology Digest* 21 (1973), 319ff.

10. Richard A. McCormick, "Notes on Moral Theology," *Theological Studies* 36 (1975), 98.

11. Williams, *Utilitarianism: For and Against*, p. 98.

12. Smart, *Utilitarianism: For and Against*, p. 4.

13. Williams, *Utilitarianism: For and Against*, pp. 82-93.

14. Lyons, *Forms and Limits of Utilitarianism*, p. xii.

15. John Rawls, *A Theory of Justice* (Cambridge, Mass.: Harvard University Press, 1971), p. 25.

16. William K. Frankena, *Ethics* (Englewood Cliffs, N.J.: Prentice Hall, 1973), pp. 13, 14. In the light of these definitions, it seems that what is often called ideal utilitarianism would not fall under this description of utilitarianism.

17. John Rawls, "Two Concepts of Rules," *The Philosophical Review* 64 (1955), 4.

18. Smart, *Utilitarianism: For and Against*, p. 72.

19. Williams, *Utilitarianism: For and Against*, pp. 108-118.

20. Brock, *American Philosophical Quarterly* 10 (1973), 261-269.

21. G. E. M. Anscombe, "Modern Moral Philosophy," *Philosophy* 33 (1958), 1-19.

22. Thomas Nagel, "War and Massacre," *Philosophy and Public Affairs* 1 (1972), 123-144.

23. Jonathan Bennett, "Whatever the Consequences," *Analysis* 26 (1965-66), 83-102.

24. R. W. Beardsmore, "Consequences and Moral Worth," *Analysis* 29 (1968-69), 177-186; R. G. Frey, "Some Aspects to the Doctrine of Double Effect," *Canadian Journal of Philosophy* 5 (1975), 259-283.

25. John Finnis, "Natural Law and Unnatural Acts," *Heythrop Journal* 11 (1970), 365-387; Finnis, "The Rights and Wrongs of Abortion," *Philosophy and Public Affairs* 2 (1973), 117-145.

26. W. D. Ross, *The Right and the Good* (Oxford: Clarendon Press, 1930); Ross, *The Foundations of Ethics* (Oxford: Clarendon Press, 1939).

27. P. Knauer, "La Détermination du bien et du mal moral par le principe du double effet," *Nouvelle Revue Théologique* 87

(1965), 356-376; Knauer, "Das rechtverstandene Prinzip von der Doppelwirkung als Grundnorm jeder Gewissensentscheidung," *Theologie und Glaube* 57 (1967), 107-133.

28. Bruno Schüller, "Zur Problematik allegemein verbindlicher ethischer Grundsätze," *Theologie und Philosophie* 45 (1970), 1-23; Schüller, "Typen ethischer Argumentation in der katholischen moral Theologie," *Theologie und Philosophie* 45 (1970), 526-550.

29. McCormick, *Ambiguity in Moral Choice*, pp. 72ff.

30. Bruno Schüller, "Neuere Beiträge zum Thema 'Begründung sittlicher Normen,'" *Theologische Berichte* 4, (Einsiedeln: Benziger, 1974), pp. 109-181.

31. Joseph Fuchs, "The Absoluteness of Moral Terms," *Gregorianum* 52 (1971), 445ff.

32. Louis Janssens, "Ontic Evil and Moral Evil," *Louvain Studies* 4 (1972), 123ff.

33. John Giles Milhaven, "Objective Moral Evaluation of Consequences," *Theological Studies* 32 (1971), 407-430.

34. John R. Connery, "Morality of Consequences: A Critical Appraisal," *Theological Studies* 34 (1973), 396-414. I do have one difficulty with many of these authors — the use of premoral evil to cover diverse realities which at best are only analogously related. For example, killing a person and contraception are not premoral evils in exactly the same way. Many people in society rightly see little or no premoral evil in contraception. Catholic authors tend to call contraception premoral evil because they want to maintain some continuity with the official teaching that contraception is morally evil. Why is contraception a premoral evil? The same is true of sterilization so that there is no practical moral difference in my judgment between direct or indirect sterilization. Also these authors must consider more questions of social ethics. Even here one might properly say, for example, that discrimination because of race, creed, or color is only a premoral evil which in extreme situations of compensatory justice to others in society might be morally overriden. One could also argue that in social ethics we are often dealing with formal and not material norms as in Rawls' concept of justice. However, these questions deserve greater attention.

35. Thomas C. Oden, *Radical Obedience: The Ethics of Rudolf Bultmann* (Philadelphia: Westminster Press, 1964).

36. For a further development of this model, see my *Catholic Moral Theology in Dialogue* (1972; reprint ed., Notre Dame, Ind.: University of Notre Dame Press, 1976), pp. 150-183.

37. These different conflict situations have been discussed in my other writings especially *Ongoing Revision: Studies in Moral Theology*, (Notre Dame, Ind.: Fides Publishers, 1976).

38. E.g., Anscombe, "Modern Moral Philosophy," p. 13.

7. Church Law

The consideration of the relationship between Church law and conscience will embrace three areas of investigation: (1) the concept of positive law in the Church; (2) the relationship between law and sin; (3) the observance of positive law in the life of the Christian. In the following discussion Church law or canon law always refers to the purely positive laws of the Roman Catholic Church and not to the restatement of other obligations.

The Concept of Positive Law in the Church

In his Epistle to the Romans, Paul explains the freedom of the Christian as a freedom from sin, death, and the law. St. Paul does not merely say that the Christian is freed from the ceremonial and juridical aspects of the law. Paul apparently uses law to mean, in this particular case, the entire Mosaic law insofar as the Mosaic law is an example of a general economy of law. The Christian is freed from living under an economy of law in the sense that salvation would depend upon the observance of certain laws or precepts. Salvation comes through faith in Christ Jesus. Freedom from law, however, does not mean that the Christian can now do whatever one pleases. Through the gift of the Spirit the Christian has received the new life in Christ Jesus. The Christian must now produce in life the fruits of the Spirit and walk according to the Spirit. The primary law for the Christian is the Spirit who dwells in the hearts of the just. The law of the Spirit is a law of freedom precisely because its demands are not imposed upon us from outside. The love of God is poured into our hearts by the Holy Spirit. The Spirit gives us the new heart which then directs all the activities of the Christian. The Spirit becomes the vital principle of Christian life and activity. The primary law for the Christian is "the law of the Spirit giving life in Christ Jesus" (Rom. 8:2).

Since the primary law of the new covenant is the Spirit who dwells in the hearts of the just, canon law and Church law necessarily assume a secondary and ancillary role. Too often in the past, the prevailing attitude has given too much importance to the role of positive law in the life of the Church. Canonical legislation should not occupy the primary role in the living of the Christian life. In discussions about eliminating Friday abstinence, some people objected that the changes are doing away with all mortification in Christian life. Such objections betray a mentality that equates the Christian life with the observance of the positive laws of the Church. The greatest mortification remains always the attempt to live out the Paschal Mystery in everyday life. The attitude of some Catholics in the past implied that laws make people holy. A proliferation of laws in many religious communities seems to bear out that understanding of law. However, the notion that more and better laws make people holy is totally inadequate. St. Paul reminds us that laws only provoke more transgressions. History indicates that positive laws have come into existence when the ebb of Christian life was already low. As long as Christians maintained a real understanding of the Eucharist, there was no need to make a law about receiving communion once a year. Positive laws are neither the source of Christian life nor an adequate sign of vitality in the Christian community.

However, there is a need for positive law in the Church. Since the Church strives to be a community of love in this world, positive law will always have its place in the life of that community. Although the community owes its continued existence primarily to the Spirit, positive law plays a secondary role in the life of the Church. Positive law is a necessity in any community for the well being of the community itself and the individuals who comprise the community. Life in a community demands a certain amount of order which positive law seeks to obtain. If just two or three people are living together, they can decide among themselves what they intend to do; but when there is a large community, there is need for established order within which the community lives and functions.

The positive law of the Church, like all other externals in the Church, has a sacramental character. The law must be a sign of the inner reality of the Church, which is above all the community of love. The whole purpose of the law of the Church must be to build up the Body of Christ in truth and love. Canon law should strive to create the climate in which the Church and its individual members can better respond to the call of the Spirit.

Law in the Church cannot be considered in exactly the same way as law in any other society, for the Church is a unique community. Naturally, there are many analogies between the Church and other communities, but the law of the Church must always manifest the unique character of the community of salvation. Church law has the somewhat negative function of preserving the necessary order in the Church so that the community and individuals can best accomplish their God-given destiny. At the same time Church law should also exercise a more positive function in pointing out some of the demands of the Spirit for the community and the individual Christian. In its more positive and even creative function, Church law must be careful not to stifle the freedom which it is trying to promote. Unfortunately, in the past positive law played too dominant a role and stifled rather than stimulated life in the Church.

Roman Catholic theological tradition has embraced two divergent understandings of positive law. The Thomistic concept defines law as the *rationis ordinatio ad bonum commune, ab eo qui curam communitatis habet, promulgata* (*I.II.*q. 91,a. 4). In the Thomistic tradition law is primarily an ordering of reason. There is another school which is more voluntaristic and is represented by Scotus and Suarez. In the voluntaristic concept, law is primarily an act of the will of the legislator. The speculative differences about the concept of law have very practical consequences. In a Thomistic understanding, something is commanded because it is good in itself. In the voluntaristic viewpoint, something is good precisely because it is commanded.

The first practical consequence concerns the obliging force of law. A voluntaristic concept derives the obliging force of law primarily from the will of the legislator. The Thomistic understanding of law derives the moral obligation of law from the ordering to the common good of the society. Notice the realism present in the Thomistic approach. The law must correspond to the reality of the situation and not just to the will of the legislator.

A second practical consequence concerns the role and function of the legislator. In a voluntaristic understanding the will of the legislator is supreme. Everything depends on the will of the legislator. Such a concept of positive law certainly represented the sociological situation of feudal and monarchical society. The legislator was supreme, and the will of the legislator determined what was right. As an example, note the axiom — *cuius regio, eius religio.* In a more Thomistic interpretation, the will of the legislator is not the last word. The legislator must conform to the needs of the society here and now. In my application of the Thomistic teaching today, I am not understanding the *ordinatio rationis* in the same sense as St. Thomas did. Nor did St. Thomas see the role of the legislator in the same way that I am envisioning the legislator today. However, Thomas has established the basic principle of realism — the law must reflect the needs of the community here and now. Consequently, the legislator is not the last word. The legislator must conform to the needs of the community and the ordering required for the common good.

An examination of the old axiom — "the will of the superior is the will of God" — will help focus the conflicting viewpoints. A voluntaristic understanding of law can accept that axiom as being true. However, a more realistic understanding must reject such an axiom. The will of the superior is not the will of God. I am not denying that the superior in some way takes the place of God. But the superior takes the place of God not in the function of willing a law, but in the function of ordering for the needs of the community. The sad lessons of history remind us that we cannot identify the will of the superior with the will of God.

The role of the legislator or superior in a realistic understanding of law corresponds very well with the biblical description of authority. Jesus emphasized the difference between the rulers of this world and his own apostles. The rulers of this world lord it over their subjects and make all subjects feel the weight of their authority. But, whoever has authority among the apostles must become the servant and the slave of all, for Christ himself came not to be served but to serve and give his life as a ransom for many (Mark 10:42-45). The legislator does not rule supreme because his or her law is the last word on the subject. Rather, as the humble servant of the community, the legislator tries to unite the service and love of all the members so they can work together for their own fulfillment and the fulfillment of the whole community.

The legislator in the Church must always see that role as the servant of the community trying to order the life of the community according to its own needs and purposes. In addition, the legislator in the Church is the servant of the Spirit. The Spirit and the law of the Spirit must always remain supreme in the Church. The legislator must always conform the will of the legislator to the call of the Spirit. The legislator can never proceed arbitrarily as if the will makes something right or wrong. The legislator rather must conform to the call of the Spirit and the needs of the community. The legislator in the Church, as well as all authority in the Church, remains always the servant of the Spirit and the servant of the community. The servant role of the legislator corresponds with the necessary but secondary role of law in the life of the Church. A Thomistic or realistic understanding of law reemphasizes the biblical notion of law and authority in the Church.

The Relationship between Law and Sin

Can Church law bind under penalty of mortal sin? On this specific point, the Code of Canon Law has been much more accurate than the teaching of some theologians. Actually, the Code of Canon Law is very discreet and does not talk in terms of sin. But too frequently, on a popular level, one hears, for example, not simply that it is a "grave matter" but that all Catholics are obliged under pain of mortal sin to participate in the Eucharist on Sunday. Sin, however, should never be conceived as a penalty for the violation of Church law. Sin is not primarily a penalty or a punishment. Rather, sin is the reality of the creature's breaking the relationship of love with God. If the Christian has not broken that relationship with God, the Church cannot say that the relationship is broken. The Church has no right to use sin as a penalty for its own laws.

The idea of sin as a penalty for the infringement of Church laws probably owes its origins to an overly slavish imitation of an earlier secular society and authority. Secular society uses penalties as threats to bring about observance of the law. The Church in the past has succumbed to the temptation to use sin as a penalty and a threat to insure the observance of a Church law. But in so doing, the Church has acted more like secular society and not in accord with her own true nature. I am not saying that Church law cannot deal with sanctions, but purely Church law can never use sin as a penalty or a punishment. Sin is the reality of one's breaking one's relationship with God and is not just an extrinsic penalty which the Church can attach to particular actions.

Can mere positive Church law propose that certain actions are mortal sins? For example, it is a mortal sin to miss the breviary or it is a mortal sin to miss Mass on Sunday. Church law should not speak in terms of sin. Church law must consider the need for certain actions to be done or others to be avoided. The commission of certain actions or the omission of others might be a sin for this particular person here and now, but the Church cannot speak about the action itself as being a sin. The manuals of moral theology mention three conditions that are required for mortal sin: (1) grave matter, (2) advertence to the gravity of the matter, and (3) perfect consent of the will. (Personally I believe that mortal sin ultimately consists in the involvement of the subject in a particular action. Mortal sin involves a fundamental option of the person in the particular choice which he makes. The three conditions mentioned above for mortal sin are presumptive guidelines and not the ultimate explanation of mortal sin. (This notion of sin has been explained earlier in some detail.) Church law only speaks about the matter itself and does not consider advertence or consent. Consequently, Church law cannot speak in terms of sin. Church law can only speak about the greater or lesser importance of a particular action for the life of the community. And this is precisely what the Code of Canon Law does. It speaks about the relative importance of a particular matter in the life of the community and the individual. The expressions, "grave matter" or "light matter", refer precisely to the greater or lesser importance which the Church attaches to a particular action.

However, the Church in this time of renewal must ask if any one particular action is really that important a matter. For example, it was commonly taught by theologians that it was grave matter to omit even a smaller hour of the breviary. Any realistic understanding must conclude that missing the recitation of the breviary is not an important matter. There are so many important matters in the world today that the Church exposes herself to ridicule by maintaining that such things are that important. In considering the importance attached to praying the breviary daily, one can see quite clearly at work the attitude that has used sin or the threat of sin to bring about compliance with the law. But the Church can never use sin as a penalty or a threatened penalty. Participation in the Eucharistic banquet is certainly an important matter for the Christian; but I think that the importance of participation every single Sunday has been exaggerated by most theologians and canonists.

By speaking merely in terms of the greater or lesser importance of certain actions, the Church can do much in the proper formation of Christian consciences. The final judgment and application in a particular situation will be left up to the individual. Unfortunately, in the past the observance of the laws of the Church has become the infallible criterion of Christian life for many Catholics. Legalism has had an adverse effect not only on the formation of individual consciences but also on the attitude of the Church as a whole. Legalism easily leads to a mediocrity that stifles all creativity and initiative.

The overemphasis on the law serves as a crutch which saves the teaching Church from exerting all its necessary efforts. It is so much easier to say that missing Mass on Sunday is a mortal sin than it is to show by our celebration that we believe the Eucharist to be an important matter in the life of the Christian. The temptation to become administrators and just cite the law has often usurped the teaching office and function in the Church. Legalism also leads to a smugness, a sterility, and an unwillingness to see the need for necessary change. I believe that for too long pastors and teachers have relied on the Sunday obligation to coerce people to "hear Mass." I am convinced that if we had to meet open competition in presenting the meaning of the Eucharist to Christian people, somewhat as a soap commercial on TV has to meet competition openly, we would not have left our presentation completely unchanged for the past four centuries. How long would an announcer last in the competitive field of TV advertising if she spoke in a foreign language, mumbled the lines, and kept her back turned to the people? Legalism has made us all a bit lazy. Yes, law will always be necessary in the Church, but its function is always secondary and dependent on the law of the Spirit.

The Observance of Positive Law in the Life of the Christian

In any society there will be a tension between the laws of the community and the rights of the individual. The Church experiences these tensions not only because it is a society like others but even because of its own peculiar nature. The fundamental law for the Christian and for the Church is the law of the Spirit, which is primarily an internal law. There is a need for external law in the Church, but this external law must be in conformity with the demands of the internal law. Obviously, here is the first source of tension in the life of the Church. The external law might not always correspond to the demands of the Spirit here and now. The external law of the Church might say that religious vows are by their very nature permanent, but for the good of an individual here and now such vows may become a positive hindrance. The Church law prescribes a certain formulary of prayers for her religious and clerics in major orders. However, perhaps the prescribed prayer does not meet the needs of a particular individual.

A second source of tension comes from the unique nature of the Church itself as the pilgrim Church. Precisely because the Church has not yet arrived at its final goal and perfection, there will always be the possibility of conflicting demands. The pilgrim Church must constantly change its laws, but actual change might lag behind the changes that have already occurred in the life of the community

itself. Even the new Code of Canon Law which went into effect in the fall of 1983 cannot claim to be totally adequate and
absolutely perfect today.

A third source of tension is common to all societies and
communities — the tension between the individual and the
society itself. Such a tension exists because the individual
is not completely subordinated to the society. Totalitarian-
ism or collectivism demands the total subordination of the
individual to society. On the other hand, only anarchy
would maintain that the individual is completely independent of the demands of society. Society and the individual
are going to exist in a constant state of tension precisely
because they are neither totally independent of nor totally
dependent on one another. A true Christian communi-
tarianism should avoid the extremes of collectivism, on the
one hand, and, on the other hand, anarchy. In this tension
one finds the theological defense of so-called civil disobedience. When the law interferes with the inalienable rights
of individuals, then it can no longer be a binding law.

A fourth source of tension is the very nature of positive
law itself. Most Catholic theologians teach with St.
Thomas that positive law admits exceptions. Positive law
obliges *ut in pluribus*. Since positive law is not based on
immutable essences but on changing circumstances, the
legislator cannot possibly foresee all the different circumstances that might arise in a particular case. There are
times when the letter of the law can become an injustice
for an individual. In fact, the very imperfection of positive
law appears more readily in the Church than it does in
many secular societies and states. Nations are more homogeneous groupings of people than the Church. For example,
here in the United States, people enjoy the same type of
climate, the same basic culture of a technological civilization, a high degree of education, a common history and
heritage. Consider the difficulties involved in framing laws
for people living all over the globe, in completely different
climates, with opposing cultural formations, with no common heritage, with differing languages and customs. A law

enacted for a greater number of people living in very disparate circumstances will necessarily admit more exceptions than a law made for a more homogeneous grouping
of people. Some canon lawyers in the process of revising the
Code of Canon Law, which was finally put into effect in 1983,
urged that the new law of the Church should give even greater
emphasis to local differences by providing for more legislation on regional and national levels.

A fifth source of tension comes from the possibility of
human error. Our nation has already admitted that prohibition was a mistake and has repealed the law. Is it possible
for the Church with the guidance of the Holy Spirit to be
led astray by human error? The Apostolic Constitution,
Veterum Sapientia, which required theology courses in
seminaries to be taught in Latin, is an excellent example of
error on the part of the lawmaker in the Church.

The rapidly changing sociological conditions of modern
life merely accentuate the inherent tensions in human law,
and consequently, in Church law. In considering the function of law in secular society official Catholic teaching today
recognizes the shrinking role that law plays in society. The
Declaration on Religious Freedom of the Second Vatican
Council explicitly taught that law has the limited purpose of
protecting public order. "For the rest, the usages of society
are to be the usages of freedom in their full range. These require that the freedom of human beings be respected as far
as possible and curtailed only when and insofar as necessary"
(n.7). It is only in the last few decades that Catholic social
teaching has given greater emphasis to human freedom and
human rights in society and thereby circumscribed the role
of law. However, contemporary discussions show that some
Catholic thinkers have not recognized the significant change
that has occurred in this Catholic teaching.

There are many and different groups within society
which must work for the common good. Law today does
not have the function of controlling and directing most of
the life within the community. Rather, the role of law is
limited to assuring that all these other smaller societies and

institutions can make their contribution towards the common good. The role and place of law in the secular society today is much less than it was in medieval society. The recent Church-State and religious liberty controversies point up the changed role of law and government in modern society. Law provides the framework within which the individuals and the different institutions within society can make their contribution for the common good. Perhaps the predominant role given to law in the life of the Church reflected the secular societies of the medieval period; but society and the role of law in society have greatly changed since that time.

The new Code of Canon Law was needed to update the older code which had been in force since 1918. This new law for the Church has tried to incorporate the newer theological emphases of Vatican II and to recognize the present sociological realities. However, the new code reflects the tensions of the times in which it was written. These are changing times in our understanding and living out the life of the Church with the different roles of all the people of God. The changing Catholic understanding of the function of law in secular society has already been mentioned. In these circumstances no code can be without some tensions and imperfections.

However, moral theology has always taught that there are built-in safeguards to deal with the possible sources of tension relating to law in the Church. Manuals of moral theology spend a great number of pages discussing excusing causes, dispensations, privileges, etc. However, there is one built-in safeguard which requires greater emphasis today — *epikeia*.

Catholic moral teaching embraces two different notions of *epikeia*. Most manuals of theology actually adopt a very restricted and Suarezian understanding of *epikeia*. *Epikeia* has usually been surrounded with many precautions and safeguards. If the obliging force of law comes from the will of the legislator, then *epikeia* must be seen in terms of the will of the legislator. In any given situation an individual must have recourse to the will of the legislator to determine if the particular law is still obliging. If in an individual situation it is impossible to approach the legislator, then the individual may act according to the presumed will of the legislator. *Epikeia* is looked upon with some suspicion because it goes against the letter of the law.

The Thomistic teaching on *epikeia* is quite different. Thomas makes the flat assertion that *epikeia* is a virtue (*II. II.* q. 120. a.l.). Despite the objections that *epikeia* might foment anarchy, cause dissensions, or harm the common good, Thomas still asserts that *epikeia* is a virtue. The Thomistic teaching maintains that *epikeia* is a part of the virtue of justice precisely because of the inherent imperfections of human law. *Epikeia* for Thomas is not a lazy attempt to escape from certain obligations, but rather *epikeia* is the response to a higher law, the law of justice. *Epikeia* has been called the crown of legal justice and the virtue of the spirit of the law. For the Christian, *epikeia* cannot be merely the wish to free oneself from a particular obligation, but rather *epikeia* must be a demand of the higher law — the law of the Spirit.

The question naturally arises about the need to have recourse to the legislator before using *epikeia*. A voluntaristic notion of law and *epikeia* stresses the need to have recourse to the will of the legislator. Since in this view the obligation stems from the will of the legislator, the individual should have recourse to the will of the legislator to see if the obligation is still existing. *Per se* the Thomistic notion of *epikeia* does not demand recourse to the legislator. A realistic interpretation of law puts the obliging force of law in the ordering for the common good (better: the public order). If the law does not contribute to the common good in these circumstances, then it no longer obliges. Thomas' own teaching on *epikeia* does at times demand the need for the determination of the ruler. Thomas maintains that in doubtful matters there is need for interpretation, and in these cases it is not permitted to go against the letter of the law without the determination of the ruler (*principis*). But in obvious cases, there is no need for interpretation, but only for execution.

I believe that the Thomistic understanding of *epikeia* is valid today with some adjustments because of the changed sociological circumstances. It is important to realize in the Thomistic understanding that *per se epikeia* does not require recourse to the will of the legislator. Thomas demands recourse only for interpretation in doubtful cases. I contend that today even in doubtful cases the interpretation of the legislator is not the last word. Certainly, the presumption must always stand for the justice of the particular law, but the presumption must cede to the truth in particular cases. The role of the individual in society has changed greatly since Thomas' time. Today both in the Church and in secular society the stress is on the freedom and responsibility of the individual. People in secular society are citizens and not subjects. The whole structure of modern society depends upon the creative contributions of individuals and institutions within society. Law contributes only a small part to the common good of society. Thomas knows only a society which is structured from the top down — everything must come from the command and word of the ruler. (The very word *princeps* used by Thomas indicates that he is not talking about the same type of society that we know.) Less than a century ago, Pope Leo XIII could refer to subjects as the unlettered masses. This is not true in modern society. Society has changed, and the role of the legislator and the individual member in society has changed since the thirteenth century. Consequently, even for interpretation, recourse to the legislator is not required. In many circumstances today such recourse would be virtually impossible.

Our present understanding of law in the Church also shows that interpretation does not demand recourse to the legislator with the final outcome depending on the legislator. The primary law for the Christian is the law of the Spirit. Every other law is secondary. The Christian is entrusted by God with the responsibility of listening to the voice of the Spirit. External law is necessary, the presumption is always with the legislator; but the ultimate decision in the particular case rests with the individual.

The twelfth chapter of Matthew's gospel offers a good illustration of the virtue of *epikeia*. Christ himself justifies the breaking of the letter of the Sabbath law to heal the person with a withered arm. Christ reminds his hearers that they too would break the letter of the law even to free a sheep that may have fallen into a ditch. Notice that no recourse for interpretation is required in these cases. Christ also recalls the story from the Old Testament in which David and his men ate the sacred loaves which according to the law could be eaten only by the priests. In cases of emergency, obviously the letter of the law is no longer binding.

The objection immediately comes to mind — *epikeia* ultimately leads to anarchy. By stressing the need for the individual to make the final decision, *epikeia* results in pure subjectivism and anarchy. However, the objection is not valid if one has a proper understanding of the virtue of *epikeia*. *Epikeia* does require that ultimate responsibility rests with the individual, but such a concept does not lead to anarchy.

First, *epikeia* is a part of the virtue of justice. *Epikeia* does not mean license and the possibility of following personal whims and selfishness. Some authors have called *epikeia* the crown of justice, for at times a literal interpretation of the law would violate justice.

Second, *epikeia* is closely connected with the virtue of prudence. Prudence is probably the most forgotten virtue in the manuals of moral theology. Prudence is basically an art. No one can really teach prudence to another, and yet all have an obligation to learn prudence in their daily life. In the past, moral theology has tried to do away with the virtue of prudence by an exaggerated casuistry that tried to solve in advance every conceivable type of problem. Today, many people are calling for prudence. However, prudence, according to St. Thomas, is always a virtue of action. Prudence does not mean an unwillingness to act, rather prudence is the virtue that is present in every risk and decision in the Christian life.

Third, *epikeia* is always a demand of the higher law, the law of the Spirit. *Epikeia* is not a mere sneaking out from some positive obligation. The law of the Spirit is the ultimate criterion in the use of *epikeia*. One is trying one's best to hear the call of the Spirit in a particular situation. Openness to the Spirit is completely incompatible with irresponsibility and a selfish seeking of the easiest way out in a given situation. Contemporary theology needs to develop the treatise on the rules for the discretion of spirits. The discernment of the Spirit is a most important factor in the moral life of the contemporary Christian.

Fourth, *agape* remains always the fundamental attitude of the Christian. Perhaps too often today one speaks of the law of love and the law of the Spirit without realizing the concrete demands of love in a given situation. *Agape* includes the willingness to give oneself for others. The attitude of the Christian toward the laws of the Christian community must be a meditation of love. Christian love demands the willingness to make personal sacrifices for the good of others. Christians must even see the inherent imperfections in Church law as an opportunity to live the Paschal Mystery in the dying to self in the service of others. *Epikeia* in the context of *agape* can never lead to selfishness and egoistic individualism.

What about abuses? There will be abuses, even glaring abuses. However, the old theological axiom remains true: *abusus non tollit usum. Epikeia* is the great virtue of Christian freedom and Christian responsibility. The Christian must stand on his or her own two feet and make the decisions with regard to the obligations of Church laws in particular circumstances. Naturally, one will be guided by the counsel and actions of others in the Christian community. However, the ultimate decision rests with the individual. The freedom and responsibility entailed in the proper understanding of *epikeia* are the same freedom and responsibility which the free call of God in Christ presupposes.

God could have corralled all people into salvation, but he chose to freely call human beings to a life of community with himself and all others. The divine plan of salvation has tried to safeguard personal responsibility and freedom. Sin is the terrible abuse of human freedom, and yet God was willing to accept the horrible consequences of sin rather than do away with human responsibility. The abuses connected with *epikeia* can never constitute a sufficient reason to deny the need for *epikeia* in the life of the Christian.

Why all the stress on *epikeia* today? There are many reasons contributing to the greater need for the virtue of *epikeia* today. As already mentioned, the tensions between the individual and the community are much greater today than in the past. Likewise, theology now realizes the ancillary role of law in the Church, but much of the present perspective reflects a mentality that practically equates life in the Christian community with the observance of positive law. Also, the stress on individual responsibility is being recognized in all of theology. When people were truly the unlettered masses, they were not able to make their own decisions. Just a few centuries ago, all life was structured from the top down. The individual person who lacked adequate knowledge and education always looked to the authorities to find out what one should do. In such circumstances, the greatest stress was put on dispensations, privileges, and recourse to the will of the legislator. Today, privileges and dispensations have no real meaning when they concern laws that affect only individuals. In fact, some of the privileges connected with certain organizations are a source of scandal, especially today. If membership in a certain society gives me the privilege of not praying the breviary under certain conditions, there is no reason why as a mature Christian I cannot make the judgment that in particular situations I am not bound to the canonical law of praying the breviary.

The complexity and responsibility which characterize modern life require that the individual Christian make the final decision in a particular situation involving a positive law of the Church. The individual Catholic must respect and follow the laws of the Church, but a true understanding recognizes the provisional and imperfect nature of Church law. The virtue of *epikeia* moderates the literalness and inapplicability of the law in the face of the very real Christian demands in a concrete situation. *Epikeia* is a virtue of Christian maturity and responsibility. A true understanding of *epikeia* should avoid false extremes of legalism and anarchy. *Epikeia* is the practical functioning of the law of the Spirit, the primary law of the Christian life, in the context of the positive law of the Church.

8. Conscience

Since conscience constitutes a very important theme in Christian morality, it is appropriate to include here a study of conscience. In addition a consideration of conscience will help synthesize, concretize, and develop many of the points made earlier. The first section will develop the meaning of conscience in the tradition of Roman Catholic theology which culminated in the treatises on conscience in the manuals of moral theology which were the usual textbooks both for theologians and for future priests. In the second section the approach of the manuals will be critiqued, and in a positive manner a different theory of conscience will be developed. The third section will bring together some practical conclusions for the formation of conscience.

Historical Development

Since conscience plays so important a role in human existence and is often discussed in Christian circles, one would expect to find a lengthy and extensive discussion about conscience in scripture. Such is not the case. The word *conscience* (the Greek συνειδησις) was introduced into the scriptures by Paul, and for all practical purposes

215

does not exist outside the Pauline corpus. Where did Paul find the term *conscience*? Again there is general agreement among scholars that Paul borrowed the word from the Greek world, but there is some discussion as to whether his source was the stoic philosophers or just the ordinary usage of the time. Scholars generally agree that the Greek usage portrayed conscience almost always as a guilty conscience — conscience as a negative judge of our actions completed or at least already initiated.[1]

There is a great disagreement about the meaning of conscience in Paul. C. H. Pierce, in a monograph entitled *Conscience in the New Testament,* indicates that the biblical notion is quite different from the notion of conscience as found among contemporary theologians. Conscience today is understood as justifying, in advance or in general principle, actions and attitudes of others as well as of oneself. But in the New Testament conscience cannot justify; it refers only to the past and the particular — and to acts of the self, not of others.[2] Conscience comes into play only after at least the initiation of a wrong act. At most conscience, according to Paul, can only indicate the act was not wrong — not that it was right, or the only act, or the best possible act in the circumstances. Above all conscience can say nothing directly about future acts.[3] According to Pierce's analysis, *conscience* appears thirty-three times in the New Testament. It never refers to an action to be placed, and only once unambiguously and in two other places ambiguously refers to a good conscience. The overwhelming number of references are to various types of a negative or morally bad conscience. Thus conscience is generally a negative judge of past behavior.[4]

There is another school of thought. Eric D'Arcy claims that Paul introduced an entirely new phase in the history of conscience by giving conscience a directive role before an action takes place. For the pagan writers conscience appeared only after the action (what we call today *consequent conscience* as distinguished from *antecedent conscience*) and in a judicial role; but for Paul conscience has a legislative function and indicates an obligation as such.[5] Ceslaus Spicq also understands conscience in the New Testament as a norm of conduct.[6] Philippe Delhaye maintains that for Paul conscience exercises both a judicial and a legislative function in reference not only to personal acts but to acts of others. Delhaye even develops the criteria of the norm of conscience as antecedent legislator.[7] Exegesis is not the only factor involved in this discussion. The authors holding the second opinion are all Roman Catholics who tend to understand Paul in the New Testament in the light of the generally accepted Catholic understanding which includes the notion of conscience as a judgment about the rightness or wrongness of actions to be placed. Pierce adopts a position more in keeping with the classical Protestant tradition which emphasized the importance of faith and downplayed works. Conscience in this perspective often plays a theological role rather than an ethical role. In conscience one recognizes that all our works, struggles, and efforts do not bring us closer to God, but rather conscience accuses us of our sinfulness and brings us to realize that salvation comes only through faith as the acceptance of God's gracious gift.[8] Many Protestant scholars, however, do not agree with Pierce's interpretation of Paul.[9]

There is no doubt that Paul places heavy emphasis on the negative and consequent aspects of conscience, stressing the pain and remorse for past actions. To what extent Paul speaks of the antecedent conscience and the function of conscience as a guide or directive for action is a matter of dispute.[10] However, there seems to be general agreement that Christians must address the question of conscience as the guide for action. There are also other concepts in the scriptures such as wisdom, heart, or choice which do include the understanding of direction and guidance for our actions.[11]

In the medieval period there is no doubt that the concept of conscience as an antecedent guide to actions is present together with the notion of the consequent conscience which judges past actions and is often synonymous with pain and remorse. Twelfth- and thirteenth-century Roman Catholic Scholastic theologians developed the notion of conscience — especially antecedent conscience as a guide to moral actions.[12]

There is one fascinating development which sets the parameters for the discussion in the twelfth and thirteenth centuries. These medieval theologians generally distinguished between *synderesis* and conscience. Where did this distinction come from? St. Jerome in his commentary on Ezechiel describes the four powers in the soul — reason, spirit, desire, and a fourth element above and beyond the other three which the Greeks called *synderesis*. This passage and its interpretation became pivotal because Peter Lombard, whose *Sentences* was the primary theological textbook of the times, referred to the text of Jerome which thus became a point of departure for any future discussion.[13] Why did St. Jerome use such a new term as *synderesis*? Why did he not use the word *syneidesis*? A widely accepted theory claims that St. Jerome himself did not use the word *synderesis*. There are different manuscripts of Jerome's commentary, some of which use the word *synderesis* and some *syneidesis*. Apparently a monk transcribing the text mistakenly employed the term *synderesis* rather than *syneidesis*. There is no other use beside Jerome's use of *synderesis*. The medievalists knew the text of Jerome primarily through the *Glossa Ordinaria* which contained the reading *synderesis*. Thus the discussion proposed by the influential Peter Lombard on the basis of the mistaken transcription of Jerome distinguished between *syneidesis* (conscience) and *synderesis*.[14]

Lombard's text became the starting point for the ensuing discussions. Jerome's text understands *synderesis* as a fourth element of the soul above and beyond reason, spirit, and desire. It makes us feel our sinfulness, and it corrects the other elements when they err. This spark of conscience was not quenched even in the heart of Cain according to Jerome, but he adds in the same paragraph that in some people it has been overcome and displaced. Such a text naturally raised questions for the Scholastics. Being like reason, spirit, and desire, is *synderesis* a faculty? Does it belong to the cognitive order or the affective order — i.e., the intellect or the will? Can it be lost? Jerome seems to be contradicting himself on this point. What is the relationship of *synderesis* to conscience? What is conscience itself? The stage is set for the future discussions.

Stephen Langton (1205) in his commentary on Lombard's *Sentences* made what became a lasting contribution in Scholastic thought. *Synderesis* is a part of the power of reason concerned with very general moral judgments (Aquinas will later call it the habit of first principles). Disagreements existed as to whether or not *synderesis* refers to the appetitive (will) or cognitive (intellect) aspect of the person. St. Bonaventure, developing the thought of Philip the Chancellor, sees *synderesis* as a habit-like faculty of the will — a natural appetite for the morally good. Bonaventure, like the theologians before him, on the basis of the authority of Jerome refers to *synderesis* as a habit-like faculty — a concept which is not very clear — rather than just a habit. Conscience for Bonaventure is a habit belonging to practical reason which is partly innate and partly acquired, referring to all moral judgments, both general principles and particular conclusions.[15]

Albert the Great, a representative of the Dominican School influenced by Jerome, understands *synderesis* as a habit-like faculty but connected not with the will but with practical reason. *Synderesis* is the knowledge of the universal principles of morality just as speculative reason has a knowledge of the self-evident truths of the speculative order. Albert logically proposes a different understanding of conscience than Bonaventure. *Synderesis* gives the first universal principles which form the major premise of a syllogism. Conscience is a judgment about a particular case that is the conclusion of a syllogism whose major premise is given by *synderesis* whose minor premise is given by reason or experience.[16]

The stage is set for the teaching of Thomas Aquinas who discusses the question first in his *Commentary on the Sentences* of Lombard, then in his *De veritate,* and finally in his *Summa Theologiae* which will be briefly summarized here.[17] In the *Pars Prima,* question 79, articles 12 and 13, Aquinas deals with the meaning and nature of conscience. Here Aquinas finally throws off the influence of Jerome and claims *synderesis* is not a faculty but a habit belonging to practical reason by which one knows the first, self-evident principles of practical moral reasoning. By this Thomas means the principle of doing good and avoiding evil and acting according to right reason. This habit, which corresponds to the knowledge of the first principles in the speculative order (e.g., principle of noncontradiction), then impels us to the good and cannot be lost as long as one enjoys the use of reason.

Conscience according to Aquinas is neither a faculty nor a habit, but an act — the act of applying knowledge to conduct. Here both the antecedent conscience as directing and guiding actions and the consequent conscience of judging are mentioned. Thomas also mentions that since the habit is the principle of the act, sometimes the name *conscience* is given to this habit which he has called *synderesis.*

Our discussion has traced the very fascinating historical development of the meaning, function, and working of conscience. Aquinas, who stands as the most influential person in the development of Catholic teaching, treats another aspect of conscience — its obliging force, especially in terms of following an erroneous conscience. Albert the Great had broken with earlier authors and asserted that conscience is binding whether it be correct or erroneous. Before his discussion in the *Summa,* Aquinas treated the question in an earlier and different way in his *Commentary on the Sentences* and in the *De veritate.*[18]

In question 5 of article 19 of the *prima secundae* of the *Summa Theologiae,* Thomas asks if a will going against an erring reason is bad and immediately adds in his response that this is the same as asking if an erroneous conscience obliges. Thomas refutes some other positions and argues that, since the object of the will is what is presented by reason, the will in pursuing what is proposed as evil incurs guilt. For example, it would be a sin to embrace the Christian faith if a person judges it to be evil. Thomas finishes his response by saying that every act of the will which is at variance with reason, whether the reason is correct or erroneous, is evil. An erroneous conscience always obliges. In question 6 he responds to the question whether an act is good if the will follows an erroneous conscience. The response hinges on the difference between vincible and invincible ignorance — is the error blameworthy or not? The question is, as Thomas himself notes in beginning his answer, whether an erroneous conscience excuses. One is obliged to follow an erroneous conscience; but it is sinful to do so if the ignorance is voluntary or vincible. An invincibly erroneous conscience excuses from guilt. In these two very short discussions Thomas considers the nature, function, and obliging force of conscience. One of the great differences between Thomas and the manuals of Catholic moral theology concerns the length of the discussion on conscience. The manuals devote a long, separate tract to conscience — much of which comes from a controversy that absorbed Catholic moral theology in the sixteenth, seventeenth, and eighteenth centuries. The problem centered on the question of a doubtful conscience. How is one to act if one's conscience cannot certainly decide what to do? The so-called moral systems, while recognizing that one cannot act with a doubtful conscience, proposed ways of moving from theoretical doubt to practical certitude about acting. How can theorectical doubt be turned into practical certitude?

This debate took place within a number of very significant contexts.[19] Moral theology had become a very practical discipline concerned with training confessors for the Sacrament of Penance especially in their role as judges about the existence and gravity of sin. Moral theology was cut off from its speculative roots as well as from dogmatic and spiritual theology. The tone was often legalistic, extrinsicist, and minimalistic. Casuistry for many takes on pejorative overtones because of the way it was used in the moral theology of this period. Within this general context there were different approaches to the problem of resolving doubts of conscience depending upon the rigidity of the authors. On the one extreme were the Jansenists many of whom embraced an absolute or rigid tutiorism. When there existed a doubt in theory, one always had to follow the safer course in practice — that is, the course asserting there was an obligation. On the other side of the debate were the laxists who in theory held that one could follow an opinion in favor of freedom from the obligation of law even if arguments in favor of such a theory were only tenuously probable or even much less probable than those in favor of the obligation.

During this debate the papal magisterium through the Holy Office entered the discussion to condemn the extreme opinions. (Incidently this was the most significant intervention up to that time by the papal office in the area of moral theology and began a trend that has continued until contemporary times.) In 1679 under Pope Innocent XI the Holy Office condemned sixty-five propositions associated with moral laxism at the instigation of the University of Louvain, which had previously condemned many of these propositions and sent their condemnation to Rome. These opinions were taken from a number of authors some of whom were Jesuits such as Thomas Tamburini.[20] The Holy Office condemned the use of the less probable opinion and of even a tenuously probable opinion (*DS* 2102, 2103). Likewise in conferring the sacraments it was forbidden to follow a probable opinion leaving aside a more safe opinion (*DS* 2101). Some of the condemned propositions show the state of moral theology at the time and the minimalistic and juridical approach to morality. The following laxist opinions were condemned as at least scandalous and dangerous in prac-

tice: We do not dare to condemn the opinion that some-
one sins mortally who only once in a lifetime elicits an act
of the love of God (*DS* 2105). It is sufficient to elicit an
act of faith only once in a lifetime (*DS* 2117). We are able
to satisfy the precept of loving our neighbor by only external acts (*DS* 2111).

Sometime after these condemnations, the opponents of
the Jansenists gathered together various opinions espoused
by theologians in Belgium. They were sent to Rome in
1682; a study by the Holy Office was finished in 1686, but
the decree containing the condemned errors was only
promulgated in 1690, under Pope Alexander VIII (*DS*
2301-2332). The principle of absolute tutiorism, that one
always had to follow the safest opinion even though the
opinion for freedom from the law was most probable, was
condemned (*DS* 2303). Other condemned opinions included the following: Although there exists invincible
ignorance of the natural law, this does not excuse from
formal sin one who in the state of fallen existence operates
on the basis of such ignorance (*DS* 2307). The intention
by which one detests evil and pursues the good merely
to obtain heavenly glory is neither right nor pleasing
to God (*DS* 2310). They are to be excluded from Holy
Communion who do not have in them the most pure
love of God which is in no way contaminated (*DS*
2323).

Although the extremes were condemned, bitter discussions still continued. Generally, at least after 1656,
the Dominicans were associated with the theory of probabiliorism according to which one could follow the opinion
for freedom only if it were more probable than the opinion in favor of the obligation. The Jesuits were generally
associated with the theory of probabilism according to
which one could follow the opinion for freedom from the
obligation provided it was probable or, as sometimes
phrased, solidly and truly probable.[21] Although some
Jesuit theologians maintained opinions which were condemned as laxist, it would be entirely false to claim, as

some have, that the Jesuits as a whole were laxists. They generally followed the opinion of probabilism.

The intensity and intrigue in the entire debate is well illustrated by the case of Thyrsus Gonzalez de Santalla, S.J., who was a professor at Salamanca. Gonzalez wrote a book dedicated to the General of the Jesuits, Father Oliva, in which he advocated probabiliorism; but he was denied permission to publish the book. Gonzalez's opinions were brought to the attention of Pope Innocent XI who issued a decree through the Holy Office in 1680. In this decree the Holy See told Gonzalez to preach, teach, and defend intrepidly with his pen the teaching about the more probable opinion. In addition the decree ordered the General of the Society of Jesus that he not only permit Jesuits to write in favor of the more probable opinion but he inform all Jesuit Universities that scholars are free to write in favor of the more probable opinion. It seems that this decree was never communicated to the members of the Society of Jesus. There exists another version of the same decree (judged by many to be not authentic) in which the Jesuits are forbidden to write in favor of probabilism. The story does not end here. Gonzalez, with some help from the Pope, was elected General of the Jesuits in 1687. But his book on the correct use of probabiliorism which he had secretly published in Bavaria around 1691 was still surpressed. In 1694, Gonzalez did succeed in publishing a version of the book he had originally written in 1671.[22]

The controversy finally came to an end with the moderate probabilism of St. Alphonsus Liguori, who worked out his moderate probabilism in the 1750s and 1760s. The opinion for freedom could be followed if it were equally probable as the opinion for the obligation. Alphonsus called his opinion equiprobabilism or moderate probabilism. In his later writings, he even changed his terminology but not his teaching in an effort to avoid being attacked by anti-Jesuits. With the demise of the Jesuits, Alphonsus became the champion of moderate probabilism.[23] St. Alphonsus was later named a doctor of the church and patron saint of confessors and of moral theologians.[24]

This long dispute had a great impact on the treatment of conscience in the manuals of moral theology. The characteristics of legalism and minimalism mentioned earlier became even more prevalent in the manuals of moral theology in the light of the long discussion. Until contemporary times the primary and most often asked question about a particular moral opinion in Roman Catholicism was whether or not such an opinion was probable and could be followed in practice. According to the theory an opinion could be probable either intrinsically, on the basis of the reasons proposed, or extrinsically, on the basis of the authority of the authors who maintained such an opinion. It was generally accepted that five or six authors of grave weight could constitute an opinion as probable.[25] Thus Catholic moral theology often "solved" moral problems by counting up the various authors who supported a particular opinion.

Unfortunately, the definitive history of the teaching on conscience still needs to be written, but this study has mentioned what appear to be the most important influences in the development of the Roman Catholic manuals of moral theology.[26] In the light of this one can both better appreciate and criticize the teaching of these manuals of moral theology on conscience.

The manuals of moral theology almost invariably divide their consideration of fundamental moral theology into the following treatises — the ultimate end (which is usually very short), human acts, law, conscience, sin, and virtue. The manual written and first published in 1952 by Marcellino Zalba, S.J., will be used for purposes of illustration. After his brief discussion of the ultimate end and a longer discussion of human acts, Zalba discusses rules, norms, or criteria which should direct our acts. These rules are basically two — the remote, objective, and extrinsic norm is law; the proximate, subjective, and intrinsic norm, which applies the law in particular cases and judges the morality of acts, is called conscience.

The first chapter under conscience treats the nature

and meaning of conscience. Moral conscience is defined as a dictate of practical reason or the ultimate practical judgment of reason about the morality of an act, here and now to be placed or omitted or already placed or omitted, according to moral principles. It is called the dictate of reason because conscience is formally an act of the intellect obtained by means of an at least virtual conclusion from general moral principles either by way of a strict reasoning process or by a certain sense and intuition of the right. Conscience is distinguished from other realities such as *synderesis* which is the innate habit of the universal principles of the moral order. Then the various distinctions of the types and kinds of conscience are given.[27]

The second chapter considers the necessity, truth, and certitude of conscience, dealing with the question of the erroneous conscience in the same general way as proposed by the theory of Thomas Aquinas — i.e., invoking the concept of vincible and invincible ignorance. Chapter 3 discusses the formation of conscience when one is doubtful. After a lengthy discussion of all the moral systems, Zalba chooses the system of probabilism according to which in cases of a law which is purely or principally preceptive, that is, about the mere liceity of an act, it is permitted to follow a less-probable opinion favoring liberty provided it is truly and solidly probable. However, probabilism cannot be used in a number of cases: a question of something probably necessary for salvation, actions concerning the validity of sacraments, acts involving the certain rights of another or, generally, a matter of the common good. The next section then discusses the various types of habitual conscience — tender, lax, perplexed, and scrupulous.[28]

In my judgment there are significant deficiencies in this understanding of conscience, which will be briefly mentioned. In the first place the basic approach is too legalistic with the resulting problems of minimalism and an extrinsic understanding of morality and the moral life. Second, conscience viewed as a faculty tends to give too little importance to the person as a whole — the subject of the action. Third, the understanding of conscience is too one-sidedly rationalistic — there is little or no mention of affectivity. Fourth, the emphasis is on a deductive reasoning process which bespeaks a classicist approach.

Toward a More Adequate Theory

Now it is time to propose a more adequate understanding of conscience which will avoid the criticisms briefly mentioned above. These criticisms of the manuals do not imply that there is nothing of value in the past Catholic tradition. It will be pointed out that the manuals, perhaps because of some aspects of the historical development mentioned earlier, do not necessarily represent the best of the Catholic tradition. On the other hand, there are changes called for in the light of contemporary understandings some of which have been mentioned in chapter 5.

As a preliminary consideration it is important to establish the different theological context within which the question of conscience is to be situated. The manuals operate almost exclusively within the realm of the natural as differentiated from and distinct from the supernatural. The stance for moral theology proposed in the second chapter criticized the older approach and argued that the natural, rather than being considered as existing apart from the supernatural, must be incorporated into the total Christian vision or stance. Such a theological context is a very necessary prerequisite for a proper understanding of conscience.

The first and primary consideration involves the ethical model within which one situates the reality of conscience. There is no doubt that the manuals understand morality primarily in terms of deontology. The objective norm is God's law as this is mediated in and through other laws — divine positive, natural, and positive law. The impression is readily given that the law spells out all one's moral obligations and conscience passively conforms to the existing law.

As mentioned earlier, there are three possible models that can be employed for understanding the moral life — deontology, teleology, and relationality — responsibility. The legalistic theology of the manuals, which sees the moral life primarily in terms of law, seems totally inadequate and accentuates the negative characteristics of minimalism and juridicism which so often characterized this morality. Interestingly, the manuals of Catholic moral theology do not follow the approach of Thomas Aquinas. They continually quote Aquinas in their discussion of law and appear to be following him but in reality they do not.

Thomas Aquinas properly belongs under the category of teleology — morality is based on the ultimate end and acts are good or bad depending on whether or not they bring us to the ultimate end or impede this progress.[29] Thomas's first consideration is the ultimate end of human beings, followed by his discussion of the human acts by which we achieve the ultimate end. His next major treatise concerns the principles of human actions. The intrinsic principles are the various powers or potencies from which our acts comes — e.g., the intellect, the appetites; but these powers can be modified by habits which are stable ways of acting inclining us either to the good or to evil. Among the good habits affecting our powers or faculties, Aquinas considers at great length the virtues and also mentions the gifts of the Holy Spirit, the beatitudes, and the fruits of the Holy Spirit. Only then does Thomas consider the external principles of actions which are both law and grace.[30] The manuals unfortunately do not follow either the whole of the Thomistic teaching or the tone of that moral teaching.

However, as mentioned in the preceding chapters, I choose a relationality-responsibility model as the basic ethical model. The use of this model was illustrated in the consideration of sin in chapter 4. For a deontological model, sin is an offense against the law of God. For a teleological model, sin, especially mortal sin which is the primary reality, involves going against one's ultimate end. For the relationality-responsibility model, sin is the breaking of our multiple relationships with God, neighbor, self, and the world. As illustrated in chapter 4, the relationality-responsibility model better corresponds with the biblical data and with a more adequate understanding of the moral life in general and of sin in particular.

There are a number of important theological and ethical considerations arguing for the acceptance of a relationality-responsibility model for moral theology. The first important impetus has come from biblical ethics. In Roman Catholic theology the renewal associated with the Second Vatican Council first appeared in the area of scripture and then grew as scriptural insights were incorporated more and more into the whole of theology so that scripture truly became the soul of theology.[31] In biblical ethics it became clear that relationality-responsibility was a very significant ethical theme. The primary ethical category even in the Old Testament is not law but covenant which is the loving relationship that God has made with the people.[32] The Gospel ethic with its call to perfection fits much better in relational categories than in deontological terms.

The understanding of the scriptures also played a significant role in leading Protestant scholars to a relationality model. Protestant ethics had always been firmly based on the Scriptures. The more critical approach to the Scriptures made theologians realize that the Scriptures could no longer be used as a source of laws or norms universally binding in the Christian life. In the Scriptures God revealed himself in his loving acts so that the concept of propositional revelation was no longer accepted. Especially in Barthian ethics the God of the Scriptures is the God who acts with his mighty deeds. In relationship to the God who acts and saves the Christian is a responder.[33] I have already negatively criticized a theological actualism which can easily develop in the light of this approach, but such an abuse does not destroy the valid understanding of the moral life in terms of relationality and responsibility.

Theological emphasis on eschatology also influences the selection of the relationality model. Contemporary eschatology no longer sees its subject as the last things but rather the Kingdom of God is already somewhat present and trying to become more present in history. The Christian then has a responsibility to make the kingdom more present and to overcome the evils of social, economic, political, and sexual oppression which too often continue to imprison many human beings. Such a theme is particularly central in the theology of liberation which in the Roman Catholic context has been developing especially in South America.[34]

Theological anthropology today understands the individual person as called to creatively make the kingdom more present in the struggle against the reality of sin in the world. Such an anthropology, highlighting the powers and capabilities of human beings, does not view the individual primarily in terms of conformity to a minutely spelled-out law or plan. Here again there is a danger of overestimating human creativity. The true realization that the individual creates one's own meaning and value can be distorted to deny the limitations that continually exist for human beings.

From a more philosophical-anthropological perspective the relationality-responsibility model fits in better with the emphasis on historicity. The tone of the manuals of moral theology with their insistence on all embracing laws characterized by universality and immutability is the product of a classicist worldview. This is not to deny that there is a place for law or for considerations of universality in ethics and the moral life of the Christian, but primary emphasis does not belong here. Historicity favors the stress on growth and development which is also much better incorporated in a relationality-responsibility model. A proper understanding of our multiple relationship with God, neighbor, self, and the world does justice to all the aspects of human existence including the political and social dimensions.

The emphasis on the person and personalism rather than the natural has also influenced the shift toward a model of relationality-responsibility. The individual as person is seen as a subject interacting with other persons. As was mentioned in chapter 5 this approach rejects an understanding of natural law as based on physical and biological processes or the innate teleologies of particular faculties seen apart from the person.

The adoption of a relationality-responsibility model rests on convincing theological and ethical arguments. Naturally it is necessary to develop at great detail what precisely is meant by relationality-responsibility. I have already pointed out in chapter 5 what I see as some erroneous approaches. In many ways I accept the basic approach of H. Richard Niebuhr to the model of relationality-responsibility. Niebuhr understands responsibility as embracing four elements — response, interpretation, accountability, and social solidarity.[35] My approach differs from Niebuhr in two important aspects. First, my understanding of relationality has a more metaphysical basis to it. Second, I want to give a greater emphasis to the subject as agent and incorporate here some of the findings of transcendental philosophical approaches. This emphasis will now be developed at much greater length in the subsequent steps of this section within the context of a relationality-responsibility model.

The second step in developing a more adequate concept of conscience in the Catholic theological tradition concerns giving greater importance to the subject or the person as agent. The legalistic and extrinsicist view of the manuals saw the moral life primarily as actions in obedience to the law. The law was recognized as an objective norm of morality to which the individual conformed one's acts. In this perspective conscience formation consisted primarily in instructing people about what is in the law. To this in practice was often added a motivational aspect emphasizing the fear of sin and hell.

In general an emphasis on the person as subject or agent

accepts the fact that the acts of the individual must be seen not in relation to an extrinsic norm but in relation to the person acting. An older axiom in Catholic thought understood this reality very well — *agere sequitur esse* — action follows from being — in other words, what we do follows from what we are. Actions are expressive and revelatory of the person. The person expresses oneself and extends oneself in and through one's actions. The biblical metaphor expresses the reality very well — the good tree brings forth good fruit while the bad tree brings forth bad fruit. Loving and compassionate actions come from a loving and compassionate person.

But there is also another important aspect to the emphasis on the person as agent. Not only are actions expressive and revelatory of the person, but by one's actions the individual shapes and constitutes the self as subject and as moral agent. By our actions we make ourselves the moral agents we are. Truly the individual human person has the opportunity and the destiny to create one's own moral self.

In more technical ethical terminology emphasis is placed on an ethics of character or of the virtues. How often we talk about the character of the person coming through in one's action. Character, as distinguished from particular character traits, emphasizes that the person is more than what happens to the self. One can determine oneself and one's character, recognizing that there are some factors over which we have no control. James Gustafson has emphasized the role of the self, virtues, and character in Christian ethics.[36] Stanley Hauerwas, influenced by Gustafson, has recently developed an ethics of character, understanding character as the qualification of self-agency which is an orientation of the self.[37] Obviously there would be many ways in which one could develop an ethics of character.

An ethics of the virtues also rests on the recognition of the importance of the subject as agent. This emphasis was present to a degree in Aquinas who saw the virtues as good habits or stable ways of acting modifying the faculties or powers and inclining them to the good.[38] Contemporary Christian ethicists are speaking again about an ethic of the virtues and some even want to develop an independent ethic of virtues with no place for an ethic of obligation.[39] An ethic of the virtues could be developed in many different ways, but all such approaches stress the importance of the person as subject and agent.

Unfortunately this emphasis is missing in the approach of the manuals and much of contemporary moral thought which often reduces ethical considerations to the moment of decision, forgetting about the self who continues from decision through decision and who actually affirms and creates one's moral self in and through those decisions. Again the Catholic tradition with the understanding of the virtues tried in some way to do justice to the importance of the subject and the person, but the manuals tended to neglect this aspect in their development. Even when treating of the virtues the manuals primarily discuss only the acts of the virtues and the obligations to place such actions.

From a theological perspective Catholic ethics possessed a strong basis for developing an ethic of the person as subject. The Catholic theory of grace maintains that grace produces an ontological change in the person. By freely responding to the gracious gift of God's love in Jesus Christ, one truly now becomes intrinsically changed, a different person mystically and really united with Jesus in the family of God. The Christian should then live in accord with the new life which has been received in Christ Jesus and grow in that life. The teaching of Aquinas can readily be understood in the light of the agent transformed by grace.[40] Some Protestant theology with its teaching on justification and the lesser emphasis on sanctification would have a greater difficulty in developing an ethic stressing the fact that the moral subject constitutes oneself as subject in and through one's actions and that the subject grows and progresses in the moral life.[41] However, Hauerwas develops an ethic of character judged to be in accord with some Protestant theories of justification.[42]

In the light of the importance of the person as agent and subject, the centrality of continual conversion in the moral life of the Christian emerges. Continual conversion has strong roots in the scriptural notion of *metanoia* and well illustrates the dynamism and call to perfection which characterizes a gospel inspired ethic. Bernard Häring has made conversion a central concept in moral theology.[43]

The Christian through responding to and accepting the gift of God's love in Jesus Christ becomes a new person, a new creature sharing in the life of Jesus. But one must continue to grow and deepen this new life. There is a true sense in which the individual remains *simul justus et peccator* — at the same time justified and a sinner. As mentioned in chapter 4 the reality of venial sin understood as the continuing sinfulness of the redeemed takes on added importance in this view, for the Christian constantly strives to overcome the sinfulness which is still present in the individual as well as in the world. The Christian continues both to express in actions the new life received in Baptism and to constitute self as a person ever more united with Jesus through the Spirit. Spiritual theology in the Catholic tradition, which unfortunately became separated from moral theology, has often insisted on the injunction to put on the Lord Jesus, to imitate Jesus and to live in union with the risen Lord. All of these notions, when made more dynamic in the light of continual conversion, underscore the personal growth of the subject who not only expresses this reality in one's actions but also constitutes one's moral self through these choices.

The biblical concept of conversion seen as the change of heart in response to the gracious gift of God in Jesus also avoids some of the dangers of Pelagianism which lurked in older approaches to morality in the Catholic tradition. With the insistence on works there was always the danger of thinking that one is saved by one's own efforts. Conversion as the opposite of sin has personal, social and cosmic dimensions and thereby views the Christian subject in the context of an ethical model of relationality-responsibility.

The virtues can be readily integrated into a theology of conversion and continual conversion. Virtues refer to the attributes and dispositions which characterize the Christian life. In the Thomistic presentation of the virtues some problems arose because of the faculty psychology on which they were based — virtues are habits modifying the individual faculties or powers of the soul. Likewise there exist some dangers of Pelagianism in the Scholastic understanding of the virtues. However, the basic concept of the virtues as the attitudes, dispositions, and inclinations characterizing the Christian person as subject must be seen as very important in the moral life of the Christian. One could develop the important virtues of the Christian on the basis of the beautitudes or the list of virtues in Paul or those characteristics such as hope, humility, mercy, and forgiveness, which so often appear in the New Testament.

The understanding of conscience must give central importance to the self — the person who acts and the characteristics of the person. Formation of conscience in this context can never settle merely for instruction in the law but rather must spur the individual to grow in wisdom, age, and grace as a follower of Jesus. What has been developed in this second step is a general emphasis on the subject and the person. The level of generality at which it was presented needs to be specified. The third and especially the fourth steps involve this process of specifying exactly how to understand the person as subject in deciding and acting.

The third step in a more adequate understanding of conscience is to overcome the one-sidedly cognitive aspect in the manuals of moral theology. Conscience should also have an affective dimension as well as a cognitive aspect. The affective dimension has taken on increased importance in light of work done in depth psychology and psychiatry. As the historical section points out there were different traditions within Roman Catholicism which saw conscience as either connected with the intellect as in the Thomistic approach or connected with the will as in the Franciscan approach.

In my judgment one of the sources for the problem in the Catholic tradition stems from an anthropology accepting a faculty-psychology approach. If conscience is viewed in terms of a particular faculty or power, then there lurks the danger of not giving enough importance to all the aspects of conscience.[44] It seems better to identify conscience with the moral consciousness of the subject as such. Bernard Lonergan shows how his intentionality analysis of the subject differs from the older faculty approach.

> The study of the subject is quite different, for it is the study of oneself inasmuch as one is conscious. It prescinds from the soul, its essence, its potencies, its habits, for none of these are given in consciousness. It attends to operations and to their center and source which is the self. It discerns the different levels of consciousness, the consciousness of the dream, of the waking subject, of the intelligently inquiring subject, of the rationally reflecting subject. It examines the different operations on the several levels and their relations to one another.[45]

A transcendental methodology which begins with the subject as conscious provides one way of overcoming the problems connected with the one-sided view of conscience as related to only one faculty or power and not to the whole subject. However, one must avoid any simplistic reduction and carefully distinguish the different levels of consciousness and operations in the subject — the levels of experiencing, understanding, judging, and deciding.

The recognition of the importance of the affective aspects and feelings in the formation of conscience have important practical ramifications. Much can be learned from all branches of psychology. Appeal must be made not only to the intellect but to the imagination and the affectivity of the person. In this connection one can mention an element which unfortunately has been lost in recent Catholic life — emphasis on the lives of the saints.[46] The saints furnished inspiration and supplied heroes for many younger Catholics in the past. These stories in their own way fired the imagination, triggered the feelings, and inflamed the hearts of those who strove to follow in the footsteps of the saints. With the passing of this emphasis on the lives of the saints, Catholic life has lost an important element in conscience formation.

A fourth step in arriving at a better understanding of conscience calls for a deeper understanding of the subject and how the subject arrives at its judgments and decisions. What do we mean by the self knowing, feeling, deciding, and how does the self do these things? Our inquiry starts with the traditionally accepted notion that a good conscience indicates that a good decision has been made. The precise question concerns what is a good conscience. When has the subject judged rightly and decided well? This question raises very fundamental issues about our understanding of human knowing, judging, and deciding. The approach developed here will differ from the considerations of the manuals which propose a heavily deductive reasoning process going from the universal to the particular and which see a correct judgment in terms of the correspondence of the mind to the objective reality existing "out there" or outside the subject.

As a preliminary note it can be pointed out that the neo-Thomist Jacques Maritain rejected the deductive reasoning process often proposed in the definitions of conscience. According to Maritain's interpretation the manner or mode in which human reason knows natural law is not rational knowledge but knowledge through inclination. Such knowledge is not clear knowledge through concepts and conceptual judgments. It is obscure, unsystematic, vital knowledge by connaturality or congeniality in which the individual in making judgments consults and listens to the inner melody that the vibrating strings of abiding tendencies make present in the subject.[47]

More radical solutions have been proposed in the context of transcendental method which sees objectivity not in conformity to the object out there but rather in terms of the human knowing, deciding, loving subject itself. Both Karl Rahner and Bernard Lonergan have made significant contributions to the understanding of conscience in this area.

Rahner has developed his approach in the context of discussions of the discernment of spirits and of a formal existential ethic.[48] The discernment of spirits has been a traditional part of Catholic spirituality.[49] There are three types of phenomena which the individual can experience — revelations and visions; internal enlightenment or impulses concerning some determinate object; general states of consolation or desolation. The discernment of spirits tries to determine the causes of these as either God and the good angels or the bad angels or human nature.[50]

Rahner develops his thought in commenting on the spiritual exercises of St. Ignatius. The whole purpose of the exercises is to bring the individual to make a vital decision — the election. According to Ignatius there are three times or occasions for making such an election. The first time arises when God moves the soul without any hesitation, as in private revelation. The second time occurs when light and understanding are derived through the experience of desolation and consolation in the discernment of spirits. The third time arises in tranquility when the soul is not agitated by different spirits and has the free and natural use of its powers. Rahner maintains that most commentators mistakenly interpret Ignatius as choosing the third time as the time for making the election. But Rahner argues, convincingly in the eyes of many, [51] that the second time is the usual time for making an election.[52]

Rahner attempts to explain the reality of discernment in the second time in light of his transcendental metaphysics. Knowledge does not mean only the conceptual knowledge of an object. In all human knowing there is also the concomitant awareness of the knowing self as the subject. This is not the knowledge of an object or even of the self as an object but is the subject's awareness as subject. Rahner interprets the Ignatian expression of consolation without previous cause as consolation without an object of that consolation. In all conscious acts the human being has an indistinct awareness of God as transcendent horizon but this awareness does not ordinarily emerge into explicit consciousness. Just as the individual is conscious to oneself as subject, so God as transcendent horizon but not as an object is present in consciousness. Now, however, in this second time the soul explicitly feels oneself totally drawn to the love of God and thus experiences this consolation, peace, and joy which is coming from God's presence. This consolation is the nonconceptual experience of God as the individual is drawn totally into his love. If this consolation perdures when the person places oneself in accord with the projection of the election to be made, the individual rightly concludes that the prospective choice harmonizes with one's own human, Godward subjectivity. Obviously this requires that the person as subject be truly open to the call of God. This experience by which the soul is wholly drawn to the love of God as God, unlike discursive or conceptual knowledge, possesses intrinsically an irreducibly self-evident, self-sufficient character.[53]

In an earlier essay Rahner proposes a formal existential ethic in addition to and in no way opposed to an essential ethic resulting in the general principles of natural law. Rahner agrees that in addition to one's essence each individual also has a positive individual reality. This positive individuality cannot be the object of reflective, objective knowledge which can be articulated in propositions. How does conscience perceive this individual moral obligation? Rahner again appeals to nonreflective, nonpropositional self-presence of the person to self in one's positive uniqueness.[54]

Rahner in this way tries to develop a theory of conscience which corresponds with the traditionally accepted idea of the peace and joy of a good conscience when a good decision has been made or is to be made.[55] Obviously there are questions that can and should be put to Rahner. One problem is that his transcendental method, while handling quite well questions primarily of a personal and individual nature such as vocation, does not even try to say anything to questions of social ethics. Perhaps this is just the appearance in the realm of moral theology of the reality that Metz criticized in Rahner's systematics for not giving enough importance to the social and political aspects of reality.[56] Likewise, in my judgment Rahner's approach does not seem to give enough importance to empirical reality.

Bernard Lonergan in his work on theological method and elsewhere has outlined a transcendental approach to ethics which seems to overcome the problems mentioned above with the theory of Karl Rahner.[57] Lonergan is opposed to deductive reasoning. He always begins with the concrete. Lonergan understands consciousness as the presence of the subject to oneself — not the presence of an object. In the following paragraphs Lonergan's approach to conscience or moral consciousness will be sketched although it is impossible to give a full and complete understanding of his complex thought.[58]

Conscience for Lonergan is seen in the context of the thrust of the personal subject for the authenticity of self-transcendence. The person shares sensitivity with the other animals, but the human individual can go beyond (transcend) this level of consciousness. In addition to the empirical level of consciousness and intentionalities, in which one perceives, senses, etc., human beings go beyond this to the intellectual level of understanding and to the rational level of judgment which not only goes beyond the subject but also affirms that which is so. On the next level self-transcendence becomes moral — in the order of deciding and doing not just knowing. By responding to questions about value we can effect in our being a moral transcendence. This moral transcendence is the possibility of becoming a person in human society. Our capacity for self-transcendence becomes fully actual when we fall in love. Being in love is of different kinds but being in love with God is the basic fulfillment of our conscious intentionality. This brings a joy and a peace that can remain despite failure, pain, betrayal, etc. The transcendental subjectivity of the person stretches forth toward the intelligible, the unconditioned, and the good of value. The reach of this intending is unrestricted.[59]

Within the context of self-transcendence Lonergan develops the three conversions which modify the horizon of the subject. Intellectual conversion denies the myth of the object out there as the criterion of objectivity and reality. This is a naive, comic-book realism. Lonergan strives for a critical realism. The real world for Lonergan is mediated by meaning and is not the world of immediate experience. The real world mediated by meaning is known by the cognitional process of experiencing, understanding, and judging, which is based on the thrust of cognitional self-transcendence. Moral conversion consists in opting for the truly good, for values against satisfactions when they conflict. Here we are no longer cajoled as children, but we freely opt for value. Thus we affect not only the object of choice but we decide for ourselves what to make of ourselves.

Religious conversion, the third conversion, is being grasped by ultimate concern. It is the total and permanent self-surrender of other-worldly falling in love.[60] Lonergan himself succinctly summarizes his understanding of the three conversions.

As intellectual and moral conversion, so also religious conversion is a modality of self-transcendence. Intellectual conversion is to truth attained by cognitional self-transcendence. Moral conversion is to values apprehended, affirmed and realized by a real self-transcendence. Religious conversion is to a total being-in-love as the efficacious ground of all self-transcendence, whether in the pursuit of truth, or in the realization of human values, or in the orientation man adopts to the universe, its ground and its goals.[61]

How do we know our judgments have attained the true and our decisions have achieved the value? In other words, what are the criteria by which we know our judging and deciding have been good and proper? In the manuals of moral theology the criterion of judgment is conformity to the objective truth out there. Lonergan firmly rejects that criterion. In a judgment one arrives at truth when there are no more pertinent questions to ask. The self-transcending thrust toward truth is satisfied. The judgment for Lonergan is thus described as virtually unconditioned because the subject seeking the truth can now rest content. Thus we have established the radical identity between genuine objectivity and authentic subjectivity.[62]

Likewise, the criterion of value judgments is not the value or reality out there; rather, it is the satisfaction of the moral subject as a self-transcending thrust toward value. A rounded moral judgment is ever the work of a fully developed self-transcending subject or, as Aristotle would put it, of a virtuous person.[63] The drive to value rewards success in self-transcendence with a happy conscience and saddens failure with an unhappy conscience.[64] Thus once again the peaceful and joyful conscience of the authentic subject understood in terms of self-transcendence becomes the criterion of objective value. One might truly say that for Lonergan the norms for the proper formation of conscience are the transcendental precepts which correspond to the basic levels of consciousness of the subject and the basic operations — be attentive, be intelligent, be reasonable, be responsible.[65]

Lonergan is well aware of the dangers and difficulties in achieving authenticity and self-transcendence. Development is not inevitable; there are many failures. In moral conversion one must overcome enticing but misleading satisfactions and fears of discomfort, pain and privation. Lonergan speaks of bias as affecting authentic transcendence on all levels and going against the transcendental precepts.[66] He applies to all levels of self-transcendence what was said about intellectual conversion in *Insight*.

Bias as a block or a distortion appears in four principal matters: the bias of unconscious motivation brought to light in depth psychology; the bias of individual egoism; the bias of group egoism; and the bias of common sense.[67] The recognition of such obstacles in the way of authentic self-transcendence continually reminds the individual to be self-critical. Human authenticity has no room for complacency and self-satisfaction. One must continually question, inquire, and be open to learn.

Again, one should critique and discuss the theory proposed by Lonergan. One set of problems arises from the nature of conversion, the order of conversion (according to Lonergan there is usually, first, religious, followed by moral, and then, and only rarely, intellectual conversion),[68] and the frequency of conversion (Lonergan admits intellectual conversion is rare and describes the other conversions, especially religious, in such a way that they would seem to be very rare in practice).

I would make two suggestions. First, I do not think there is that great a difference or distinction between moral and religious conversion. The strictly theological data (love of God and neighbor) and existential experience seem to see the two conversions as basically one.[69] Second, Lonergan could introduce a variant of the notion of continual conversion to indicate that both conversions involve a continual growth and that these conversions might take place on a fundamental and beginning level even though the radical description of conversion has not yet been fully achieved.[70]

I have tried to develop through various steps a basic understanding of the reality of conscience and how it functions in the Christian life. First, conscience must be understood in the context of a relationality-responsibility model of the Christian life — never forgetting the multiple relationships within which one lives. The second step affirmed the importance of the self as agent and subject who expresses oneself in actions and also by those very actions constitutes oneself as subject. The third step insisted on seeing conscience as more than merely cognitive and strove to bring together the cognitive, the affective, and the moral aspects of conscience. Finally, the fourth step proposed specific metaphysical theories explaining the reality of conscience and how one arrives at good judgments and decisions. Lonergan's basic theory has advantages over Rahner's for three reasons: (1) it deals more adequately with the empirical; (2) it can handle better the social aspect as well as the personal aspect of moral existence; (3) it is a unified theory explaining all knowing and deciding and does not distinguish between the essential and the existential aspects of conscience formation. This theory attempts to explain in a more systematic and reflective way the traditionally accepted notion that joy and peace mark the good conscience which is the adequate criterion of good moral judgment and decision.

One further point deserves mention. This understanding of conscience recognizes the importance of the development of conscience. The approach proposed here calls for and readily incorporates within its philosophical context the work of developmental psychologists in describing the way in which conscience itself develops and grows.[71] What has to be remembered is that development occurs not only in childhood, although it is obviously more dramatic in childhood, but continues to occur throughout adult life. Theologians must take the biblical concept of continual conversion and see how this can be psychologically understood in terms of the development of conscience.

Practical Conclusions

The first practical conclusion of the discussion on conscience reaffirms the traditionally accepted teaching that conscience is the norm of personal action. Yes, the conscience judgment and decision might be wrong, but the individual must be true to one's own self. Authentic subjectivity excludes the possibility of error, but authentic subjectivity is not always present. Many abuses have existed in the past in the name of conscience, and there will continue to be many abuses in the future. But this does not take away the basic realization that the individual must decide and act in accord with conscience. Christians and the Church should learn from the divine wisdom both to accept the freedom and responsibility of the individual to decide in conscience despite all the abuses of that freedom and to challenge the individual to achieve authenticity. God's loving gift of self to human beings respects human freedom and the choices made by human beings, even though God's gift is often spurned.

Second, however, one must be well aware of the dangers involved in judgments and decisions of conscience. Yes, the ultimate decision and judgment rest with the individual, but the individual must recognize the limitations and dangers involved in trying to achieve subjective authenticity which is synonymous with objectivity. In a practical way human experience reminds us of the many horrendous realities that have been done in the name of conscience — slavery, torture, atrocities, and deprival of basic human rights. The realization of the dangers involved becomes even more acute when recognizing how seemingly even good people can disagree over such basic issues as the use of force in the service of justice, abortion, or the just ordering of the economic system for the good of all. The authentic development of self-transcendence is threatened on every level.

The Christian can and should recognize the two basic sources of this danger as human finitude and sinfulness. Finitude is different from sinfulness. As a result of our finitude we are limited; we see only a partial aspect of reality; we cannot achieve all possible goods or values. Human sinfulness, on the other hand, stems not from creation itself but from the actions of ourselves or others and can be seen in the sinfulness both of the individual and of the society in which we live.

Although the basic sources of the dangers in a theological perspective are easy to identify, the actual dangers can take many different forms. Again, these dangers exist in the cognitive, affective, and moral levels and operations. Bias and prejudice can easily affect our judgments and decisions. Why is it that those who espouse the just-war theory generally judge wars of their own country to be just while rejecting the justice of the wars of their opponents? An examination of conscience reveals the lack of courage which prevents us from acting upon what we believe to be right or the lack of ardor which weakens our pursuit of value.

One example will well illustrate the complexity of the problem of how limitation and sinfulness can affect our judgments and decisions of conscience. Will better conscience decisions result if a person is involved in the problem or if a person is an "objective" observer? Frankly, there are pluses and minuses to both approaches. The one who is intimately involved in the struggle knows and appreciates the problem. One must honestly admit that white, male, middle-class theologians have not been as aware as we should be of the problems of racism, poverty, and sexism in our society. On the other hand, personal involvement in an issue might prejudice one's judgments and decisions. Do the heads of powerful governments or people desperately fighting for the rights of the poor and oppressed tend to resort too quickly to violence? Do people involved in equal rights and opportunities for women tend to overlook the fetus? Yes, it is not too difficult to become aware of the difficulties and dangers in making judgments and decisions of conscience.

Third, one must not only be aware of the dangers but strive to overcome them. This is what it means to live out a theory of critical self-transcendence. From the Christian perspective the basic disposition that we all need to cultivate is openness to the gift of God and the needs of our neighbor. The Christian should try to put aside all prejudice, bias, and egoism. There is much talk today about openness, but to be truly open is not easy. The fundamental importance of openness stems from the theory of conscience proposed on the basis of critical self-transcendence which sees the individual person in terms of an unrestricted thrust toward truth, value, love, and the unconditioned. The proof of a good conscience is had when one affirms the true and embraces the value. A false conscience arises from a lack of authenticity on the cognitive, affective, and moral levels of our existence. Openness therefore keeps one truly open to the truth, value, and love which alone can satisfy the unrestricted thrust toward the unconditioned. Openness also seems to be a very good understanding of the biblical attitude of humility of spirit. The humble in spirit are truly those who are open to the gift of God and the needs of neighbor. Openness aptly describes the primary disposition in conscience formation.

The individual should be critically alert to the many different ways of trying to guarantee that openness characterizes our existence in the quest for truth, value, and love. Many ways have been proposed but one must remember that they are usually only prudential specifications of the basic disposition of openness. The Gospel gives us a very significant way of trying to overcome our finitude and sinfulness — love your neighbor as yourself. To put ourselves in the position of the other person remains an excellent way to overcome our own finitude and sinfulness. This same wisdom is found in the golden rule — do unto others as you would have them do unto you. Some contemporary philosophers speak of the veil of ignorance. In choosing what social system should be in existence all individuals must choose from behind the veil of ignorance — that is, not knowing which of the various positions in society might be theirs.[72] Other philosophers speak of the ideal observer as the way of overcoming the prejudice and bias of any one individual.[73] The philosophical principle of universalization based on the understanding that one must always be willing to see all others act in a similar way in similar circumstances also serves as a strong antidote to individual bias, prejudice, and sinfulness.

Above all openness for the Christian calls for one to be an authentic self with all those attitudes and dispositions which should characterize a human and Christian person. In this way the person develops the feeling for the true and the good as well as the yearning and inclination to affirm and embrace them. The good conscience remains the work of a virtuous person.[74]

Fourth, community and especially the Christian community of the Church are very important in the formation of conscience. The discussion thus far has concerned only the individual, but the insistence on multiple relations and on the social aspects of morality recalls that the individual judges and decides in dialogue with other individuals and as members of various communities in which one lives. The various communities to which we belong play a very important role in personal conscience formation. These considerations will be limited to what for the Christian must be the most important community — that of the Church.

The Church as the people of God, called together to live in the risen Lord and to bear witness to that life, has a very significant role to play in the formation of the conscience of the individual Christian. The Church as the mediator and sign of the Gospel strives to have its own people become signs of that Gospel to others. From an ethical perspective, the Church is a great help in the formation of conscience precisely because it can overcome the two basic dangers of finitude and sinfulness which always threaten the individual. Because of our finitude we are limited historically, spatially, and temporally. The Church as a universal community existing in different cultures, in different times, and in different places is thus able to help overcome the limitations of finitude. The Church as the community of Gospel and grace also tries to overcome human sinfulness and egoism. Although the Church remains a sinful Church still in need of continual redemption, the believer sees in the Church the presence of redeeming grace and a power to overcome sin and its ramifications.

Take a particular example of how the Church is able to help conscience. In my judgment some Protestant clergy deserve great credit for the leadershp role they played through early opposition to the recent American involvement in the war in Viet Nam. Many of these people suffered greatly because their stand was far from popular when they first took it. Some of these clergy admitted that at the very beginning they favored American participation in the war, but their early opposition was greatly influenced by the questions posed to them by Christians from other countries. These other Christians in the light of a broader perspective could overcome the narrowness, limitations, and group egoism of Americans.

The Church by every means possible — challenging, accusing, approving, questioning, supporting, teaching — helps in the formation of the conscience of the individual Christian. There are myriad ways in which this formation can and should take place in the Christian community. The Roman Catholic believer also recognizes the God given function of the hierarchical magisterium as one mode in which the Church teaches and forms consciences. One way in which the whole Church and the hierarchical magisterium can inform conscience is by giving specific directions for specific actions. The following chapter will discuss the fact that the hierarchical magisterium must go through a proper discernment process to understand just what these specific directives are. Likewise, it was also pointed out that the Roman Catholic Church has recognized that this teaching of the hierarchical magisterium on specific moral matters cannot claim the certitude that excludes the possibility of error. At times the individual Christian, conscious of all the dangers, can rightly dissent from such teaching in theory and practice. Here again in making that decision one must carefully follow all the available approaches to conscience formation mentioned above. Here again, too, the ultimate criterion is the peace and joy of a good conscience.

This rather lengthy, but still unfortunately sketchy, consideration of conscience attempts to understand conscience in the light of recent developments in fundamental moral theology. The concept of conscience proposed here overcomes the criticisms proposed against the theory of conscience found in the manuals of moral theology. Above all this theory of conscience incorporates an understanding of the Christian life which highlights its Gospel, personal, dynamic, historical, and social characteristics.

NOTES

1. C. A. Pierce, *Conscience in the New Testament* (London: SCM Press, 1955), pp. 13-53.

2. Ibid., p. 117.

3. Ibid., p. 109

4. Ibid., p. 62.

5. Eric D'Arcy, *Conscience and Its Right to Freedom* (New York: Sheed and Ward, 1962), pp. 11-12.

6. Ceslaus Spicq, *Théologie morale du Nouveau Testament,* vol. 2 (Paris: J. Gabalda, 1965), p. 603. See also C. Spicq, "La Conscience dans le Nouveau Testament," *Revue Biblique* 47 (1938), 50-80.

7. Philippe Delhaye, *The Christian Conscience* (New York: Desclée, 1968), pp. 37-50.

8. Emil Brunner, *The Divine Imperative* (Philadelphia: Westminster Press, 1947), pp. 156ff.

9. Ronald Preston, "Conscience," in *Dictionary of Christian Ethics,* ed. John Macquarrie (Philadelphia: Westminster Press, 1967), pp. 66-68. For a view of conscience in the Protestant tradition which recognizes a positive and antecedent function, see David Little, "A View of Conscience within the Protestant Tradition," in *Conscience: Its Freedom and Limitations,* ed. William C. Bier (New York: Fordham University Press, 1971), pp. 20-28.

10. For a Catholic scholar who sees the legislative and positive role of conscience in the New Testament as exceptional and differing from the usual usage, see James C. Turro, "Conscience in the Bible," in Bier, *Conscience,* p. 7.

11. Eric Mount, Jr., *Conscience and Responsibility* (Richmond: John Knox Press, 1969), p. 26.

12. For the development of the teaching in the scholastic period, see Odon Lottin, *Psychologie et morale aux XIIe et XIIIe siècles,* vol. 2 (Louvain: Abbaye du Mont César, 1948) pp. 103-350. For a shorter treatment in English which acknowledges a great debt to Lottin, see D'Arcy, pp. 20-48. My summary discussion is dependent on both of them.

13. *Liber IV Sententiarum,* lib. 2, dist. 39.

14. J. de Blic, "Syndérèse ou conscience? " *Revue d'Ascétique et de Mystique* 25 (1949), 146-157.

15. The question is whether *synderesis* is a faculty or power like reason or the will or whether it is a habit or disposition which modifies the reason or will. Philip the Chancellor, obviously influenced by Jerome, cannot say it is merely a habit. The Latin term he employs is *potentia habitualis,* which Lottin (pp. 140-142) translates as "faculté doublé d'habitus" and D'Arcy (p. 27) as "habit-like faculty." For Bonaventure's position see his *In II Sent.,* dist. 39, art, 1 and 2.

16. *Summa de Creaturis, secunda pars* q. 71, a 1; q. 72 a. 1.

17. *In II Sent.,* dist. 24, qu. 2 art. 3.; *Quaestiones Disputatae De Veritate,* q. 16.

18. For a brief historical summary of this discussion, see D'Arcy, pp. 76-105.

19. The source generally cited for this debate is Th. Deman, O.P., "Probabilisme," in *Dictionnaire de théologie catholique* (Paris, 1936), vol. 13, col. 417-619. (Hereafter referred to as *D.T.C.*). However, in my judgment this account is somewhat biased in favor of the probabiliorist approach against the probabilist approach. In this connection note Deman's dependence on a strong proponent of probabiliorism, Daniel Concina, *Della storia del probabilismo e del rigorismo,* 2 vols. (Lucca, 1743).

20. *Enchiridion Symbolorum Definitionum et Declarationum de Rebus Fidei et Morum,* ed. H. Denzinger, A. Schönmetzer, 32nd ed. (Barcelona: Herder, 1963), nn. 2101-2167. Hereafter referred to as *DS.*

21. Deman, *D.T.C.,* vol. 13, col. 502-510, 523-530.

22. *DS* nn. 2175-2177; Deman *D.T.C.,* vol. 13, col. 534-547; P. Bernard, "Gonzalez de Santalla, Thyrse," *D.T.C.,* vol. 6, col. 1493-1496.

23. For a recent and very accurate study of the development of St. Alphonsus's thought on probabilism, see the three part study of Domenico Capone, "Dissertazioni e note di S. Alfonso sulla probabilità e la conscienza." *Studia Moralia* 1 (1963), 265-343; 2 (1964), 89-155; 3 (1965), 82-149. The documentary evidence of how he changes his terminology in the light of political and religious pressures is found in *Studia Moralia* 2 (1964), 123ff.

24. I. Aertnys-C. Damen, *Theologia Moralis*, ed. J. Visser, 17th ed. (Rome: Marietti, 1956), 1: n. 95, pp. 103-105.

25. Marcellino Zalba, *Theologiae Moralis, Summa I: Theologia Moralis Fundamentalis* (Madrid: Biblioteca de Autores Cristianos, 1952), p. 306.

26. Recently there have appeared a number of anthologies bringing together different articles on conscience. In addition to the work edited by Bier which has already been mentioned, see *Conscience: Theological and Psychological Perspectives*, ed. C. Ellis Nelson (New York: Newman Press, 1973); *Conscience*, ed. John Donnelly and Leonard Lyons (Staten Island: Alba House, 1973); *Conscience*, ed. Curatorium of the C. G. Jung Institute, Zurich (Evanston, Ill.: Northwestern University Press, 1970).

27. Zalba, pp. 241-253.

28. Ibid., pp. 253-328.

29. For a categorization of Aquinas as belonging to a deliberative rather than a prescriptive motif, see Edward LeRoy Long, Jr., *A Survey of Christian Ethics* (New York: Oxford University Press, 1967), pp. 45-49.

30. This paragraph merely summarizes the outline of the *prima pars* of the *Summa Theologiae*.

31. Dogmatic Constitution on Divine Revelation, n. 24; Decree on Priestly Formation, n. 16.

32. Robert Koch, "Vers une morale de l'alliance," *Studia Moralia* 6 (1968), 7-58.

33. James M. Gustafson, "Christian Ethics," in *Religion*, ed. Paul Ramsey (Englewood Cliffs, N.J.: Prentice Hall, 1965), pp. 309-320.

34. For the best theological explanation of liberation theology stressing especially the changed understanding of eschatology, see Gustavo Gutierrez, *A Theology of Liberation: History, Politics and Liberation* (Maryknoll, N.Y.: Orbis Books, 1973).

35. H. Richard Niebuhr, *The Responsible Self* (New York: Harper and Row, 1963), pp. 55-68.

36. James M. Gustafson, *Christ and the Moral Life* (New York: Harper and Row, 1968), pp. 1-5 and throughout the book; James M. Gustafson, *Christian Ethics and the Community* (Philadelphia: Pilgrim Press, 1971), pp. 151-216.

37. Stanley Hauerwas, *Character and the Christian Life: A Study in Theological Ethics* (San Antonio, Texas: Trinity University Press, 1975).

38. For a development of the Thomistic concept of the virtues, see George P. Klubertanz, *Habits and Virtues* (New York: Appleton-Century-Crofts, 1965). In the next step I will express my disagreement with the faculty psychology on which the Thomistic approach is based.

39. For example, see the following articles in the first issue (1973) of *The Journal of Religious Ethics:* Frederick Carney, "The Virtue-Obligation Controversy," pp. 5-19; William K. Frankena, "The Ethics of Love Conceived as an Ethics of Virtue," pp. 21-36; Arthur J. Dyck, "A Unified Theory of Virtue and Obligation," pp. 37-52.

40. Yves Congar, "Le saint Ésprit dans la théologie thomiste de l'agir morale," in *Tommaso D'Aquino nel suo VII Centenario, Congresso Internazionale, Roma-Napoli, 17-24 aprile, 1974,* pp. 175-187.

41. As an illustration of an unwillingness to accept such an approach, see Victor Paul Furnish, *Theology and Ethics in Paul* (Nashville: Abingdon Press, 1968), pp. 176, 239, 240.

42. Hauerwas, *Character and the Christian Life,* pp. 183-195.

43. Bernard Häring, *The Law of Christ* (Westminster, Md.: Newman Press, 1961) 1: 287-481; Bernard Häring, *Pastoral Treatment of Sin,* ed. P. Delhaye et al. (New York: Desclée, 1968), pp. 87-176.

44. For an illustration of the faculty-psychology approach to conscience, see Ralph McInerny, "Prudence and Conscience," *The Thomist* 38 (1974), 291-305. McInerny restricts conscience to the cognitive, but he recognizes other important affective aspects in the moral life.

45. Bernard Lonergan, *The Subject* (Milwaukee: Marquette University Press, 1968), pp. 7, 8.

46. Berard L. Marthaler, "A Traditional and Necessary Ingredient in Religious Education: Hagiography," *The Living Light* 11 (1974), 580-591.

47. Jacques Maritain, *Man and the State* (Chicago: University of Chicago Press, 1951), pp. 91, 92.

48. Karl Rahner, "The Logic of Concrete Individual Knowledge," in *The Dynamic Element in the Church* (New York: Herder and Herder, 1964), pp. 84-170; Karl Rahner, "On the Question of a Formal Existential Ethic," *Theological Investigations,* vol. 2 (Baltimore: Helicon Press, 1963), pp. 217-234.

49. For an overall view of this question, see Jacques Guillet, et al., *Discernment of Spirits* (Collegeville, Minnesota: Liturgical Press, 1970). This book is the authorized English edition of the article in the *Dictionnaire de spiritualité.* For a contemporary theological discussion, see Philip S. Keane, "Discernment of Spirits: A Theological Reflection," *American Ecclesiastical Review* 168 (1974), 43-61.

50. Joseph de Guibert, *The Theology of the Spiritual Life* (London: Sheed and Ward, 1956), pp. 130ff.

51. See, for example, the special issue of *The Way Supplement* 24 (1975), which is devoted to the spiritual exercises of Ignatius.

52. Rahner, *Dynamic Element in the Church*, pp. 89-106.

53. Ibid., pp. 129-170.

54. Rahner, *Theological Investigations*, vol. 2, pp. 217-234.

55. For an interpretation of Rahner's entire ethical theory, see James F. Bresnahan, "Rahner's Ethic: Critical Natural Law in Relation to Contemporary Ethical Methodology," *The Journal of Religion* 56 (1976):36-60. For a fuller development, see James F. Bresnahan, "The Methodology of Natural Law: Ethical Reasoning in the Theology of Karl Rahner and its Supplementary Development Using the Legal Philosophy of Lon L. Fuller" (Ph.D. Diss., Yale University [Ann Arbor, Mich.: University Microfilms, 1972, no. 72-29520]).

56. Johannes B. Metz, "Foreword: An Essay on Karl Rahner," in Karl Rahner, *Spirit in the World* (New York: Herder and Herder, 1968), pp. xvi-xviii.

57. The two major works of Bernard Lonergan are: *Insight: A Study of Human Understanding* (New York: Philosophical Library, 1957); *Method in Theology* (New York: Herder and Herder, 1972).

58. Of great value are two, unfortunately unpublished, dissertations: Walter Eugene Conn, "Conscience and Self-Transcendence" (Ph.D. diss., Columbia University [Ann Arbor, Mich.: University Microfilms, 1973, no. 73-26600]); John P. Boyle, "Faith and Community in the Ethical Theory of Karl Rahner and Bernard Lonergan" (Ph.D. diss., Fordham University [Ann Arbor, Mich.: University Microfilms, 1972, no. 72-20554]).

59. Lonergan, *Method in Theology*, pp. 103-105.

60. Ibid., pp. 239-241.

61. Ibid., p. 241.

62. Lonergan, *Insight*, pp. 279-316.

63. Lonergan, *Method in Theology*, p. 41.

64. Ibid., p. 35.

65. Ibid., pp. 53, 231.

66. Ibid., pp. 51-55.

67. Ibid., p. 231.

68. Ibid., pp. 243, 267.

69. Charles E. Curran, "Christian Conversion in the Writings of Bernard Lonergan," in *Foundations of Theology: Papers from the International Lonergan Congress 1970*, ed. Philip McShane (Notre Dame, Ind.: University of Notre Dame Press, 1972), pp. 41-59.

70. For different criticisms of the questions involving conversion in Lonergan's approach, see Conn, pp. 526ff.

71. Conn develops at great length the theories of Piaget, Erikson, and Kohlberg incorporating their findings in a critical way into his understanding of conscience.

72. E.g., John Rawls, *A Theory of Justice* (Cambridge, Mass.: Harvard University Press, 1971), pp. 136-142.

73. E.g., F. C. Sharp, *Good and Ill Will* (Chicago: University of Chicago Press, 1950), pp. 156-162.

74. For a discussion of discernment from the viewpoint of a Protestant ethician who approaches the question in a nonmetaphysical way, see James M. Gustafson, "Moral Discernment in the Christian Life," in *Norm and Context in Christian Ethics*, ed. Gene Outka and Paul Ramsey (New York: Charles Scribner's Sons, 1968), pp. 17-36.

9. The Pastoral Minister, the Moral Demands of Discipleship, and the Conscience of the Believer

The question of dissent, diversity, and pluralism within Roman Catholicism has come to the fore in the last fifteen years. Sociological studies have proved the existence of such diversity. Archbishop John R. Quinn of San Francisco, for example, in addressing the International Synod of Bishops in 1980 cited without comment one study of fertile married couples which "concluded that 76.5 percent of American Catholic women (as compared with 79.9 percent of all U.S. women) were using some form of birth regulation, and that 94 percent of these Catholic women were using methods condemned by the encyclical."[1] Especially in the Western world there are many divorced and remarried Catholics who still consider themselves good Catholics and frequent the sacraments of the church. The report of the 1980 National Pastoral Congress of England and Wales recognized this reality and asked the bishops to consider with compassion the desires of such divorced and remarried people to establish unity with the church through the sacraments.[2] In Africa there is much discussion about polygamy and the relationship of polygamists to the eucharist and the church.[3] In many third-world nations there is the question of the relationship of the Christian to the Marxist and revolutionary groups.[4] These are only some of the many practical issues highlighting the fundamental question of the problem of unity and diversity in the church. In addition there are many other questions of a more doctrinal nature, but this chapter will concentrate primarily on questions in the realm of morality and practice.

In many ways there already exists a somewhat abundant literature both on the fundamental problem of unity and diversity in the church and on the particular issues under discussion. The basic problem is often addressed in terms of the question of authority in the church, the role of the hierarchical magisterium, the role of theologians, and the possibility of dissent. Despite this abundant literature in general there has been little or nothing written or discussed about the role of the pastoral minister in the midst of this problem. How does the minister, baptized and/or ordained, in counseling, sacramental preparation, teaching, and sacramental celebration deal with the question of unity and diversity in the church, especially as it affects the conscience of the person the minister is dealing with? No one can deny the tensions which the theoretical issue also creates for the pastoral minister. How does one minister to the divorced and remarried in the parish? How does the minister react to the couple preparing for marriage who casually mention that they have been and are living together now? What does one say to a homosexual couple who want to join the parish? How does one counsel a married man thinking about a vasectomy?

In addition to these issues in the area of sexual ethics problems also arise in the area of social and political ethics. Many Roman Catholics in the United States have expressed their dissatisfaction with some aspects of the American bishops' letter on nuclear weapons, such as the bishops being against any first use of such weapons or their rejection of a limited nuclear war. In Canada there has been disagreement with the statement from a bishops' committee which includes the insistence that "unemployment rather than inflation should be recognized as the number one problem to be tackled in overcoming the present crisis."[5] Perhaps it is a sign of maturity that the questions about dissent and diversity facing the pastoral minister in the first world are no longer only sexual questions.

The results of one survey bear out the significance of this issue of pluralism and dissent for pastoral ministers. A survey of the pastors in the diocese of Chur, Switzerland, reveals that "in the opinion of the pastors, it was they themselves who suffered the most from the publication of the encyclical [*Humanae Vitae*]."[6] In some ways the problem for the pastoral minister is much more difficult than for others because the pastoral minister cannot avoid the issues. One in pastoral ministry necessarily deals with questions of this type every single day. Theologians and others living more in the theoretical realm have the luxury of not dealing with these issues if they do not choose to. The editorial staff of *Le Supplément*, a French journal dealing explicitly with issues in moral theology and associated with the French Association of Moral Theologians, planned their last issue of 1979 to deal with the subject of contemporary Christian sexuality. The editor was quite surprised by the number of authors who turned down requests to write articles on this subject. In the end the journal appeared with only two articles on sexuality and five other articles dealing with different subjects in moral theology. The editor attributes the unwillingness of authors to contribute articles on this subject to the significant cleavage between the official teaching of the church and pastoral practice, between the traditional rules of the church and the actual behavior of Christians.[7] Even if the theologians and others might avoid dealing with the thorny issues involving possible dissent and diversity, the pastoral minister does not have the luxury of being able to ignore them.

I. Understanding the Problem

What precisely is the basic problem and how should one understand it? Often the issue for the pastoral minister is experienced in terms of the tension between the authoritative teaching of the church and the conscience of the individual. Throughout this chapter the discussion will be confined to what is technically called authoritative, noninfallible teaching. The pastoral minister is not merely a private individual, but in the various functions of counseling, teaching, preparing and celebrating the sacraments the pastoral minister truly is a representative of the church and must act and teach in accord with the church. The pastor must be true to the church and at the same time respectful of the conscience of the individual. This experience of the problem is certainly true, but one must understand this experience in a broader perspective.

The Christian is called to be and to live as a disciple of the Lord, to change one's heart and be converted. Christian life involves the living out of this converted existence. The subjective reality of the Christian as a disciple of Christ in the community of the disciples of the church is strongly underscored in all objective sources of theology. The Scriptures call for a fundamental change of heart and the need to produce the fruits of the Spirit. Christianity in the very beginning was often called "the Way." The Didache, one of the oldest and most revered pieces in the patristic literature, talks about the two ways—the way to life and the way to death. Throughout history belonging to the church has meant that the baptized disciples are to act in a special way in accord with their union through the Spirit with Jesus and with one another. The Christian life is the reality which the church proclaims, celebrates in its liturgy, and strives to live in its daily life. Truth is not merely something to be contemplated but something to be done. Praxis has become very important in much of contemporary theology. Too often in the past the emphasis has been only on orthodoxy, but now theology emphasizes also the need for orthopraxis. The individual believer belongs to the church, or community of the disciples of the Lord, and is committed to being truly converted and living in accord with the meaning of discipleship.

There is no doubt that the pastor often experiences the problem in terms of the tension between church teaching and the conscience of the individual. However, a third term must be considered which in a true sense is superior to both the authoritative teaching of the church and the conscience of the individual. This term is the truth and practice of the Christian faith. The Christian conscience is committed to seeking the Christian truth and practice. The hierarchical teaching office in the church exists in the service of Christian truth and practice.

Yves Congar has pointed out a significant development in the understanding of the rule of faith in Catholic history. In modern times the rule of faith as the *quod* (that which is handed down) has been replaced by the *quo* (that by which it has been handed down; namely, the teaching authority of the church). Such an approach gives too much independent weight to the teaching authority in the church and does not see that this teaching office is always in the service of Christian truth and praxis. My understanding of the problem experienced by the pastoral minister is analogous to and based on Congar's understanding of the relationship between the hierarchical teaching office and theologians. Congar insists that the problem of hierarchical magisterium and theologians should not be limited to these two terms but must include a very important third term to which both the others are related and subordinate. "We must think in three terms: above, the truth, the transmitted apostolic faith, confessed, preached, and celebrated. Beneath this, at its service, the 'magisterium' of the apostolic ministry, and the work or the teaching of the theologians, as well as the faith of the faithful."[8]

In an analogous manner in the question we are discussing, the most important reality is the transmitted apostolic faith, confessed, preached, celebrated, and lived. Beneath this, at its service, and committed to it, are both the hierarchical teaching authority of the church and the conscience of the individual believer. Such an understanding in no way calls for a perfect equality between the hierarchical teaching authority and the individual conscience, for the teaching office is a special gift of the Spirit. Traditional Roman Catholic theology has recognized this point by speaking of a presumption in favor of the teaching office. One cannot deny that on a pastoral level the problem is often experienced in terms of the tension between the teaching authority and the conscience of the individual, but both in theory and in practice these two realities are at the service of Christian truth and practice.

Is this really a new problem? The answer is both yes and no. There can be no doubt that to some extent there have always been tensions in the church between church moral teaching and the conscience of the individual members. Individual believers have often had difficulties in living up to the meaning of discipleship. The whole penitential practice in the church attests to some gap between Christian commitment and Christian living. But there are new dimensions today. In many areas some individuals in the church are contesting a particular teaching and disagreeing with it. They will not accept the proposed teaching as a moral norm whether it might be the ban on artificial contraception or the ban on first use of nuclear weapons. In addition the frequency of the tension is much more apparent today.

How can the pastoral minister deal with this underlying tension and the many specific issues which are aspects of it? In some situations the individual person is morally bound to separate oneself from the community of the church. Think, for example, of a young couple who really have no faith but feel they should be married in the church for the sake of their parents. Here the pastoral minister can offer to help them to see the contradiction in their situation and perhaps even explain their situation to their parents, so that they too will understand and accept the decision of the couple not to be married in the church. However, there are other cases in which the individual can and should continue to belong to the community of the church. In all these situations the minister above all needs the great pastoral virtue of prudence.

The purpose of this chapter is not to discuss all these various instances or problems, but rather to supply the pastoral minister with two important tools that might help one deal with the questions. These two tools are the distinction between the realm of pastoral counseling and the realm of moral theology, on the one hand, and the possibility of dissent in the church, on the other hand. The following two sections will develop these two approaches.

II. Pastoral Counseling As Distinct from Moral Theology

The perspective of pastoral counseling is not the same as that of moral theology. Moral theology looks at the objective morality of particular actions. Pastoral counseling must include the data of moral theology but also looks at the subjective culpability, responsibility, and possibilities of the subject.

The distinction between the realm of pastoral counseling and of moral theology is rooted in the complexity of the human act and in the traditional distinction between the objective morality of the act and the subjective responsibility or culpability of the person performing the act. Traditional Catholic moral theology recognized that many factors might reduce, diminish, or even take away subjective culpability. Take the case of drunkenness. All agree that drunkenness is morally wrong, but the alcoholic is not necessarily subjectively culpable and responsible.[9] This traditional distinction in Catholic moral theology is recognized by many others. Philosophy speaks of the causes that justify an act as distinguished from the causes that excuse an act. The justifying causes make the act morally good; the excusing causes diminish or take away subjective culpability and responsibility. Our legal system recognizes the same distinction, since punishments are less when culpability is diminished for any number of reasons.

The prudent confessor has always recognized and employed this distinction. As a result, in practice one could deal with some difficult cases even though one still maintained the objective wrongness of a particular act. In this light the differences between some proposals of situation ethics and traditional Catholic morality are not as great in practice as they might seem at first sight. Joseph Fletcher, the Protes-

tant situation ethicist, made famous in the 1960s the case of
Mrs. Bergmeier. Mrs. Bergmeier was imprisoned in Russia
after the war while her husband and three children were
finally together in postwar Germany, desperately hoping to
be reunited with her. She learned that if she became seriously ill or pregnant, she would be released from the prison
camp as a liability and sent home. After much thought and
prayer she asked a friendly guard to impregnate her. Mrs.
Bergmeier became pregnant, was released and reunited with
her family, and gave birth to a son, whom they loved more
than all the rest with the view that little Dietrich had done
more for them than anybody.[10] What would a confessor say
to Mrs. Bergmeier? Even the most rigid Jansenistic confessor would probably do no more than assign a nominal
penance and tell her not to do it again! But pastoral counseling comes into play before the act. What should Mrs. Bergmeier do? How should a pastoral minister counsel her?

The exact distinction between the level of pastoral
counseling and the level of moral theology has really been
proposed only briefly and in contemporary times by the
noted German moral theologian Bernard Häring. However,
this distinction is basically rooted in the subjective and objective aspects of the human act. One very important development in the tradition of moral theology which is especially
relevant for this contemporary understanding of the realm of
pastoral counseling is the discussion about invincible ignorance even of the natural law. In the eighteenth century
the more rigorous and objectivist position maintained there
could be no invincible ignorance of even the more remote
conclusions of the natural law. The natural law is given, and
the individual cannot be invincibly ignorant of its demands.
St. Alphonsus, who subsequently became the patron of confessors and of moral theology, defended the possibility of
such invincible ignorance by insisting that the law is not
promulgated unless the person has certain knowledge of that
law. But such certain knowledge of the remote aspects of the
moral law can be lacking without any fault.[11]

For Alphonsus an act done in invincible ignorance even against the remote principles of the natural law is formally a good and meritorious act. His reason is that the goodness of an act is determined by the goodness apprehended by the intellect to which the will consents and not by the mere material object of the act. Alphonsus' theological opponents such as Patuzzi and Concina disagree both with his position on this matter and with his invoking the authority of Thomas Aquinas for his position. According to their interpretation of Aquinas whatever is against the law is always bad and is not excused by the fact that it is in accord with conscience. Alphonsus attributes great importance to the human person's apprehension of the law and to the distinction between formal adherence to the divine law and material adherence. A person acting in invincible ignorance is materially violating the law but is formally in accord with it. Since the formal aspect is what determines the moral goodness or badness of an act, such an act for Alphonsus is thus morally good.[12]

On the contemporary theological scene Bernard Häring, a true spiritual son of St. Alphonsus, has made the distinction between the realm of pastoral counseling and the realm of moral theology. In developing his position Häring builds on Alphonsus' concept of invincible ignorance. Alphonsus in the light of his own times understood ignorance in a rather abstract and intellectual sense, but Häring wants to understand invincible ignorance in a more existential sense that embraces the total person. In accord with such an understanding, invincible ignorance is expanded to mean the existential inability of the person to realize a moral obligation.[13]

Bernard Häring understands the modern distinction between pastoral counseling and moral theology in the light of his heavy emphasis on the law of growth in Christian life. The call to conversion and to continual conversion has always been the central part of Häring's moral theology. The dynamism of the Christian life cannot be dealt with by an ethics based only on static external norms. The Christian is called to grow in the change of heart and in one's union of love with God, neighbor, and the world. All the followers of Jesus are called to holiness and to be perfect even as the heavenly Parent is perfect. This emphasis on growth will logically call people to go on beyond the minimal requirements of universal law, but at the same time the principle of growth can and should be applied to those who are unable to realize concretely the objective moral good in a particular situation. The German Redemptorist theologian sees this situation in the light of the way Jesus dealt with his disciples. There are many other things I could say to you, but the burden is too great for you to bear at the present time.[14]

Häring not only explains theoretically the difference between pastoral counseling and moral theology but also gives an example or application. In a symposium on abortion James M. Gustafson, the American Protestant ethicist, brought up the case of a pregnant woman in her late twenties. This woman, a lapsed and divorced Catholic, was raped by her former husband and some of his friends. She had experienced perduring emotional problems and now was without a steady job or source of income. Gustafson uses the case to argue against what he describes as the traditional Catholic approach which views the situation as an external judge and does not seem to consider the person and all the other aspects of the case. The Protestant ethicist wants to consider all these aspects — the medical, the legal, the spiritual, and the emotional. Gustafson is opposed to abortion in most cases, but here he concludes with an analogy to killing in war. The conscientious soldier is convinced that he may kill the enemy if necessary in a just war, but such a killing is always mournful. In this abortion case Gustafson is convinced that the life of the defenseless fetus may be taken less justly but more mournfully.[15]

In response to Gustafson's treatment Häring appeals to the different levels of moral discourse which Gustafson himself developed in an earlier article. Following Henry D.

Aiken, Gustafson distinguishes four levels of moral discourse — the expressive-evocative level, the moral level, the ethical level, and the postmoral level. The moral level answers the question: What ought I to do in the situation? The third level, or ethical level, raises the question about the rules or other considerations that justify a particular moral judgment. Most Catholic treatments of the rules governing abortion are on the third or ethical level, but most of Gustafson's consideration in the particular article is on the second or the moral level. Häring sees these different levels as corresponding to the level of pastoral counseling and the level of moral theology.

The Redemptorist theologian claims that on the level of pastoral counseling a Catholic moralist might come to almost the same conclusions and even to almost the same way of friendly discourse as Gustafson. Häring explicitly refers to Alphonsus' teaching that the confessor can leave the penitent in good faith when confronted with an invincible error if pastoral prudence suggests that one's admonition would do more harm than good for the penitent. If owing to the psychological effects of her traumatic experience, this woman cannot accept the moral teaching not to abort, it is possible to leave her in invincible ignorance. While refraining from any rigid judgments, Häring would not advise the person to abort and would not say this is the right decision if the person has made up her mind to abort.[16]

It seems to me that perhaps Häring's closing remarks are not totally in keeping with what he said earlier. He maintains there can be no formal sin in this particular case and quotes his patron to show that God punishes only formal sin. It seems, then, if he is convinced in this case there is no formal sin, he should be willing to say at least this to the person involved.

In my judgment Häring has creatively developed the Catholic tradition in his insistence on the distinction between the level of pastoral counseling and the level of moral theology. Unfortunately, other theologians have not paid much attention to this very significant question, especially for the pastoral minister.[17] However, the hierarchical magisterium has recognized and even employed a distinction of sorts between the moral level and the pastoral level. The occasion for this consideration and distinction by the hierarchical magisterium was the teaching of the papal encyclical *Humanae Vitae* issued by Pope Paul VI in 1968. In this context I am not primarily concerned with what the encyclical says about the specific issue of the morality of contraception, but rather with the emphasis the encyclical gives to the difference between the moral and the pastoral level. This distinction which is found in the encyclical and exists even to a greater degree in the later commentaries by different national groups of bishops can be applied in many other areas by the prudent pastoral minister today.

The distinction between the moral level and the pastoral level is made by the encyclical itself. Section II is entitled "Doctrinal Principles" and discusses the moral teaching, while Section III, "Pastoral Directives," considers the many different pastoral aspects. Among these pastoral aspects is the recognition that the teaching itself will appear to many as difficult or even impossible to follow. The pastoral section directly addresses different people—public authorities, scientists, doctors, bishops, priests, and Christian couples themselves. Couples are reminded of the serious difficulties that they face in trying to live up to God's law. Even if sin should still keep its hold over them, they should not be discouraged but have recourse with humble perseverance to the mercy of God which is poured forth in the sacrament of penance. Priests are advised to proclaim the full Catholic teaching but also to show the patience and goodness the Lord himself showed to people in need. The Lord came not to condemn but to save; he was intransigent with evil but merciful toward individuals.[18]

The encyclical differs from its predecessor *Casti Connubii* issued by Pope Pius XI in 1930 precisely because of its heavy emphasis on the pastoral aspect. Even more than the encyclical itself, the subsequent commentaries by different national conferences of bishops give even more attention to the pastoral level and definitely go beyond, although not necessarily against, what was said in the pastoral section of the encyclical itself. Since our purpose is not a thoroughgoing treatment of the encyclical and its aftermath, our discussion will be limited to examining the statements of two different bishops' conferences insofar as they deal with the pastoral aspects of the question.[19]

The commentary issued by the Italian bishops follows the two parts of *Humanae Vitae*—doctrinal reflection and spiritual and pastoral directives. The document accepts and praises the papal teaching and then in the second or pastoral section addresses a number of different groups—theologians, priests, and married couples. Couples who experience difficulty in living up to the teaching of the church should not become discouraged. The church, whose function it is to declare the total and perfect good, does not ignore the fact that there are laws of growth in doing the good. In striving for the ideal one will go through imperfect steps and stages.[20] Note that this position follows Häring's insistence on the law of growth in the Christian life. One can conclude, although the Italian bishops do not explicitly draw the conclusion, that such imperfect acts, while falling short of the ideal and perfect good and not in material conformity with the moral norm, can still be formally good acts.

The response of the French bishops to *Humanae Vitae* addresses in a pastoral way both those who accept the encyclical but find themselves unable to respond to its demands and those who are unable to accept the teaching. In speaking to the first group the French bishops maintain that contraception can never be a good. It is always a disorder, but this disorder is not always culpable. The document explains that the spouses consider themselves confronted by a true conflict of duties. When one faces a dilemma of duties where one cannot avoid any evil no matter what is done, traditional wisdom requires the individual to pursue the greater duty.[21]

There has been much discussion about the exact meaning of this part of the French bishops' statement. Some understand this approach as going beyond the traditional subjective-objective distinction as applied to ignorance and lack of freedom. Josef Fuchs sees here a moral theory according to which the sin of the world as concupiscence in the acting subject brings it about that the choice of evil (not the evil itself) does not count as morally wrong and in the proper sense sinful.[22] I am not too sure if Fuchs' interpretation differs that much from the distinction between the orders of pastoral counseling and of moral theology developed above. However, at the very minimum one can legitimately understand the approach of the French bishops in the light of the pastoral counseling–moral theology distinction.

One resolution of the 1980 Synod of Bishops reminds pastoral ministers to keep in mind the law of gradualness in dealing with married couples. However, there can be no false dichotomy between Catholic teaching and pastoral practice.[23] Pope John Paul II in his homily at the close of the synod and in his apostolic exhortation *Familiaris Consortio* recognizes the pastoral significance of the law of gradualness but also warns against confusing "the law of gradualness" with "the gradualness of the law."[24] In other words, the Pope does not want this pastoral approach to affect the objective order of morality.

At the present time within Roman Catholicism there exists a recognition even by the hierarchical magisterium that there are differences between the moral order and the pastoral order. Bernard Häring has made a most creative and satisfying distinction between the order of pastoral counseling and the order of moral theology. This section has tried to develop this distinction and show its roots in traditional and official Catholic teaching. Even if an act is objectively morally wrong, the formal act or choice of the individual who is existentially unable to realize the moral obligation is morally good. The dangers of abuse of such a distinction are obvious, but abuse does not take away use. The prudent pastor thus has a very significant tool to use in dealing with many of the tensions arising in ministry.

III. Dissent

A second tool that a prudent pastoral minister can use in some situations is the legitimate possibility of dissent within the church. The question centers on the authoritative, noninfallible hierarchical teaching. All would admit that much of the church's moral teaching on specific moral norms (e.g., masturbation is always wrong; the direct killing of the innocent is always wrong) falls into this category. With others I maintain that there has never been and never can be an infallible church teaching on a specific moral issue. However, the difference between these two positions is not all that great in practice.

Much has been written about dissent in the church.[25] This discussion will not attempt to break any new ground from a theoretical perspective but rather will relate the question of dissent to the work of the pastoral minister. The first part will consider the possibility of such dissent in general, and then the second part will briefly discuss the feasibility of dissent in particular situations.

In discussing the possibility of dissent, again it is important to understand the question properly and not merely in terms of opposition between the authoritative church teaching and the conscience of the individual believer. Here too there is the all-important third term — the Christian moral truth to which both the hierarchical teaching role and the individual conscience are subordinated. However, such an understanding does not mean that the teaching of the hierarchical magisterium and the conscience of the individual believer are on exactly the same level. Traditionally Catholic theology has talked about a presumption in favor of the teaching of the hierarchical magisterium on noninfallible issues precisely because of the gift of the Spirit given to the hierarchical office of the church. This presumption itself, however, always cedes to the truth.

There are both theological and ecclesiological reasons grounding the possibility of dissent from authoritative, non-infallible teaching on specific moral issues. The theological reason primarily concerns the area of epistemology. The more specific and complex the problem, the more difficult it is to claim a certitude that excludes the possibility of error. There can be and should be certitude and unanimity in talking about general values and goals such as the right to life. However, the solution of difficult cases by invoking the principle of double effect necessarily involves complex philosophical notions which by their nature are open to development, discussion, and error. It is a basic principle of logic that the more specific and complex the reality, the greater the difficulty in being able to claim certitude.

The ecclesiological grounding of dissent comes from the fact that the hierarchical magisterium itself is the servant of the saving moral truth of the gospel. Recall that we are dealing here only with what has since the nineteenth century been called authoritative or authentic, noninfallible church teaching. The word infallible should make one pause. What is the opposite of infallible? The most obvious response is fallible. By definition this type of teaching has always recognized its fallible nature.

Within recent Catholic theology the Second Vatican Council has insisted on recognizing the hierarchy of truths.[26] An older Catholic theology emphasized the importance of theological notes which in a certain sense tried to indicate how a particular truth related to the core of faith.[27] Specific moral norms by their very nature are not that core and central to the Christian belief within the Roman Catholic community. Thus, one can disagree with such a specific moral norm and not deny the faith. The Canadian bishops specifically mention that those who disagree with some of the conclusions of *Humanae Vitae* are not denying a point of divine and Catholic faith and should not be considered nor consider themselves cut off from the body of the faithful.[28]

The very nature of the hierarchical teaching office in the church and of authoritative, noninfallible teaching together with a recognition that such specific moral norms are not central to divine and Catholic faith grounds the possibility of dissent.

One important point needs to be mentioned. Too often the whole discussion about dissent seems to imply that those in favor of dissent are "liberals" in the church, whereas the "conservatives" are opposed to all dissent. All realize the problems and difficulties with labels such as those of "conservative" and "liberal," but also pastoral ministers are very aware of a reality corresponding somewhat to these terms. There can be no doubt that especially in the areas of sexual morality it has been a case of the "liberals" in the church dissenting from the official hierarchical church teaching. However, now that there has been so much more discussion about social issues, it is interesting to see that the "conservatives" are now talking about dissent from church teaching.

In the United States the first case of public dissent from official, noninfallible hierarchical church teaching was from a "conservative" point of view. In the July 29, 1961, issue of *The National Review* the editor, Mr. William Buckley, criticized the teaching of the encyclical *Mater et Magistra*. Two weeks later the magazine reported the epigrammatic response of some Catholic conservatives to the encyclical: "Mater, si; magistra, no."[29] Buckley's comments touched off some debate within the church about dissent, although the debate quickly subsided. One important contribution to the debate was the book published in 1964 by Gary Wills, *Politics and Catholic Freedom*, which reviewed the controversy over *Mater et Magistra* and ultimately supported the position about the possibility of dissent for Roman Catholics in social and political matters. It is very interesting to note that at that time what might be called the "liberal" position demanded that there be no such thing as dissent from the papal encyclical.[30] In this whole issue of the possibility of dissent the issue is unfortunately too often decided on the basis of whose ox is being gored. The possibility of dissent is ultimately not a question of "liberal" versus "conservative" but the recognition by all that one can disagree with such noninfallible teaching on specific moral questions and still belong to the one, true church of Jesus Christ. My whole thrust is to insist on the catholicity of the church—the church by its very nature is catholic and big. It must have room for "conservatives" and "liberals" within it. There must be room for possible dissent on such issues. The unity of the church found in the area of specific moral norms or issues. A venerable axiom provides guidance in this area: *in necessariis unitas, in dubiis libertas, in omnibus caritas* (in necessary matters, unity; in doubtful matters, freedom; in all things, charity). pluralism in the church on such specific issues.

Can the pastoral minister who represents the church dissent from official church teaching? The minister, even though not always ordained, is not speaking and acting in one's own name but in the name of the church. In addition, in the celebration of sacramental reconciliation the priest receives faculties from the bishop and absolves in the name of the church. The pastoral minister is not just a private person. Some would maintain that the pastoral minister because of one's role must always teach and act in accord with the official teaching. I disagree. The pastoral minister is a representative of the total church with its hierarchical structure, and such a role demands that the pastor be true to one's calling. The pastoral minister must be true to the self-understanding of the church.

If dissent is a legitimate possibility within the church, then the minister must recognize this fact and explain it to the people. The pastor's responsible action must be based on the many aspects of the pastoral role in the church. The teaching of the hierarchical magisterium must always be presented in a clear and objective way. However, the pastor can at times indicate that in this particular area there is some dissent within the total church. The pastoral minister can at times express in the proper manner one's own personal conviction on the matter.

What about the possibility of dissent on the part of the individual believer who is not a trained theologian? Our discussion is dealing with questions in the moral order, but the ordinary Catholic is not a moral theologian and does not seem to have the necessary expertise to dissent. Such an approach unfortunately overemphasizes the role of the theologian and downplays the role of the individual believer. One does not have to be a theologian or an ethicist in order to make good moral decisions. The primary teacher in the church is the Holy Spirit, and the Spirit dwells in the hearts of all the faithful. The expertise of the theologian is more in the theoretical and systematic realms, but in the practical realm the ordinary Catholic is at no disadvantage when compared to the theologian. I often use the analogy with the relationship of the psychiatrist and the ordinary person to understand better the relationship between the theologian and the baptized Christian. One does not have to be a psychiatrist in order to be a balanced, mature human being. (There are even those who would say that being a psychiatrist might make it more difficult!) The psychiatrist, like the theological ethicist, makes a contribution on the level of theory, systematization, and second-order discourse.

To its great credit the Catholic tradition has never claimed that one has to be a theologian in order to get to heaven or to do the right things in this world. Yes, the individual Christian must be aware of one's limitation, finitude, and sinfulness. Yes, there is a presumption in favor of the hierarchical teaching; but in good conscience an individual Catholic can come to the conclusion to act against a specific moral teaching of the hierarchical magisterium. In making such a decision the individual person would often consult the theologian as the prudent person often consults experts before making one's decision. But the final decision rests with the individual. Is this not what is actually happening in the way in which Catholic married couples are deciding about contraception?

Does not dissent and especially frequent dissent go against the unity of the church and cause scandal? Unfortunately, sociological conditions in countries in which

Roman Catholicism existed in a pluralistic religious situation have tended to identify Roman Catholics precisely in terms of specific moral norms or practices — Mass on Sunday, no meat on Friday, and no contraception. However, all must admit these are not truths pertaining to the core of our faith. As mentioned earlier, the unity of the faith should not be found ultimately on these particular specific moral issues.

What about scandal? Many of those who oppose the possibility of dissent frequently bring up the problem of scandal. Yes, some people are scandalized by dissent in the church. The solution to the problem, however, is to explain to them exactly what is involved and why such dissent is a possibility within the church. There has been an unfortunate tendency in the church to exaggerate the scandal of the weak and not to give enough importance to what might be called the scandal of the strong. According to Andrew M. Greeley a one-third decline in American Catholic religious practice between 1963 and 1974 is linked mostly to the encyclical *Humanae Vitae*. Even those who might not agree with this statistic must recognize that many Catholics have been estranged from the church precisely because of the teaching of *Humanae Vitae*.[31] It would indeed be a scandal if these people thought this cut them off from the church. There is a great need to explain to these and to all the possibility of dissent.

Undoubtedly there are many parishioners who are scandalized by such a possibility, but others are scandalized by the unwillingness to recognize and deal with the actual problem. The prudent pastoral minister must come up with ways to deal with all God's people. Such pastoral approaches should be based on the understanding explained above.

The discussion thus far has considered only the possibility of dissent from authoritative, noninfallible church teaching. The more practical question involves the legitimacy of dissent in a given particular case. Since it is impossible to study in depth all the individual issues, the remainder of this section will briefly mention the more general aspects involved in discerning the legitimacy of dissent in a particular issue or case. Here too one must avoid facile and one-sided solutions. The controlling factor must always be the call of the gospel and moral truth. The very fact that something is only a part of the noninfallible church teaching and is not a matter of divine faith does not mean that it can be dismissed. The failure to give great importance to such teachings would also result in a practical denial of the historical and incarnational nature of the church. The contemporary emphasis on praxis reminds us that historical and concrete moral action is an essential dimension of our Christian belief. The legitimacy of dissent must be proved in every case.

The judgment about the acceptance of dissent in a particular case should follow the process and rules involved in any good conscience decision. Since the individual is striving to know and live the moral truth of discipleship, the basic biblical attitude of readiness to hear the call of God should be the most important attitude of the baptized disciple of the Lord. The individual must ultimately take responsibility for one's own decision, but one must also honestly recognize the limitations that beset all of us — our finitude and our sinfulness. The recognition of these limitations means that the person must be ever vigilant to the need to be truly open to the call of God. The discernment process involves giving a privileged place to the official hierarchical teaching. In addition, the praxis of believers in the community and the work of theologians and ethicists as well as the experience of all people of good will can furnish some wisdom to the individual decision-maker. The individual is never alone but exists primarily in and through the church which is called to be a community of disciples of the Lord. My theory of conscience stresses that the peace and joy of a good conscience constitute the ultimate sign of a good decision, but one must recognize the many pitfalls and dangers that exist in the way of arriving at such true peace of conscience.

In conclusion, the pastoral minister today is faced with many difficulties, not least of which is the more frequently occurring experience of dealing with the tension between the conscience of the individual and the official teaching of the church. This study has tried to understand the problem properly and to suggest two approaches which at times might be used. However, these approaches or tools are quite delicate and call for great prudence on the part of the pastoral minister. Such prudence can never be taught in an article, a textbook, or in a classroom but can only be learned by a prayerful and respectful minister of the gospel and the church in and through one's own experience.

There is another aspect which the prudent minister of the church cannot forget. Part of the consideration here has been based on the law of growth in the Christian life. The entire discussion of this study has considered primarily the lower floor of the level of growth. The prudent and prayerful pastor must recognize the full range of the law of growth in the life of the disciples of the Lord. The minister in the name of the gospel and of the church must challenge and urge all the disciples of the Lord to live out the fullness of the gospel message but at the same time never forget the mercy, forgiveness, and compassion which likewise characterize the gospel and the church.

NOTES

1. Archbishop John R. Quinn, "New Context for Contraception Teaching," *Origins* 10 (October 9, 1980): 263.

2. *Congress Report: The Principal Documents of the 1980 National Pastoral Congress of England and Wales* (London: Catholic Truth Society, 1980), p. 22.

3. See, for example, for both sides of the debate Francisco Javier Urrutia, "Can Polygamy Be Compatible with Christianity?" *AFER: African Ecclesial Review* 23 (1981): 275-291; Eugene Hillman, "Reply," *AFER* 23 (1981): 292-307.

4. John Eagleson, ed., *Christians and Socialism: The Christians for Socialism Movement in Latin America* (Maryknoll, NY: Orbis Books, 1975).

5. Canadian Bishops' Commission, "Alternatives to Present Economic Structures," *Origins* 12 (January 27, 1983): 523.

6. Kajetan Kriech, "A Firsthand Report on the Current Crisis in Catholic Sexual Morality," *Concilium* 100 (1976): 43.

7. F. Refoulé, "Liminaire," *Le Supplément* 131 (Novembre 1979): 425-427.

8. Yves Congar, "A Brief History of the Forms of the Magisterium and Its Relations with Scholars," in *Readings in Moral Theology No. 3: The Magisterium and Morality*, eds. Charles E. Curran and Richard A. McCormick (New York: Paulist Press, 1982), p. 328.

9. Marcellino Zalba, *Theologiae Moralis Summa*, vol. 1: *Theologia Moralis Fundamentalis* (Madrid: Biblioteca de Autores Cristianos, 1952), pp. 103-220.

10. Joseph Fletcher, *Situation Ethics: The New Morality* (Philadelphia: Westminster Press, 1966), pp. 164, 165.

11. Charles E. Curran, *Invincible Ignorance of the Natural Law according to St. Alphonsus* (Rome: Academia Alfonsiana, 1961).

12. Ibid; Zalba, *Theologiae Moralis Summa*, pp. 258, 259. Recall that Catholic moral theology also counseled the confessor to leave the invincibly erroneous penitent in good faith if there was no harm to others, no scandal, and if warning the penitent would do more harm than good.

13. Bernard Häring, "A Theological Evaluation," in *The Morality of Abortion: Legal and Historical Perspectives*, ed. John T. Noonan, Jr. (Cambridge, MA: Harvard University Press, 1970), pp. 139, 140.

14. Bernard Häring, *Shalom: Peace — The Sacrament of Reconciliation* (New York: Farrar, Straus and Giroux, 1968), pp. 39-49.

15. James M. Gustafson, "A Protestant Ethical Approach," in Noonan, *The Morality of Abortion*, pp. 101-122.

16. Häring, "A Theological Evaluation," pp. 140-142.

17. One moral theologian who briefly develops the traditional notion of invincible ignorance along the same lines as Häring is Louis Monden, *Sin, Liberty, and Law* (New York: Sheed and Ward, 1965), pp. 136-141.

18. Pope Paul VI, *On the Regulation of Birth: Humanae Vitae* (Washington: United States Catholic Conference, 1968), pp. 12-19.

19. Some bishops' conferences recognized the possibility of dissent in practice, while others asserted that disobedience to the encyclical is morally wrong. A center group often emphasized pastoral sympathy and consideration for those struggling with the decision. For the development of these categories see William H.

Shannon, *The Lively Debate: Responses to Humanae Vitae* (New York: Sheed and Ward, 1970); Joseph A. Selling, "The Reaction to *Humanae Vitae*: A Study in Special and Fundamental Theology" (S.T.D. dissertation, Catholic University of Louvain, 1977).

20. *N.C. News Service*, September 21, 1968; Shannon, *The Lively Debate*, pp. 122-124.

21. *N.C. News Service*, November 22, 1968; Shannon, *The Lively Debate*, pp. 135, 136.

22. Joseph Fuchs, "The 'Sin of the World' and Normative Morality," *Gregorianum* 61 (1980): 62-68.

23. These resolutions were not officially released, but a version was published in *National Catholic Reporter* 16 (December 12, 1980): 22.

24. Pope John Paul II, *The Role of the Christian Family in the Modern World: Familiaris Consortio* (Boston: St. Paul Editions, 1982), n. 34, p. 56.

25. For reactions to *Humanae Vitae* by bishops and theologians, including the recognition of the possibility of dissent on this issue, see Shannon and Selling. For a collection of articles giving different positions see Charles E. Curran and Richard A. McCormick, eds., *Readings in Moral Theology No. 3: The Magisterium and Morality* (New York: Paulist Press, 1982).

26. Decree on Ecumenism, n. 11.

27. Sixtus Cartechini, *De Valore Notarum Theologicarum* (Rome: Gregorian University Press, 1951).

28. *N.C. News Service*, October 11, 1968; Shannon, *The Lively Debate,* pp. 128-130.

29. "The Week," *National Review* 11 (July 29, 1961): 38; "For the Record," *National Review* 11 (August 12, 1961): 77.

30. Gary Wills, *Politics and Catholic Freedom* (Chicago: Henry Regnery, 1964).

31. Andrew M. Greeley, William C. McCready, Kathleen McCourt, *Catholic Schools in a Declining Church* (Kansas City: Sheed and Ward, 1976), pp. 103-154.

Index